Zola and Film

Zola and Film

*Essays in the
Art of Adaptation*

Edited by Anna Gural-Migdal
and Robert Singer

with a foreword by Brigitte Émile-Zola

McFarland & Company, Inc., Publishers
Jefferson, North Carolina, and London

LIBRARY OF CONGRESS CATALOGUING-IN-PUBLICATION DATA

Zola and film : essays in the art of adaptation / edited by Anna
   Gural-Migdal and Robert Singer ; with a foreword by Brigitte
   Émile-Zola.
       p.   cm.
   Includes bibliographical references and index.

   ISBN-13: 978-0-7864-2115-2
   softcover : 50# alkaline paper ∞

   1. Zola, Emile, 1840–1902—Film and video adaptations.
   2. Motion pictures and literature—France. I. Gural, Anna,
   1955–   II. Singer, Robert, 1953–
   PQ2538.Z64   2005
   791.43'6—dc22   2005000094

British Library cataloguing data are available

©2005 Anna Gural-Migdal and Robert Singer. All rights reserved

*No part of this book may be reproduced or transmitted in any form
or by any means, electronic or mechanical, including photocopying
or recording, or by any information storage and retrieval system,
without permission in writing from the publisher.*

Cover photograph: Mexican film poster of *Nana*, starring Lupe
Velez and Miguel Ángel Ferriz (1944)

Manufactured in the United States of America

McFarland & Company, Inc., Publishers
   Box 611, Jefferson, North Carolina 28640
   www.mcfarlandpub.com

Acknowledgments

A generous thank you to Dr. Brigitte Émile-Zola for having had the kindness to write a foreword to this book, and for her support, from its very beginnings, of the "Association Internationale Zola et le Naturalisme" (AIZEN). I would like to express my sincere thanks to my student Alexandra Miekus for her excellent translation work from French to English. I thank her in particular for having had the kindness to translate my article on Claude Berri's *Germinal* published in this volume. Thank you also to Mrs. Anna Chilewska from the Department of Modern Languages and Cultural Studies at the University of Alberta for having carefully translated from Polish to English an article by Professor Alicja Helman, and to Professor Waclaw Osadnik. I am grateful to Dr. Carolyn Snipes-Hoyt for having reread and corrected several articles from this book. Finally, I thank my husband, Andrew Migdal, for his everyday support.

—Anna Gural-Migdal

I would like to extend a very special "thank you" to Alexandra Miekus and Dr. Carolyn Snipes-Hoyt for their support and work as translators. All of the contributors have made this a wonderful experience for me, and I thank them individually—they are the vanguard. Special recognition is extended to the British Film Institute film stills division, in particular to Simone Potter for her enthusiastic support, and also to Jan-Hein Bal, of the Nederlands Filmmuseum. Thanks to Adam Klein for indexing this text. A very special "thank you" to the PSC-CUNY Research, Grants and Development Office for the generous grant and released time. I especially wish to recognize Prof. Diane Smith for proofreading and editorial suggestions.

—Robert Singer

Table of Contents

Acknowledgments   v

Foreword   Brigitte Émile-Zola   1

Introduction   Robert Singer   5

1. Antoine's Version of *La Terre*: An Experiment in Naturalist Cinema   *Russell Cousins*   15

2. Eisenstein and Zola: Naturalism, Cinema, and Mythography   *Tony Williams*   27

3. Staging the Courtesan: Taking Zola's *Nana* to the Movies   *Heather Howard*   45

4. From Theater to Cinema: Jean Renoir's Adaptation of *Nana*   *Katherine Golsan*   62

5. The Eye Behind the Writing Hand: Surveillance and Adaptation in *La Bête humaine*   *Monica Filimon*   69

6. "La Rançon du progrès": Naturalistic Discourse and Two Adaptations of Zola's *Au Bonheur des Dames*   *Klaus Peter Walter*   89

7. Viewing *Au Bonheur des Dames* in the Context of Occupied France   *Jennifer Wolter*   103

8. *Thérèse Raquin* in a Fog-Covered Corner   *Alicja Helman*   117

9. Ideology and Focalization in *Gervaise*:
   The Aurenchébost/René Clément Treatment
   Russell Cousins 132

10. The Female Reader in *Pot-Bouille* and
    Duvivier's Cinematic Representation
    Elisabeth-Christine Muelsch 148

11. The Fabrication of Claude Berri's *Germinal*
    Anna Gural-Migdal 163

12. Nostalgia Is Hard to Let Go: The French
    Communist Party's Reception of Claude Berri's
    Filmic Adaptation of *Germinal*   *Laurent Marie* 182

13. "At the Still Point": Framing the Naturalist *Moment*
    Robert Singer 194

Select Filmography 207
About the Contributors 211
Index 215

Foreword
Brigitte Émile-Zola

La première question que me posèrent les auteurs de cet ouvrage fut celle-ci: "Etes-vous surprise du nombre important des adap-tations cinématographiques des romans de Zola?" Eh bien, non! Elevée depuis mon plus jeune âge par mes grand-parents Jacques et Marguerite Émile-Zola, j'ai toujours été avec Zola, grâce à la mémoire de son fils Jacques et, au courant de tout ce qui se passait ou s'était passé concernant mon célèbre bisaïeul. Dans l'appartement du bas de la rue Pigalle, non loin des divers appartements de Jeanne et de l'Hôtel particulier de la rue de Bruxelles, j'étais dans le 19ème siècle. Dehors était le 20ème. Partout, les murs étaient couverts de bibliothèques rassemblant livres et souvenirs. Le salon était un véritable musée, quant au cabinet de travail, tous les murs sans exception étaient couverts de livres et plus particulièrement,

The first question I was asked by the authors of this work was this one: "Are you surprised by the considerable amount of cinematic adaptations of Zola's novels?" Well, no! Raised by my grandparents Jacques and Marguerite Émile-Zola from a very young age, I have always lived with Zola, thanks to his son Jacques' memory, and knew of all that was happening or happened concerning my famous great-grandfather. In the downstairs apartment on Pigalle street, not far from Jeanne's various apartments and from the distinctive Hotel on Bruxelles Street, I was in the 19th century. Outside it was the 20th. Everywhere, the walls were covered with bookcases gathering up books and memories. The living room was a true museum; as for the study, all walls without exception were covered with books and, particularly, with the novels but also their trans-

pour les romans mais aussi leurs traductions: non seulement dans toutes les langues européennes, mais aussi en russe, en hébreu ... et même en japonais! Que les cinéastes aient été nombreux à adapter les romans et souvent dans des versions différentes m'apparaissaient la logique même; fillette d'une dizaine d'années, j'avais accompagné mon grand-père Jacques sur le lieu de tournage de *Gervaise* (tiré de *l'Assommoir*) et avais assisté aux différents essais de la fameuse scène de la "fessée" Maria Schell interprétait Gervaise; mon grand-père fût content de constater qu'elle représentait bien physiquement et nerveusement le personnage de Gervaise. Il bavarda avec elle et j'étais toute ouïe.

Un peu plus tôt, en 1952, à l'âge de huit ans, j'avais tourné moi-même aux côtés de Jacques Zola dans le très beau documentaire de Jean Vidal sur la vie de Zola. J'ouvrais la porte aux spectateurs, les conduisais au salon où mon grand-père leur expliquait soit directement, soit en s'adressant à moi et en me montrant des albums de photos, ses souvenirs, avec son Père et Jeanne sa Mère. Cela me paraissait tout naturel et j'étais fière de me montrer déjà utile!

Par contre, j'ai été très tôt déçue par certains films, le plus souvent, lorsque les cinéastes disposaient d'un budget limité qui entraînait une représentation minimaliste de la Foule. Or, chez Zola, je dirais que c'est le personnage le

lations: not only in all the European languages, but also in Russian, in Hebrew ... and even in Japanese! That numerous directors had adapted the novels and often in different versions seemed natural to me; as a little girl of about ten I had accompanied my grandfather Jacques on the set of *Gervaise* (based on *L'Assommoir*) and had seen the different rehearsals of the famous "spanking" scene. Maria Schell played Gervaise; my grandfather was pleased to note that she represented the character of Gervaise well, physically and psychologically. He chatted with her, and I was all ears.

A little earlier, at the age of eight, alongside Jacques Zola, I participated in the filming of Jean Vidal's beautiful documentary on Zola's life. I was opening the doors for the viewers, leading them to the living room where my grandfather explained either directly, or by speaking to me and showing me photo albums, his memories of his father and Jeanne his mother. That seemed very natural to me and I was proud to already make myself useful!

On the other hand, certain films disappointed me very early, most often when the film directors had a limited budget that generated minimalist representations of the crowd. Yet, in Zola, I would say that it is the most important character, the one best described: with the miners' strikes, the soldiers of 1870, the events of Plassans, etc. Only the most recent *Germinal*,

plus important, le mieux décrit : avec les grèves des mineurs, les soldats de 1870, les événements de Plassans, etc. Seul le dernier *Germinal* de 1993, possédait les moyens mais tout était gâché par le manque de solidité du personnage d'Etienne Lantier: ce n'était pas l'homme de Zola, à mon avis. Il faut rappeler que de son vivant, Zola lui même avait porté à la scène nombre de ses romans et avait remporté de beaux succès.

Sa collaboration avec le musicien Alfred Bruneau, avait également été fructueuse et je suis sûre que s'il avait vécu 15 ou 20 ans de plus, il se serait senti attiré par le cinéma, tout comme il l'avait été par la photographie, art où il est reconnu comme un maître.

Il faut rappeler que si l'écrivain ne s'est pas intéressé vraiment aux premiers balbutiements du 7ème art, c'est que les événements concomitants de l'Affaire Dreyfus, son exil en Angleterre et sa préoccupation, dès son retour, de travailler à la réhabilitation de Dreyfus, que malheureusement il n'a pas pu connaître, l'éternel chercheur aurait, j'en suis convaincue, touché aussi à ce nouvel art.

Il existe encore beaucoup de romans qui n'ont pas été adaptés, j'espère avoir la joie de voir d'autres films inspirés par l'oeuvre colossale d'Émile Zola.

La maison natale champenoise, où était née Marguerite Émile-Zola, vite adoptée par Jacques, m'appartient désormais, j'y ai tous mes souvenirs: nous y

made in 1993, had the means, but everything was spoiled by the lack of solidity of Etienne Lantier's character: he was not Zola's man, in my opinion. It must be mentioned that while he was alive, Zola had himself staged a number of his novels and had achieved great successes. His collaboration with the musician Alfred Bruneau had also been fruitful and I am sure that if he had lived 15 or 20 more years, he would have been attracted by cinema, just as he had been by photography, an art in which he is recognized as a master.

It must be mentioned that if the writer was not really interested in the beginnings of cinema, it is because of the events concomitant with the Dreyfus Affair; his exile in England and his preoccupation upon his return with the rehabilitation of Dreyfus, whom unfortunately he did not know. Had it not been for these factors, the eternal investigator, I am convinced, would have also experienced this new art. There still are a large number of novels that have not been adapted; I hope to have the joy to see other films inspired by Émile Zola's colossal collection of works.

The native house in Champagne, where Marguerite Émile-Zola was born, quickly adopted by Jacques, belongs to me from now on; it is where I have all my memories; it is where we spend all our vacations. It is also where all books and documents passed on by my grandfather can be found. I also

passions toutes les vacances. S'y trouvent aussi tous les livres et documents transmis par mon aïeul. Moi aussi, j'ai installé des bibliothèques partout: les murs de notre salle à manger sont complètement couverts de volumes!

J'y reçoit les chercheurs qui, comme Anna Gural-Migdal et Robert Singer, viennent trouver des informations pour leurs travaux. Ils y seront toujours les bienvenus.

had bookcases installed everywhere: the walls of our dining room are completely covered with volumes!

It is where I receive researchers who, like Anna Gural-Migdal and Robert Singer, come to gather information for their works. They will always be welcome there.

—Translation by
Alexandra Miekus

Introduction
Robert Singer

Leo Braudy, in his seminal essay "Zola on Film: Ambiguities of Naturalism," asked, "Why should Zola provide such a fertile field for directors and scriptwriters in search of material?"[1] Braudy's question is still germane to the field of literary and film studies some thirty years later. The reader may already know that Zola has been one of the most adapted authors in world literature, with approximately eighty adaptations of his novels and select short stories, many of which occur during the silent era of international film production (1895–1927). These films were not solely the product of French filmmakers. Directors as diverse as Griffith, Sjöström, Guy-Blaché, and Lupu-Pick all created adaptations based on Zola's texts, and these were all produced before 1923. As Zola scholar Russell Cousins has stated, "[T]here are many Zolas abroad, and not all of them appear in the medium of print.... Arguably, some of the most provocative and productive new readings of the author have originated in dramatizations of his work for the cinema and television."[2] There is, in fact, an extensive and complex history of literary and film interrelations emanating from the singular figure of Émile Zola.

Why Zola? Why this study of French novelist Émile Zola (1840–1902) and the art of cinematic adaptation? Shakespeare, with his magisterial language and psychologically complex figures, or Dickens, with his alternately humorous and serious critiques of nineteenth-century society and his colorful, memorable characters, have received the attention of film and literary scholars in countless articles and texts. In fact, many authors other than Zola might, and justifiably should, be the subject of a volume of critical studies devoted to cinematic adaptation. Other novelists were "better" prose practitioners, more stylish, poetic, and even more experimental. Film scholars such as Robert Stam have referred to Zola's literary theories and practice as "shallow, reductionist, and obsessively veristic,"³ and the historical arguments against naturalism, Zola, and the products of this movement are manifold and amply documented. Although Zola has been recognized as an author of international stature, he seems to have been eclipsed in the university setting and even for the general reader by figures such as Joyce, Proust, Kafka, and even Zola's predecessor, Flaubert, greater gods of modernism. However, in the field of film adaptation, Zola has eclipsed all of these authors.⁴

If the reader selects well-known characters created by Zola, such as Etienne Lantier, Nana, Gervaise (so many women), and other participants in the *Rougon-Macquart* cycle of twenty novels,⁵ a common link might be their "ordinariness." There is no Romeo, Hamlet, Tiny Tim, or Uriah Heep annually recycled by the various media outlets on holidays or for basic box-office appeal, to account for Zola's prominence in film adaptation. Who or what, then, is the typical "Zola character" and what makes this character significant to the reader and to the cinema? When Zola writes about "Le Naturalisme au Théâtre," he expresses his conception of a more sophisticated form of personal psychology, either innate or environmental in origin, which shapes the identity and "drive" of individuals:

> J'attends qu'on plante debout au théâtre des hommes en chair et en os, pris dans la réalité et analysés scientifiquement, san un mensonge.
> J'attends qu'on nous débarrasse des personages fictifs, de ces symbols convenus de la vertu et du vice qui n'ont aucune valeur commes documents humains. J'attends que les milieux déterminent les personages et que les personnages agissent d'après la logique des faits combinée avec la logique de leur proper tempérament ... notre théâtre sera naturaliste ou il ne sera pas.⁶

If the reader substitutes the word "cinema" for "stage," an important insight is provided into how character, plot, and the overall narrative process is formulated: environment, genetics, and the influence of an era/milieu are the prominent agencies that shape a post-supernatural human destiny in naturalist fiction and film.⁷ Characters are motivated by a pre–Freudian determinist psychology, the surfacing of repressed instincts, animal in origin. For example, in Renoir's *La Bête humaine* (1938), Jacques Lantier, a vision of working class atavism becomes sexually aroused and then nearly strangles young Flore, only to be interrupted by the passing of a train, a sign of civilization. Jacques is "the human beast," responding to near-genetic impulses he cannot control or totally understand, only experience. The train, which plays a critical role in Zola's *La Bête humaine* and its subsequent film adaptations, is an ideal claustrophobic naturalist setting, with enclosed compartments and compressed passageways; it is a laboratory for the examination of predatory behavior. The constant motion, power, and presence of the train are visually juxtaposed with literal and encoded images of Jacques' physical and biological entrapment. Self and the world he inhabits trap Jacques. These are moments in the life of the human animal.

The image connotes the naturalist moment of experience. Antonin Artaud has commented on this form of aesthetic representation: "The human skin of things, the epidermis of reality: this is the primary raw material of cinema. Cinema exalts matter and reveals it to us in its profound spirituality, in its relation with the spirit from which it has emerged."[8] The substance of the surface of things, the image, "[imposes] an objective synthesis more penetrating than any abstraction ... that moves the mind by osmosis ... [and] rediscovers the original order of things."[9] For example, in Roger Vadim's *The Game Is Over* (1966), father, husband, and industrialist Alexandre Saccard is depicted as the "leader of the pack" of guard dogs that protect his mansion and family. In one early shot sequence, he playfully sets these dogs on his son, but nobody is hurt. In a later shot, after leaving his wife's room, and strongly suspecting her of adultery with his son (her stepson), the shot cuts to Alexandre feeding the anxious dogs. Alexandre's power over his family/animals, initially represented by an act of playful aggressiveness, now involves a re-assertion of male control, represented by the active and primal consumption of meat. These contrasting images from the human and animal world are suggestive and direct, without abstraction. This is the essential reason why Zola appeals to the visual medium of film: one *sees* as a demarcation point to observe, reflect, conclude, and even to learn.

It is a visual and material process of motion that, for the artist and man, Zola has been informed by history, science, art, and a world of experience. Zola's life incorporates the evolution of the photographic arts; the redesigning of Paris during the Second Empire; the failed "glory" of the Second Empire; the revolt and suppression of the Paris Commune; significant debates in the scientific community involving evolution, medicine, criminal anthropology, and overall clinical methodologies; the emerging trends in modern art of realism and impressionism; the rise of a public, consumer culture predicated on sociological, economic, gender and class-bound practices; and ultimately, the Dreyfus Affair. This was Zola's France of the nineteenth century. The milieu is not an affected prop; it is a complex signifying system. In regard to film narrative practice, Claude Aveline has stated that "the milieu is never simply a décor; rather it plays an essential role ... milieu determines everything."[10] For Zola, social and historical experiences were immediately referential. These are not influences but absorptions, layers of experience to be recalled and revised as a narrative, intertextual practice.

This intertextual frame of reference suggests a model for the reception and analysis of Zola's literary and adapted film texts. According to Laurent Jenny, intertextuality situates the reader/viewer as the agency that unites a text. The reader/viewer superimposes meaning upon meaning, text upon text, thus transforming the narrative into interrelated perceptions and quotations. The intertextual "does not imply a confused and mysterious accumulation of influences, but a work of transformation and assimilation of several texts performed by a centering text."[11] For example, when the informed viewer witnesses the abusive behavior and struggle of the alcoholic father in D.W. Griffith's *A Drunkard's Reformation* (1909), s/he actively recalls Zola's *L'Assommoir*, as well possessing an awareness of subsequent stage adaptations and numerous social, historical and literary texts, which form a core, linking set of narratives.[12]

Zola's naturalist novels and their subsequent film adaptations invoke the primacy of the senses, particularly the visual, to engage the reader/audience in the act of *seeing*. The typical Zola narrative involves an affected authorial distancing, a process of posed clinical observation and experimentation in the immediate environment to examine both the local and broader social and biological systems of (dis)order. It is an art and science of the dynamic, suggestive surface that actively connotes an ideological set of assumptions. Of course, these theoretical assumptions are privileged acts; Zola's art is no more objective or scientific than that of any other practitioner of a modern system of representation. The *"truth"* is in the positioning of the author as spectator. In practice, however imperfect, Zola's theories inform Zola's art, and his naturalist, experimental novels are representative moments of a determinist process. For example, in a lesser-known short story by Zola, "Celle Qui M'aime," (1864), his first published work, a young woman informs a male admirer how she makes her living:

> Je m'habille chaque soir de mousseline blanche. Seule dans une sorte de réduit, appuyée au dossier d'un facteuil, j'ai pour tout travail à sourire depuis six heures jusqu'à minuit.
> ... En face de moi, derrière une petite vitre enchâssée dans la cloison, je vois sans cesse un oeil qui me regarde. Il est tantôt noir, tantôt bleu.... Par moments, à le recontrer toujours seul et fixe, il me prend de folles terreurs ... [M]ais il faut bien travailler pour vivre. Je souris, je salue, j'envoie un baiser.[13]

This young working class female, subject of a pervasive and paying unscrupulous male gaze, is spied upon in the act of being "adorable." She is an object of desire and willingly participates in this voyeuristic performance, like her fictional successor, Nana. Her audience knowingly accepts the illusion. In essence, she is watched, *seen*, as she plays an idealized, sexual image of herself; it's what the male audience wants to believe, what she connotes.

With Zola's fiction, the reader is the observer who interprets phenomena, a form of intellectual postulating, in the naturalist narrative, the process and product of his experimental fiction. Zola's "scientific methodology," as delineated in his theoretical writings and "put to practice" initially in the preface and text of *Thérèse Raquin* (1887), suggests that the reader observes/gazes at the naturalist human experiment, from a clinical, generally voyeuristic, and privileged position of knowing. The author is engaged in the process of grounding what is ideological into the discerned narrative, and this is linked to the social and biological sciences.

This signals a theoretical shift from realism's myth of the "invisibility of the author," a narrative presence of controlling absence, invoked, for example, in Flaubert's *Madame Bovary*, in which notions of verisimilitude are given a historical and social context in bourgeois society to examine the inherent state and conditions of authorial and fictive disillusionment. In the realist novel, the failure of the modern world to formulate ideological and empirical coherence for human experience is linked with historical and social issues involving capital and consumerism, class and consciousness, and a commitment to the surface of the "real," that is, how life is lived.

The naturalist author, Zola in particular, encodes in his fiction the system of seeing = knowing. This suggests a context of interpretation of the social constructions depicted in the realist and subsequent naturalist novel and its film adaptation. It is not the "truth" but an explanation and exploration of the idea of truth. Zola's naturalism, the theory and practice, is not a substitute revealed religion or even clinically objective as the scientific process it alleges to imitate. Naturalist literature and its film adaptation build upon this textual practice; the visual is the connotative "real" in modern consciousness. This suggests why Zola consistently appeals to the technological and aesthetic practice of international cinema. The theoretical foundation of his naturalist art continues the process, the visual agenda that realism proposes. Zola's naturalism adds an informing ideological framework, incorporating art, science, and history. Zola's appeal to international cinema has proven to be consistent in the new millennium, and this includes stage versions of the novels and other artistic venues.[14]

Zola and Film: Essays in the Art of Adaptation has been a collaborative, decade-long process in the making. Since 1991, the AIZEN, the International Association for Multidisciplinary Approaches and Comparative

Studies Related to Émile Zola and his Time, Naturalism, Naturalist Writers and Artists, Naturalism and the Cinema around the World, has been dedicated to the purpose of discovering, promoting, and expanding the study of Émile Zola, naturalism, film interrelations, and of facilitating communication amongst the academic disciplines. This collection of essays, the product of the collective and individual research and scholarship produced by the AIZEN, explores the dynamic relationship between Zola's fiction and its film adaptations. This text makes available, for the first time in English or any language, essays that examine critically significant cinematic adaptations of Zola's novels from a variety of theoretical and interdisciplinary perspectives, and it is prepared for a twenty-first century audience in search of new, lost, or even unknown titles from international cinema. In order to appeal to a wide range of readership, these essays will provide, as endnote references, translations of all French and other languages. Unless noted, the respective author of the article is responsible for all translations appearing in the text.

No text on Zola and film adaptation would be complete without the contribution of Russell Cousins, who has graciously submitted two essays. The first, "Antoine's Version of *La Terre*: An Experiment in Naturalist Cinema," discusses how this filmmaker worked within the limitations of the silent cinema to produce *La Terre* (1921). This adaptation posed several challenges, not only involving film technique but also film censorship, considering the notoriety of Zola's naturalist text. Cousins' essay provides the reader with a look into Antoine's approach to filmmaking, and Antoine's experience as a theatre director committed to Zola's naturalist concepts.

In a more experimental vein, with an emphasis on a theoretical exchange rather than a more traditional adaptation process, Tony Williams' "Eisenstein and Zola: Naturalism, Cinema, and Mythography" discusses the affinity between Zola and Eisenstein and reveals Zola's importance to Eisenstein's cinematic aesthetic and practice. Williams examines how both talents never adhered exclusively to the principles they affirmed in their different eras but how they often creatively interacted and transcended the boundaries they set for themselves.

Heather Howard's "Staging the Courtesan: Taking Zola's *Nana* to the Movies" comparatively explores Zola's novel *Nana* and Jean Renoir's 1926 silent film adaptation. It focuses on the manner in which the courtesan is affected by the male gaze while immersed in interplay between presence/visibility, as well as absence/occlusion, thus demonstrating the dynamics of the "specular side" of prostitution.

The second essay concerned with Zola's and Renoir's *Nana*, Katherine Golsan's "From Theater to Cinema: Jean Renoir's Adaptation of *Nana*," presents an analysis of the spatial dynamics manifest in Zola's novel, particularly as concrete and symbolic manifestations of the interpenetration of classes during the Second Empire. In this adaptation of *Nana*, Golsan examines the failure of class barriers to protect against biological and social forms of conflict, which occur in many scenes leading up to Nana's deathbed.

In "The Eye Behind the Writing Hand: Surveillance and Adaptation in *La Bête humaine*," Monica Filimon discusses Renoir's second adaptation of a Zola novel and concludes that while the text may be interpreted as traditional thriller, whose characters cannot escape the entanglements of their nature and milieu, one may read both texts as the expression of power relations and the role played by seeing and being seen in the development of the events.

Klaus Peter Walter's "La Rançon du progrès: Naturalistic Discourse and Two Adaptations of Zola's *Au Bonheur des Dames*" closely reads both film adaptations of the eleventh volume of *Rougon-Macquart*, published in 1883. This article examines Julien Duvivier's *Au Bonheur des Dames* (1930), a silent film whose effects are derived from powerful visual impressions, while the 1943 version of the same title, directed by André Cayatte, utilizes a soundtrack and an effective mise-en-scène, typical of the "qualité française." This essay explores significant characteristics of both films as models of naturalist discourse and economics.

Jennifer Wolter's "Viewing *Au Bonheur des Dames* in the Context of Occupied France" takes a comprehensive look at André Cayatte's 1943 film adaptation of Zola's novel. Although largely overlooked by critics and the public alike, this film, according to Wolter, is a worthy subject for study on two levels: as a film produced under the German Occupation during World War II, containing encoded anti-Nazi sentiment as well as more overt signs of French national pride, and because the film revisits many of the issues brought to light in Zola's novel involving the struggle of the small business enterprise with the emergence of big business, "*le grand magasin.*"

Alicja Helman's essay, "*Thérèse Raquin* in a Fog-Covered Corner," provides a comparative analysis and interpretation of the relationship between Zola's novel *Thérèse Raquin* and Marcel Carné's adaptation (1953). This essay examines the difficulties associated with classification of the latter text. Carné's unusually personal film is independent of its literary prototype, which it transforms in a manner characteristic of twentieth-century culture.

In Russell Cousins' second essay, "Ideology and Focalization in *Gervaise*: The Aurenchébost/René Clément Treatment," he examines the critical acclaim accorded to *Gervaise* (1956), directed by René Clément, from a script by Jean Aurenche and Pierre Bost. Cousins discusses the writers' contribution to *Gervaise*, not only in terms of the ideological inflection given to Zola's working class narrative but also in terms of the film's dramatic development and the cinematic deployment of *focalization*.

Elisabeth-Christine Muelsch's essay, "The Female Reader in *Pot-Bouille* and Duvivier's Cinematic Representation," concludes that Duvivier addresses Zola's concern for female education through his attention to the practice of reading. Female literacy becomes a structuring element of the film. Muelsch's article investigates Duvivier's reading scenes, focusing on multiple representations of the reading woman and the active female reader of the text/film.

Anna Gural-Migdal's "The Fabrication of Claude Berri's *Germinal*" analyzes the critical reception/misreading of Berri's (1993) film, viewed by some as ideologically reductive, and the manner in which Berri's adaptation respects the way the novelist thought out and "manufactured" his novel. According to Gural-Migdal, Berri was strongly influenced by the reserve of memories established by Zola in his catalogue of character sketches for the novel. Gural-Migdal maintains that Berri's film differs from Zola's novel in its pessimistic view of the world and awareness of loss at hand.

Laurent Marie's study, "Nostalgia Is Hard to Let Go: The French Communist Party's Reception of Claude Berri's Filmic Adaptation of *Germinal*," explores one of the most expensive productions in the history of French cinema. Berri's adaptation received an enormous amount of media coverage, particularly in the French Communist Party (PCF) daily newspaper *L'Humanité*. Marie analyzes the reception of the Communist press, within a historical dimension, as well as discussing its views on previous film adaptations of *Germinal* and other related mining films.

My essay, "'At the Still Point': Framing the Naturalist *Moment*," examines the critical framing of the naturalist experience in the shot analysis of select stills from various Zola adaptations. I link the dynamic of the still, its aesthetic composition, to a broader theoretical practice of intertextual naturalist precepts.

When Zola asserted: "Si le dix-septième siècle est resté le siècle du théâtre, le dix-neuvième siècle sera le siècle du roman,"[15] then it does not strain the imagination of the reader to conclude that the twentieth century, as *Zola and Film: Essays in the Art of Adaptation* suggests, has been the century of the cinema. As for the twenty-first century, the editors of this text anticipate new adaptations, more "found footage," and alternative forms of media interpretation to keep naturalist theory and fiction, the art of Zola, in the foreground of representation.

Notes

1. Leo Braudy, "Zola on Film: Ambiguities of Naturalism," *Yale French Studies*, no.42 (New Haven: Yale University Press, 1969): 68.

2. Russell Cousins, "Was Judas a Woman? Re-Inventing Zola for the Cinema," *New Approaches to Zola*, ed. Hannah Thompson (London: The Émile Zola Society, 2003), 111–112.
3. Robert Stam, *Film Theory* (Massachusetts: Blackwell Publishers, 2000), 16.
4. This is not the place to mount a defensive strategy in support of Zola, his theories or practice, since both historical and contemporary debates among literary and film scholars concerning realism, naturalism, and the value of taxonomy and classification are most often relegated to theoretical dogma or personal taste that excludes the more objective and dispassionate form of scholarship that avoids the "divide and conquer" syndrome in favor of textual explorations. Admittedly, taste and theory inform one's critical perspective and overall judgment, but must they dominate or subvert the exploration of the text, especially in its capacity to lead to and reveal other systems of narrative representation? Adjectives aside, the "ranking" of the author and his/her related production excludes the due process of historical reception and intertextual analysis.
5. Of course, not all of Zola's fiction was part of the famous cycle of twenty novels; for example, *Thérèse Raquin* was published prior to the series. In addition to this, the reader should be aware of Zola's theatrical adaptations of his own work, short stories, art criticism, and his various forays into reportage and even the photographic arts.
6. Émile Zola, "Le Naturalisme au Théatre," *Le Roman Expérimental* (Paris: Garnier Flammarion, 1971), 163, 173. "I am waiting for the [dramatists], in the first place, to put a man of flesh and bones on the stage, taken from reality, scientifically analyzed, without one lie. I am waiting for them to rid us of fictitious characters, of conventional symbols of virtue and vice which possess no value as human data. I am waiting for the surroundings to determine the characters, and for the characters to act according to the logic of facts.... Our stage will be naturalistic, or it will cease to exist." Émile Zola, "The Experimental Novel," *The Experimental Novel and Other Essays*, trans. Belle Sherman (New York: Haskell House, 1964), 142,157.
7. This is an obvious paraphrase of Hippolyte Taine's theoretical overview of naturalism.
8. Antonin Artaud, "Cinema and Reality," *French Film Theory and Criticism, 1907–1939*, vol.1, ed. Richard Abel, trans. Helen Weaver (Princeton: Princeton University Press, 1988), 412.
9. *Ibid.*, 412.
10. Claude Aveline, "Film and Milieux," *French Film Theory and Criticism, 1907–1939*, vol.2, ed. Richard Abel (Princeton: Princeton University Press, 1988), 246.
11. Laurent Jenny, "La Stratégie de la Forme," quoted in Mikhail Iampolski, *The Memory of Tiresias: Intertextuality and Film*, trans. Harsah Ram (Berkeley, University of California Press, 1995), 36.
12. The reader may wish to read about *A Drunkard's Reformation* and other Griffith appropriations of Zola's naturalist aesthetic in the article by Diane Smith and Robert Singer, "A Drunkard's Representation: The Appropriation of Naturalism in D.W. Griffith's Biograph Films," *Griffithiana*, no.65 (1999): 97–125.
13. Émile Zola, "Celle Qui M'aime," *Contes a Ninon* (Saint-Amand: Imprimerie Bussière, 1955), 66–67. "Every evening I dress up in white muslin. Then I stand leaning over the back of an armchair, all alone in a tiny room, and the only thing I have to do is to smile from six o'clock until midnight.... All the time I can see an eye watching me through a little pane of glass in the partition. Sometimes it's blue, sometimes, it's brown.... There are times, as I watch that solitary eye staring at me, when I feel quite terrified ... but you've got to work to stay alive and so I smile, wave my hand and throw kisses." Émile Zola, "The Girl Who Loves Me," *The Attack on the Mill and Other Stories*, trans. Douglas Parmée (Oxford: Oxford University Press, 1989), 12.

14. Some recent examples: In New York, the Classic Stage Company produced Neal Bell's "off–Broadway" adaptation of *Thérèse Raquin* (1997), which removed all naturalist tensions and references. A Broadway musical production of *Thérèse Raquin*, entitled, *Thou Shalt Not*, was produced in 2001. This production set Zola's narrative in the WWII era, in New Orleans, and it was directed by Susan Stroman, with music/lyrics composed by Harry Connick, Jr. As recently as 2003, the Aurora Theatre Company of Berkeley, CA, produced *The Lives of Thérèse Raquin*, developed by dramaturge Daniel Olmstead. Malcolm McKay's *Cruel Train*, an adaptation of *La Bête humaine*, was produced for television in 1995.

15. Zola, "Le Naturalisme au Théatre," 165. "If the seventeenth century was the century of the stage, the nineteenth will belong to the novel." "Naturalism on the Stage," Zola, "The Experimental Novel," Sherman trans., 146.

1

Antoine's Version of *La Terre*: An Experiment in Naturalist Cinema

RUSSELL COUSINS

For the filmmaker working within the limitations of the silent cinema, a screen version of *La Terre* (1921) inevitably posed several challenges in terms not only of filming technique, but also of censorship thresholds.[1] Given the notorious reputation of Zola's naturalist epic of brutish farming mores, any production company would have to be wary about the film's potential content, while a script which necessitated extensive location work would itself create difficulties for an industry much more accustomed to studio-based productions. For André Antoine, however, questions of propriety and creative convention were precisely the issues he sought to confront as a self-declared naturalist filmmaker.[2] Indeed, his projected version of *La Terre* would provide a further opportunity to experiment with an approach to filmmaking rooted in his years of experience as a theatre director committed to Zola's naturalist concepts.[3] His first task, however, was to devise a viable film treatment which would meet the studio values of Pierre Decourcelle's respected production company, the *Société des Auteurs et des Gens de Lettres* (*S.C.A.G.L.*) and, in this respect, his earlier experience of producing a stage version of the novel in 1902 was invaluable.[4] An outline of Zola's problematic source text and Antoine's censored screen version is required before consideration can be given to the defining characteristics of the naturalist film style instituted by Antoine.

Antoine's Source Material: Zola's La Terre *(1887)*

Though evoking the beauty of the countryside and subscribing to a pantheistic vision of mother Earth, Zola provides a less than flattering portrait of the farming community.[5] His decidedly unsentimental account of brutish, tight-fisted farmers driven by greed and primitive survival instincts was intended to puncture rose-tinted romantic images of the utopian ideal. His morally debased, godless characters are strangers to altruism and will stop at nothing to retain their hold on their land, readily resorting to violence and even to murder where necessary. The main illustration of these primitive values is provided by the tragic story of the aging Père Fouan, whose foolish decision to divide his land between his uncaring children turns him into a peasant version of Shakespeare's King Lear. The once powerful figure is reduced to spending his remaining unhappy years with his three ungrateful and mercenary offspring: his daughters Lise and Fanny, married to Buteau and Delhomme, respectively, and his dissolute son Hyacinthe, nicknamed Jésus-Christ. Newcomers, such as the former soldier Jean Macquart or Hourdequin, seeking to mechanize farming, or those, such as priests and schoolteachers, with less materialistic concerns, find integration into this self-interested, closed community all but impossible.

In a carefully documented narrative, Zola follows the farming calendar, setting his action within the seasonal patterns of sowing and harvesting and in terms of animal husbandry. His narrative seeks to illustrate the farmer's relationship with the earth and explores issues such as free trade and collective farming. His treatment is both bluntly realistic and lyrical in its evocation of nature and the cyclical patterns of birth, death, and regeneration. In his epic vision, man is constantly depicted against the vast rolling plains of La Beauce as an insignificant being, haplessly engaged in a timeless life-and-death struggle with the forces of nature.

Contemporary critics normally hostile to Zola were further outraged by his unvarnished account of country life, and even his most fervent supporters were moved to condemn the novel as a betrayal of naturalist values. His explicit account of degraded human behavior, including rape, incest, and murder, not to mention erotic imagery, animal reproduction, and several scatological episodes, provoked expressions of moral indignation. Previously accepted notions of realism were considered to have been transgressed, and five of his former unquestioning disciples took Zola to task in a highly critical article published in *Le Figaro*.[6] Clearly, a screen version of such a contentious novel would not be without difficulties.

Antoine's Screen Adaptation[7]

Understandably, Antoine's reworked narrative reveals a number of changes, some of which were doubtless required to satisfy commercial imperatives and censorship norms.[8] Zola's wide-ranging thematic exploration of attitudes and issues is narrowed to Père Fouan's treatment at the hands of his heartless family. Character studies are foreground at the expense of the author's original conception, which focused on the land itself as the principal protagonist,[9] while further dramatic concentration is achieved by reducing the enormous range of individuals to key family members and those essential to plot development. In terms of Zola's explicitness, Antoine's answer to anticipated censorship appears to have been self-censorship, with the novel's more notorious episodes judiciously modified or omitted.

In his paring down of Zola's original narrative, Antoine discards characters and situations having little direct relevance to Père Fouan's tragedy, with the inevitable loss of the sense of the wider community achieved in the novel. There is no place for the despairing village priest l'Abbé Godard or his replacement l'Abbé Madeleine, the undervalued schoolteacher Lequeue, or local politicians such as Chédeville. Though a number of humorous episodes are retained, those involving the Charles' brothel at Chartres are discarded with the corresponding omission of Estelle and Elodie. Doubtless with an eye on propriety, scatological elements disappear with the suppression of La mère Caca and the memorable flatulence of Jésus-Christ, notably in his explosive dismissal of the bailiff seeking to evict him. A chorus of mocking village children replaces the poacher's celebrated cannonade. Neither is there place for an account of the wine harvest with the associated drunken behavior and the comedy involving Gideon, the ass.

To remain within more self-evident censorship constraints, the number of violent or sexually motivated episodes is also greatly reduced. Buteau's repeated sexual harassment of Françoise is less explicit, while her fatal rape at his hands becomes an accidental death, when she falls on her scythe. The declining Père Fouan no longer exposes himself, and his death results from callous neglect rather than the brutal murder and incineration by Buteau and Lise. In the same vein, the omission of Palmyre and her brother Hilarion removes both the treatment of incest and Hilarion's attempted rape of La Grande. Finally Tron's jealous killing of Hourdequin and his subsequent burning down of La Borderie have no part to play in the reworked conclusion. In Antoine's less apocalyptic ending, Fouan's lonely death in the fields is set against positive images of renewal, as La Cognette greets the dawn as the newly installed mistress of La Borderie.

Antoine's refashioning of Zola's material reveals the degree of compromise required by even the most dedicated of naturalist disciples in producing an acceptable screen adaptation of *La Terre* in the early twenties. It will be recalled that Zola himself had recognized such difficulties when reflecting on the differences between the private experience of reading and the theatrical adaptation of the same narrative. In *Le Naturalisme au théâtre* he readily conceded that the creative artist was inevitably subjected to greater moral and aesthetic constraints in the shaping of material for public performance: "le lecteur isolé tolère tout ... même lorsqu'il se fâche, tandis que les spectateurs pris en masse ont des pudeurs, des effarements, des sensibilités dont il faut tenir compte, sous peine de chute certaine."[10]

The Evolution of Antoine's Naturalist Film Style

Before turning his attention to filmmaking, Antoine had championed Zola's cause for naturalist drama through a series of experimental productions at his *Théâtre libre* and later at the *Théâtre Antoine*. Here, realist plays, which included adaptations of Zola's novels, were performed in a style that attempted to be as close to lived experience as was possible. Serious attempts were made with the mise-en-scène to convey Zola's posited interplay between character and environment with a more realistic rather than a stylized setting in which authentic objects replaced the traditionally painted objects of theatrical trompe-l'œil. In his production of *La Terre* (1902), for example, Antoine brought to the stage mounds of earth with planted corn, live animals and genuine farm implements.[11] In terms of dialogue, writers were expected to reflect more closely the register and rhythms of everyday speech. Actors were required to adopt a more natural delivery thus abandoning the declamatory style of Boulevard theatre. Perhaps Antoine's greatest innovation, however, was to train his actors to perform as though the traditional proscenium arch had been replaced by a "fourth wall" that screened them from the audience, thus turning their public performance into a more private and intimate drama. It followed from this that the expressive theatrical gestures normally deployed by actors to reach out to spectators should be minimized and rather than deliver their lines to the audience they should now address each other directly.[12] The intended effect was to turn the audience from public spectators into unseen witnesses of a drama played out in private.

Despite these innovations in performance, Antoine was still acutely aware of the limitations of the stage and with cinema's greater flexibility in terms of scene setting, scene changes, and the potential of shifting viewpoint, he was determined to extend further Zola's notions of naturalist drama into the realms of filmmaking. However, contemporary filmmaking practices tended to perpetuate embedded theatrical traditions rather than develop the possibilities of the new medium.[13] Although initially established as an essentially realistic medium, which provided documentary recordings of everyday actions, the cinema, as it evolved into a studio-based industry, had increasingly aligned itself with theatrical practice. Technically sophisticated studios, now lit by electric light, could ensure continuity of production whatever the weather, so that many producers preferred to reconstruct outside settings in the studio rather than film on location. At the same time, established actors, tempted away from theatre companies such as the Comédie Française brought with them years of stage craft which led them, naturally enough, to address the usually fixed camera as though they were acting to the front rows of the stalls. For many, cinema had come to mean a perfected form of theatre not an artistic medium in its own right. In short, it was in danger of remaining no more than a means of making filmed theatre available to a larger audience.

Antoine sought to break this relationship with theatrical conventions and insisted, wherever possible, on location shooting so that a greater sense of authenticity could be achieved. He also brought with him the acting style he had evolved with his own company so that actors addressed each other directly rather than the camera-as-audience. Furthermore, to get away from the filmed theatre conventions of the static camera, and to reflect more completely the reality of changing perspectives in everyday existence, he experimented with mobile cameras and point of view shots. In his hands, the camera ceased to be simply a recording instrument for rehearsed action and became part of the process of creating meaning.[14]

Towards a Definition of Naturalist Film Style: Antoine's La Terre *(1921)*

Although much reduced in its scale of treatment, Antoine's film is memorable as a technically sophisticated achievement, which manages to convey elements of Zola's social documentary together with his epic vision of man's place in nature. A number of general features will be considered before focusing on a more detailed examination of selected sequences.

In the absence of sound, and therefore spoken dialogue, intertitles guide the viewer by establishing locations and characters while also ensuring an understanding of narrative developments within the various plot strands.[15] In the opening sequence, for example, titles introduce the main characters as the camera establishes each of them in a context that reveals their occupation and their nature. The slight, solitary figure of Père Fouan is framed against the vast landscape as, single-handed, he energetically toils his land; Jean arrives, sweating from the heat of the day, and pauses to marvel at a butterfly on a blossom, a point-of-view close-up capturing his appreciation of natural beauty, a response which immediately differentiates him from the farmer concerned only with exploiting the land; a smiling, matter-of-fact Françoise arrives leading a cow, explaining that the animal is in heat and must be taken to the bull at Hourdequin's farm. Throughout, image and intertitle work in close conjunction to carry forward narrative development and character analysis.

Antoine also emulates Zola's documentary intentions. In the course of the narrative, the filmmaker provides a series of contemporary social images, including documentary footage of the market at Cloyes, women washing clothes at the riverside, local inhabitants buying and selling produce. The everyday work of the community is observed, whether in the fields, as the land is ploughed or the harvest gathered in, or as Soulas the shepherd tends his sheep from his caravan. In various farmyards the winnowing of corn or the churning of milk is recorded along with the everyday domestic duties of the farmer's wife, such as preparing food for the family meals observed in different households. The illicit activities of the poacher Jésus-Christ are similarly closely detailed as he sets traps for birds, prepares to snare animals or introduces his ferret into rabbit warrens. In episodes such as these, Antoine was satisfying a particular conception of realist film, shaped by Zola's notion of documentary literature and the Lumière brothers' pioneering work with the camera as an unrivalled means of recording everyday events.

In achieving these documentary images, Antoine was well served by his cameramen, Paul Castanet, Léonce-Henri Burel and René Gaveau. The fixed camera of the early cinema providing images of filmed theatre is here a distant memory. Traveling shots, with cameras mounted on barges and carriages, provide dynamic images of movement; sweeping panoramas survey the immensity of the land and the scale of the challenge confronting the farmer; long shots with considerable depth of field convey the smallness of the human beings engaged in their epic struggle with nature. The importance of camerawork in developing the narrative is crucial. Character motivation and reaction are captured in close-ups of faces often confirming intentions or emotions previously signaled by the intertitles, while point of view shots and subjective shots are deployed to convey personal involvement or intimate thoughts. Reaction shots invite audience identification when, for example, Père Fouan's hurt expressions follow successive rejections by his children or when he and others register pain as Jean breaks Buteau's arm during the argument over Françoise. These variable camera perspectives that mirror human perception are Antoine's cinematic equivalent to his theatrical "fourth wall," which had challenged the artificiality of the posited single audience perspective from the orchestra stalls.[16]

In his staging of plays, Antoine had often sought natural light sources to enhance the sense of reality. Interiors in the theatrical version of *La Terre*, for example, were lit primarily by on-stage household candles rather than by electric lamps. In the film version, lighting also has a considerable part to play in determining the expressiveness of particular sequences. Again, a break with the powerful studio lighting required for filming is observed with a more natural level of illumination. Dramatic, contrastive effects are achieved as silhouetted figures leave darkened interiors for sun-filled courtyards or are framed against the wide-open spaces of the land. An expressionist exploitation of light comes in the sequence depicting Lise's theft of Père Fouan's papers in the middle of the night. With Buteau keeping watch, she creeps, candle in hand, into Père Fouan's adjacent room with long shadows signaling her criminal approach and, in the tense half-light, treachery is seen to triumph under the cover of darkness.

Antoine's style is also marked by a creative use of editing. When Jésus-Christ threatens Françoise over her relationship with Jean, a series of intercut images link the conditions of Père Fouan's will, the notary's office, and Jean in the fields, conveying his realization that he must remain on good terms with her. While Jean slumbers in the hay, his romantic thoughts of Françoise are evoked as a dissolve links him to his fiancée down at the stream. Finally, a lengthy flashback sequence shows how La Trouille has snared the duck she has provided for the meal, which she now enjoys with Jésus-Christ and Père Fouan.

A more detailed analysis of two sequences serves to demonstrate more fully Antoine's cinematic approach to Zola's text, together with the growing sophistication of his naturalist film technique.

Market Day

Zola's account of market day provides Antoine with a perfect opportunity for location filming in a working village and to experiment with mobile cameras.[17] Here the director reflects Zola's aims by blending narrative development with documentary as professional actors play out their roles alongside ordinary market traders selling their wares. The customary intertitles set the scene and convey the unheard dialogue.

The sequence, which lasts three minutes and twenty seconds, is narrated through seven intertitles and composed of twenty-seven different camera shots. The action begins with Jean, Lise, and Françoise arriving by horse and trap with a group of village washerwomen by the riverside, commenting, chorus-like, on the sisters' recent good financial fortune which has spurred Buteau to marry Lise. Buteau is duly seen arriving at market on foot, shortly to be followed by La Cognette in another trap. The ensuing action is developed within the context of market activity as the fictional characters move amongst the local traders around the main village square. A second mise-en-abyme[18] narrative strand is developed within a single fixed shot showing La Trouille with her amorous rivals Delphin and Nénesse. Apart from this scene and the one with the chorus of washerwomen where a degree of theatricality is noted, the naturalness of the acting style required by Antoine has a remarkable degree of consistency and authenticity, with professional performers almost indistinguishable from genuine villagers.

Antoine's second important innovation, it will be recalled, was to tell the action through the camera rather than use the camera simply to record the action. His mobile camera moves with the characters, includes point of view shots and draws attention to objects and expressive faces in a series of creative close-ups. This participatory camera style transforms the viewer into an involved witness with privileged access to the events unfolding. Françoise's jealousy at La Cognette's apparent interest in Jean is conveyed in close shots of her hurt observation, while Jean's self-congratulation at the attention he receives is suggested by an associative montage close-up shot of a content turkey. Here, as in other sequences, Antoine deploys creative editing to convey non-verbally dramatic significance. His use of several cameras to relate different narrative elements and changing perspectives within a sequence reproduces in the cinema the effect he had sought to achieve in the theatre, albeit imperfectly, by seeking to abolish the single perspective of the framing proscenium arch. The experimental deployment of the mobile camera is particularly apparent in the final moments of the sequence as the trap leaves the village. Here, a camera mounted at the front of the trap conveys the forward motion while two further high-angled cameras, one fixed, one mobile, show the trap leaving the village behind. As Susan Hayward notes:

Naturalism as an effect ... places the spectator voyeuristically. We take up the position of the mediating camera. The characters seem so natural, their dialogue or verbal interchanges so real, the setting and mise-en-scène so totally realistic that an easy identification takes place. We are there alongside the characters.[19]

Closure

Any *Zolian* narrative works, not only in terms of accurately observed reality, but also in terms of the writer's transforming symbolism. Antoine, too, produced from his naturalist film style a defining degree of symbolic suggestion, as has been already instanced in our account of lighting, framing, and expressive montage.

The film's most developed montage sequence is reserved for the denouement with the narrative virtually dispensing with intertitles. As night falls, the outcast Père Fouan is pictured as a solitary figure lost in the vast fields he once owned and, as snow begins to fall, the bent figure of the old man supporting himself on sticks is pictured looking in vain for shelter. The sequence is punctuated by pointed associative montage images as the homeless Père Fouan is turned away in turn by each member of his family. The shepherd has his hut and the dog its kennel, but Père Fouan has nowhere; even the church is locked, denying the godless old man sanctuary.

Images of cruel defeat and joyful triumph mark the film's closure as Père Fouan is left to die in the fields and La Cognette celebrates the new day and her new beginning as mistress of La Borderie. A series of alternating contrastive images shows this double narrative. Dawn brings out the farmyard animals: in a series of intercut shots, geese, chickens, the farm cat and dog, and, later, rabbits are seen emerging from their slumbers. A smiling La Cognette rises from her bed and prepares herself for the day ahead. Meanwhile, Père Fouan is seen as an insignificant stumbling figure against the vast landscape, appearing to bend ever closer to the earth as his days draw to a close. The two narrative lines are drawn together by a linked image. Framed at her window, La Cognette stretches out her arms to embrace the new day as Père Fouan, mirroring these gestures, falls to the ground he has so loved, his arms outstretched as though crucified. A final intertitle echoes in part the concluding message of Zola's novel: "And only the earth is immortal, the Mother from whom we all spring and to whom we all return."[20]

Zola's writing is full of color, sounds, realistic dialogue, erotic imagery, poetic evocations of the forces of nature, and constantly changing perspectives. For the filmmaker working with monochrome film in the silent era, with cameramen more accustomed to the static framing of the studios, a version of *La Terre* shot on location required a considerable degree of creative imagination and technical inventiveness. Antoine was more than prepared to meet the challenge of Zola's naturalist material and his solutions effectively contribute to a definition of naturalist cinema. Actors are seen to adopt a more realistic, less theatrical performance style and, in shooting his film, Antoine readily opts for location work with mobile cameras and, wherever possible, natural lighting. Cameras are used creatively to provide shifting perspectives and to trace different threads of the narrative in a blend of documentary social observation and dramatic fiction. At the editing stage, as a good disciple of Zola, Antoine goes beyond surface reality to convey concepts symbolically through associative montage. His commitment to a naturalist style of filmmaking necessitated an experimental approach that challenged the dominant theatrical conventions and constraints of predominantly studio-bound productions. By calling these practices into question, Antoine not only advanced the cause of naturalist cinema but of cinema itself.

Notes

1. Antoine's film was two years in the making (1919–1921), with location work in and around the village of Cloyes in the Beauce region during 1920. Credits: director, André Antoine; screenplay, André Antoine; assistant directors, Georges Denola and Julien Duvivier; photography, Paul Castanet, Léonce-Henry Burel, René Gaveau and René Guychard; production, Société des Auteurs et Gens de Lettres (S.C.A.G.L), Silent, B/W, 97 mins. The film was released on 29 September 1921. Cast: Armand Bour (Père Fouan); Jean Hervé (Louis known as "Buteau"); René Alexandre (Jean); Jeanne Briey (Lise); Germaine Rouer (Françoise); René Hiéronimus (Nénesse); Berthe Bovy (Olympe known as "La Trouille"); Milo (Hyacinthe known as "Jésus-Christ"); Jeanne Grumbach (La Cognette); Max Charlier (Bécu); Emile Desjardins (Soulas, the shepherd); Léon Malavier; Armand Numès. For contemporary critical reviews, see *Le Courrier cinématographique* 36 (1921): 71; *La Cinématographie française* (3 Sept. 1921): 29–31; Hebdo-Film 36 (3 Sept. 1921): 41–43. For many years it was thought that Antoine's film had been destroyed. However, Philippe Ensault traced a copy to Russian archives and after restoration work at the Cinémathèque française, the film was screened at the Pompidou Center on 7 June 1990. This study is based on the same Moscow Gosfilmofond copy, which was made available to the Royal Belgian Film Archive and screened on British Television by Thames TV with English intertitles. The music that accompanies this version was composed by Adrian Johnston. The film was recently released on DVD by the Milestone Company, USA.

2. For a discussion of Zola's influence on early film aesthetics, see G. Sadoul, "Zola et le cinéma français," *Europe XXX* (1952): 169.

3. André Antoine (1858–1943) founded the Théatre libre, dedicated to the performance of naturalist plays, in 1887. After the theatre closed in 1894, Antoine tried to reach a larger audience with his Théâtre Antoine in 1897, but this venture too failed, and in 1906 he became director of the Odéon until 1914. He successfully turned to the cinema with the help of his former theatrical associate, Albert Capellani, and produced a number of films adapted from literary sources for Pierre Decourcelle's production company S.C.A.G.L. These included *Les Frères corses* (1915) from Alexandre Dumas, *Les Travailleurs de la mer* (1917) from Hugo, *La Terre* (1919–1921) from Zola and *L'Arlésienne* (1921) from Daudet. Antoine continued to promote his naturalist conception of cinema as film critic for *Le Journal* from 1925 to 1929. For an account of Antoine's practice as a theatre and film director, see Jean Clothia, *André Antoine* (Cambridge University Press, 1991).

4. Antoine's production of the stage adaptation in five acts and ten scenes by Saint-Arroman and Hugot opened at the Théâtre Antoine on 21 Jan 1902. Cast:

Buteau (Signoret); Lise (Fleury); Fouan (Antoine); Delhomme (Leubas); Jean (Kemm); Francoise (Becker); La Grande (Marie Laurent); Fanny (Andrée); Jésus Christ (Degeorge); Bécu (Matral); Soulas (Desfontaines).

5. Émile Zola, *La Terre* (1887). Initially serialized in *Le Gil Blas* (29 May–16 September 1887), the novel created a storm of protest not only from Zola's detractors but also from his disciples. (See below, note 6). In England, Henry Vizetelly was prosecuted under the Obscene Publications Act for publishing his translation, *The Soil* (1888).

6. *Le Manifeste des Cinq* was published above the names of Paul Bonnetain, J-H. Rosny, Lucien Descaves, Paul Margueritte, Gustave Guiches in *Le Figaro* (18 August 1887).

7. The text of the stage version was never published and the degree to which Antoine borrowed from his working knowledge of this version remains uncertain. Clothia discusses the play in *André Antoine*, 128–132.

8. In an article published in *Le Monde* celebrating Antoine's work in the cinema, it is attested that "*La Terre* (1919) jugée trop torride, est censurée." ("*La Terre* [1919] judged as too torrid, is censored"). "A le maudit," *Le Monde* (31 May 1990). No further details are provided.

9. In the *ébauche* Zola identified the land itself as the protagonist: "*La Terre*" ... C'est l'héroïne de mon livre. La terre nourricière, la terre qui donne la vie et qui la reprend, impassible. Un personnage énorme, toujours présent, emplissant le livre. L'homme, le paysan, n'est qu'un insecte s'agitant sur elle, peinant pour lui arracher sa vie; il est courbé, il ne voit que le gain à en tirer, il ne voit pas le paysage" *Ébauche*, Ms 10, 328 fol. 484. ("It is the heroine of my book. The nourishing earth, the earth that gives life and takes it back, impassive. An enormous character, always present, filling up the book. The man, the peasant, is merely an insect wriggling on her, struggling to take away her life; he is bent, he sees only the profits to be made, he does not see the scenery").

10. Émile Zola, "Le Naturalisme au théâtre," *Le Roman expérimental*, ed. Aimé Guedj (Paris, Garnier-Flammarion, 1971), 165. "The isolated reader tolerates everything ... even when he gets angry, however, spectators caught in a crowd have restraints, trepidations, and sensitivities that need to be taken into account to avoid a downfall."

11. Antoine imitated Zola's insistence on the importance of milieu in his staging of plays. He would make the décor as realistic as possible with authentic artifacts and in the case of *La Terre* used live farmyard animals and real earth. His methods already anticipated location shooting.

12. "French actors are unable to speak a word without asking you to be witness. They speak not facing but turning their backs or sides to each other. If the tenor or young premier has a declaration to make to the young première he will stand behind her in order to remain completely visible, not to her to whom he addresses himself, but to you." *Conferencia* (1 March 1923). Quoted in Clothia, *André Antoine*, 23.

13. At the time when he was working on *La Terre*, Antoine was also formulating important distinctions between the nature of the theatre and the cinema. In an article "Propos sur le cinématographe," he seeks to banish from filmmaking the following: stage acting styles, unnatural theatrical props, the tendency to recreate settings in studios rather than work on location, and the fixed camera which actors saw as a replacement audience. The article, published in *Le Film 166* (Dec. 1919), is reproduced in an English translation in Richard Abel, *French Film Theory and Criticism 1907–1939* (Princeton UP, 1993), 189–92.

14. An illustration of a more theatrical acting style and a single-take static camera is readily found in Capellani's version of *Germinal* filmed some six years earlier. In the sequence where Souvarine advocates extreme measures against the employers, he is placed in the foreground with the miners in rows behind him. They remain facing

the camera throughout in an arrangement recalling a theatrical production in which actors are advised never to turn their backs on the audience. Despite violent exchanges of views there are no point-of-view shots or close-ups as the drama unfolds. The sequence is viewed as though from the front row of the orchestra seats.

15. The narrative of *La Terre* is developed through 141 intertitles, which not only preface sequences, foreground characters and situations, but also serve to convey the unheard dialogue.

16. "Already, the camera is being handled with more independence and freedom; it is ceasing to be the fixed and immutable point around which everything is organized. Just as in the theatre it was necessary to get the actors to consent to accept the fourth wall as real and to live in the ensemble of decors instead of constantly turning toward the listener, so it ought to become necessary for the actors in the cinema to make a strict rule of ignoring the cameraman. Instead, it is he who should follow them step by step to catch all their aspects unawares, from which ever side they are presented." Quoted in Clothia, *André Antoine*, 191.

17. Zola's account of the market day appears in part 2, chapter 6, of the novel. Antoine's version is considerably condensed both in documentary description and narrative elements, though the main development concerning Buteau's plans to marry Lise is retained.

18. Mise-en-abyme refers to the film process in which an image is "placed within itself," a form of metatextual reference.

19. Susan Hayward, *Cinema Studies: The Key Concepts* (London: Routledge, 2000), 259.

20. The final intertitle is taken from Zola's closing observations in the novel: "Et la terre seule demeure l'immortelle, la mère d'où nous sortons et où nous retournons, elle qu'on aime jusqu'au crime, qui refait continuellement de la vie pour son but ignoré, même avec nos abominations et nos misères." ("And the earth alone stays immortal, the mother from whom we come out and to which we come back, her whom we love up to a crime, who recreates life continuously for her ignored purpose, even with our abominations and miseries.") *La Terre*, vol. 4 (Paris: Gallimard, "Bibliothèque de la Pléiade," 1966), 811.

2

Eisenstein and Zola: Naturalism, Cinema, and Mythography

TONY WILLIAMS

During his lifetime the Soviet director Sergei Eisenstein (1898–1948) expressed a great appreciation for the achievements of French naturalist writer Émile Zola. As youthful reader, film director, teacher, and cinema theorist, Eisenstein revealed a far greater awareness of Zola's importance than most Western and Eastern literary critics. Eisenstein and Zola both affirmed a particular *Weltanschauung*. While Eisenstein remained a committed Marxist throughout his life adapting himself to the various changes in his society, Zola affirmed his adherence to a set of principles outlined in his didactic thesis, *Le Roman expérimental* (1880). Fortunately, both talents never adhered exclusively to the principles they affirmed in their different eras but often creatively interacted and transcended the boundaries they set for themselves. Although Eisenstein's "politically correct" 1928-1929 VGIK seminar students initially criticized his interest in a writer frowned upon by one of the founding fathers of Marxism as "perverse," the director's interest in Zola was neither perverse nor limited to what we term today cinematic mise-en-scène.[1]

Eisenstein's interest formed part of his vision of a cinematic art paralleling Richard Wagner's nineteenth century definition of the *Gesamstkunstwerk*, a total work of art including opera, set design, and dramatic performance. During the thirties and forties Eisenstein moved towards a similar definition involving the combination of cinematic units of image, sound, editing, music, and color in an inclusive concept of vertical montage defined in an era antithetical to modernist, anti-realist influences shaping his earlier definition of montage as "collision." During the twenties Eisenstein reacted against *Proletkult* tendencies denying the relevance of past cultural traditions to the present, a reaction also characteristic of Leon Trotsky. Eisenstein's theoretical writings of the thirties and forties relied heavily upon past creative traditions of art, music, and literature to construct a new type of cinema based upon a synthetic conception of "organic unity and pathos." However, his interest in Émile Zola was not totally outside the parameters of brief references to the writer by the founding fathers of Marxism which reveal a much more complex picture.

Although Engels proclaimed Balzac's superiority over Zola, he does not seem to have wielded the equivalent of a papal imprimatur against the writer.[2] In an earlier letter, he describes future founder of the French Socialist Worker's Party, Paul Lafargue, (1842–1911) as young and naive. But he does not explicitly condemn his interest in a Zola in whom "he has discovered the materialist conception of history."[3] During his Siberian exile, Lenin had a photo of Zola in an album also containing images of Russian writers Herzen and Pisarev.[4] Although Lenin's political rival G.V. Plekhanov regarded Zola's "so-called experimental method" as ill-suited for a scientific study and description of great social movements since its natural-scientific methodology "fails to realize that the actions, inclinations, tastes and habits of mind of *social* man cannot be adequately explained by *physiology* or *pathology,* since they are determined by *social relationships,*"[5] neither are mutually exclusive. Leon Trotsky proclaimed Zola's superiority to the French writer Jules Romains. Unlike Romains, Zola was both spectator and participant in the events of his day. Trotsky commented, "Only a participant can be a profound spectator. Zola was a participant. That is why, with all his vulgarities and lapses, he is far above Romains: deeper, warmer, more human."[6] Although Plekhanov and Trotsky criticized the naturalist writers of Zola's day, their brief literary explorations never engage in total condemnation of Zola.[7]

Young Eisenstein avidly devoured the entire cycle of Zola's Rougon-Macquart novels at the age of ten. His autobiography mentions the great impression it made on him at the time and the influence on his future career. At the same time he discovered Daumier's lithographs in a picture book of the Paris Commune.[8] During his early period of revolutionary artistic involvement he designed sets for theatrical productions of Zola's "Les Heritiers Rabourdin" and *Pot-Bouille* in 1920.[9] Before his ill-fated Hollywood venture, Eisenstein entered into unsuccessful negotiations with Paramount to make a film about Zola and the Dreyfus case, one he intended to direct in his own inimitable way.[10] Eisenstein's inability to film a direct adaptation of the "organically felt beauty of my beloved

Zola"[11] belongs among many unrealized film projects of his career also including Karl Marx's *Kapital* and James Joyce's *Ulysses*. However, the spirit of Zola indirectly influences the films he did make as Eisenstein admits. In his 1928 reply to a questionnaire on literature and cinema, Eisenstein affirmed that, "Zola did more than anyone else for cinema" in his role as a literary "fellow traveler." He admitted an affinity between his films and key works in the Rougon-Macquart cycle claiming he reread an appropriate Zola volume before he began any new project. Eisenstein affirmed the respective influences of *Germinal*, *La Terre*, and *La Debacle* on *Strike* (1924), *The General Line* (1928), and *October* (1927). He also cited *Au Bonheur des Dames* as a key factor influencing his depiction of the Women's Death Battalion occupying the Winter Palace in *October*. Eisenstein also suggested that his enthusiasm for Zola influenced other colleagues. He claimed that the FEKS work-in-progress by Grigori Kozintsev and Leonid Trauberg which later became *The New Babylon* (1929) would be modeled upon *Le Ventre du Paris*. However, the final film contained affinities with a changed version of *Au Bonheur des Dames*, its heroine executed by reactionaries after the fall of the Paris Commune. Eisenstein also criticized V.I. Pudovkin for failing to reread Zola's *L'Argent* before filming the Stock Exchange scene in *The End of Saint Petersburg*. Eisenstein regarded Zola as being "in the methodological sense the greatest school for a filmmaker (his pages read like complete cue sheets)" or as a writer supplying directors with concrete examples of purely cinematic mise-en-scène.[12]

In his essay "On Imagery," Eisenstein criticizes devotees of the American writer John Dos Passos who believe his cinematic novels provide an ideal foundation for films. He regards the writer as borrowing exclusively from the cinema. Hence his devices are "film devices, borrowed, second-hand" using a method equivalent to reproducing one's reflection in a mirror.[13] As an alternative, he cites writers who write in a directly cinematic manner particularly Émile Zola. Zola is a writer arranging images cinematically and depicting concrete situations. Unlike Balzac who categorizes his characters and social situations in a manner inappropriate for cinematic utilization, Zola "sees concretely. He writes in terms of people, windows, shadows, temperatures."[14] While Balzac's literary depictions of social movements and people remain unsurpassed within the techniques he chooses, such techniques are insufficiently expository to lend themselves to direct cinematic adaptation in a visual medium which is far cruder and less sophisticated than the literary medium.[15] In comparison to Balzac's literary assets concerning social observation, "Zola's deficits in terms of the scope of images of people or social schematization and rationalization, which often border on oversimplification, turn out to be assets in terms of their embodiment of their details and exposition along a cinematic line."[16] In "Lessons from Literature" he compares the rich visual detail of the notary's physical environment in *La Terre* with the literary grandiose but visually schematic description of a scene in Balzac's *La Peau de Chagrin*, which is not *directly* transferable to cinema.[17] Eisenstein also recognized concrete aspects of literary description, which would ideally transfer to the more limited but visually and emotionally expressive confines of the cinema screen. Zola provides a prototype for later twentieth century practices by novelists such as Graham Greene who depicts abstract ideas by embodying them within concrete situations and directors such as Alfred Hitchcock who elevates the marginalized description of the merry-go-round in Patricia Highsmith's cerebral novel *Strangers on a Train* into a more expressive image.

Eisenstein also notes a significant relationship Zola has with French impressionist painters such as Cezanne, Degas, and Manet lending itself to cinematic treatment. He sees images of the young bar girl in Manet's painting as representing both "clots" of real detail and a "close-up."[18] Rather than attempting to represent the whole context of the social environment to which the girl belongs, Manet provides the viewer with significant, fragmented details all relevant towards understanding the nature of the entire scene. This type of impressionism is not meant to be a "method of cognizance of concrete reality" but rather "the laconic (or partial) transmission of detail moving the viewer towards a sense of unity, but a unity not necessarily philosophical."[19] Various parts, all-important in themselves, are meant to lead towards a visual and meaningful unity. Zola's literary technique of using a part to express a whole may be sketchy and lacking Balzac's "unsurpassed sculpture of images of an epoch." But it easily lends itself to shot breakdown technique. Zola, a writer who "was never condemned by Engels,"[20] lends himself to the specifics of visual embodiment in cinema. Eisenstein cites the pince-nez hanging from the hawser in *Battleship Potemkin* as one significant example of a cinematically laconic detail. As well as embodying a concrete meaning, it also lends itself to the expressive and intellectual associations of Eisenstein's montage theories.

However, Eisenstein regarded Zola's influence as extending far beyond the merely visual or metaphoric aspects of his writing. The ideal organic unity of conception necessarily needed the successful execution of an emotional effect or "pathos" for its appropriate realization. Eisenstein compared two examples from Zola's writings. He acclaimed the horse race where the mare "Nana" triumphs as being the highest point of a novel in realizing pertinent emotional tensions achieving appropriate culmination. By contrast, the deer-hunt scene concluding the first part of *Son Excellence Eugène Rougon* lacks the relevant emotional resonance to rescue it from being an artificially simplistic parallel to the savage nature of the watching courtiers. Eisenstein believes his stone lion metaphor in *Battleship Potemkin* would have been equally unsuccessful had he not preceded it with the emotionally tense Odessa Steps sequence.

In 1928 Eisenstein encouraged his students to consider the emotional effects of certain scenes in Zola's novels. He cited the sensual erotic nuances structuring the harvesting sequences in *La Terre,* the sensual atmosphere of the graveyard environment where the young lovers meet in *La Fortune des Rougons,* the hot steamy laundry environment determining the erotic relationships in *L'Assommoir,* the colossal Parisian market witnessing scenes of attempted rape and violence in *Le Ventre du Paris,* and the neglected intoxicating garden creating a sensual atmosphere in *La Faute de l'Abbé Mouret.* Observing Zola's precise descriptive powers and technical achievement, Eisenstein noted, "in each of these novels, the theme of love and its elaboration is attached to some definite material."[21] Eisenstein urged his students to pay close attention to unique situations flowing out of the given material such as noting how Nana functions in her first theatrical appearance as basic material in the same way as the market in *Le Ventre du Paris* and the particular ways in which Zola creates tension in the scenes he depicts. Whether a damp laundry with dirty linen as in *L'Assommoir,* or a warm down in the cellars of *Le Ventre du Paris,* every scene contains an accumulation of relevant details contributing to its overall nature. Thus, he urged his students to consider not only the violent nature of the harvesting scene in *La Terre* when the man throws himself on the girl but also the contributory nature of individual details such as the heat, the machines, and the surrounding workers leading up to this moment of eroticism.[22] It is a particular organic unity made up of individual competing tensions all relevant to the particular whole. Although written in 1928, this lecture is particularly relevant to Eisenstein's supposed "epistemological leap" away from the modernist montage experiments towards the more narrative confines of Socialist Realism.[23] The ideas were already present in the early writings. Changing political, economic, and industrial circumstances affecting Eisenstein led him to develop these ideas in different ways but not in a radically altered manner.

His 1939 essay rethinking the construction of *Battleship Potemkin,* "Organic Unity and Pathos in the Composition of *Potemkin,*" conceives of the film as a united whole dialectically composed of competing tensions all leading towards the successful conclusion. Emotional involvement of the spectator was paramount in this process.[24] Viewing Eisenstein's essay according to the changed cultural climate in which it appeared, the collision aspect of montage now plays a subordinate role. However, it still exists as an element of tension leading to the spectator's emotional involvement and stimulation towards experiencing the narrative. This new concept owes much to Zola's writing.

During the late thirties Eisenstein rigorously explored all aspects of artistic achievements for material relevant to his conception of cinema. In his essay "Laoccon," he notices Zola's own organic unity device of the family tree influencing the entire twenty novels. But he sees "the whole collective organism of his novels" made up of intertwining varieties of nuances and details all significantly contributing to the generalized theme of each novel whether artistic creativity in *L'Oeuvre*, lust for life in *La Joie de Vivre*, or political intrigue as in *Son Excellence Eugène Rougon*. These various tensions all lead to a unity of sorts.

> The separate features of the generalized image are so skillfully distributed throughout the cast of characters in each single novel, and so subtle and precise is his writing in depicting each bearer of these features as a living, plausible human being, that since the characters are endowed with such frankness, these features do not prevent individual features from merging into a unified generalization of an individual exhibiting all those characteristics, bringing together all the specific variants.[25]

As David Bordwell shows, Eisenstein applied the concept of montage far more broadly than in his Constructivist days finding it in works by Zola and Joyce as he explored the concept further during his career.[26] His later work explored Zola's relevance to cinema even further. In the more complete version of "Organic Unity and Pathos," Eisenstein further championed Zola's work as involving "the selection of phenomena which by themselves flow ecstatically, which of themselves are 'beside themselves,'" coinciding with "a transition from one intensity to another, from one 'dimension' to another."[27] It is a concept he applies to his perceptions of the Odessa Steps sequence in *Potemkin*, a sequence dependent upon a highly frenzied organization of shots, rhythm, movement, and tempo. Pathos and emotional tension leading to the intensity of affect in the Odessa Steps sequence characterize a Zola Eisenstein sees not as the father-figure of a scientific experimental novel but as a compiler of intense emotional sequences designed to move the reader into tensions experienced by his individual characters. Zola selects features from the real world such as the hot animal atmosphere of a Parisian market, the sultry harvest environment of Earth, and the burning hot stove of *La Bête humaine* to build particular descriptions up into emotional crescendos.

Opposite, top: **Man anxiously awaits the rampaging Cossacks:** *Battleship Potemkin* **(1925).** *Bottom:* **Man and machine are one in labor:** *Battleship Potemkin* **(1925).**

> To what extent the emotional intoxication of the atmosphere would be diminished after having lost the elements of animal warmth and heat—is for the reader himself to judge! In exactly the same way Zola builds up the desired crescendo of any nuance of expression, of any range of phenomena, increasing according to their effect. He will achieve this, not by increasing the employment of stylistic devices, but mainly by stringing out such realistic, everyday (and mostly naturalistic) details that, by their nature, as signs of everyday reality, increase proportionally to the impression they produce.[28]

Eisenstein sees Zola as anticipating the role of an editor well before the invention of the editing table. In *Le Ventre du Paris,* Eisenstein sees Zola describe women turning into fruit anticipating the visual device of a cinematic dissolve. He sees many examples in Zola's writing making it "already apparent that the method of achieving the style of *pathos* in literature is not different from the ecstatic formula we discovered in film."[29] The payday tavern scene in *Germinal* presents imagery equivalent not just to Rabelais but the "carnivalesque" devices familiar to grotesque realism.[30] However, Eisenstein insists that pathos becomes "even more inflammatory in those cases where the scenes are thematically suffused with the *pathos* of social protest, even if it were in those limited representations by means of which Zola was able to draw the images of revolution and its victory."[31] Eisenstein cites the night attack by the small army of insurgents against Plassans as one example. The director believes that Zola sees the literary significance not in the number of the insurgents but in the social nature of an event he wishes to transmit to his readers. The method is similar to Eisenstein's construction of *Battleship Potemkin.* In reality, the historical Potemkin mutiny eventually ended in miserable failure. But what was important for Eisenstein's vision was its anticipation of more successful strategies both in 1917 and beyond. Delirium, hallucination, and ecstatic excitement also characterize particular scenes in Zola's novels such as the destruction of the city in *La Debacle,* and Father Mouret's hallucination of the victory of sensual nature over the church in *La Faute de l'Abbé Mouret* when the description transcends the boundaries of both everyday reality and naturalism. Eisenstein cites a letter Zola wrote in 1894 where he sees analogies between this musical-poetic excessiveness and the techniques of Richard Wagner.[32]

Towards the end of his life Eisenstein was moving towards a definition of art emphasizing creative emotional ecstasy and seeing figures such as El Greco, Pushkin, Piranesi, Gogol, Whitman, Dostoyevsky, Tolstoy, and Zola as historical links in an artistic chain leading towards his view of cinema. In his final postscript to *Non-Indifferent Nature* written in 1945, Eisenstein ironically noted how very few Zola films captured the musical-cinematographic feature of a great French writer also acclaimed as "an astonishing master of color."³³ Renoir's *La Bête humaine* lacked "the astonishing symphony of railroads, steamships, rails, machine oil, coal, steam, and semaphores that are so attractive in the rhythm, tempo, color, texture, and sound in the novel itself."³⁴ None of the range of fervor, passion, and lyricism remained in a film necessitating an appropriate application of an impressionistically minded organic unity and emotional excess characterizing the unfulfilled legacy for a writer whose visual images anticipated the very heights of a creative cinema Eisenstein wished to achieve.

Possibly, Eisenstein wrote much more about Zola than the material currently available. Until more writings appear the following instances within Zola's writing anticipate later developments in cinema and montage.

Since Laura Mulvey's essay, "Visual Pleasure and Narrative Cinema," the concept of the gaze has occupied an important role in film studies. As originally formulated by Mulvey but since revised by her and others, the gaze formed a crucial part of the patriarchal order where the male dominated the female.³⁵ However, Zola's fiction presents a different picture. Although Abbé Faujas begins *La Conquête du Plassans* (1874) by dominating the small village, he is soon undermined by the forces he has unleashed around him.³⁶ Furthermore, Zola's fiction often presents females as powerful controllers of the gaze dominating the men around them. The most notable example is Nana's theatrical performance in the opening chapter of *Nana* (1880) where she dominates the enraptured male audience by the power of her body. Similarly, Clorinda in *Son Excellence Eugène Rougon* (1876) sensually dominates the small group of her male admirers seeking to control affairs by her body as a symbol of political capital.³⁷ Eugène Rougon, like Abbé Faujas, Brother Archangius and Aristide Saccard, attempts to repress his sexuality by finding other means of powerful sexual sublimation. He thus achieves the pinnacle of success at the end of the novel by avoiding the charms of a *femme fatale* political groupie. He does gain her admiration at the climax: "Her hand outstretched, she went up to him, her eyes moist and so deeply moved that her mere glance was a caress, and cried: 'Oh, you! After all, how beautifully strong you are!'"³⁸

Several of Zola's female characters in *La Joie de Vivre* (1884), *L'Argent* (1891) and *Dr. Pascal* (1893) emerge as among the most attractive and often well rounded of his creations. Zola perhaps recognizes that the male's acquisition of gentle, feminine qualities may be the solution towards a better society. But he is also realistic and pessimistic about this possibility. The gentle Jean Macquart becomes a sacrificial victim to the vicious "rural idiocy of country life" in *La Terre* (1887). As the best example of the Rougon family tree, Dr. Pascal is too generous and improvident for everyday life while the young Marxist revolutionary in *L'Argent* is clearly too utopian for his world. No matter how much Zola may sympathize with his idealistic creations such as Pauline Quenu in *La Joie de Vivre* who understands that "joy lies in action," both her unconscious pride, hereditary defects, and hopeless generosity limit the potentials of her action. In *La Fortune des Rougons,* Zola clearly sees that any worthwhile revolution must be one totally antithetical to bourgeois acquisitiveness, sexual excess, and personal repression. Hereditary factors influence Silvere's utopian ideals. But Zola also notes the influence of Miette. "Miette became in his mind quite essential to the abolition of pauperism and the definite triumph of the revolution."[39] Like Maxime and Renée in *La Curée,* their sexuality is stunted in the society they inhabit: "Her sweetheart treated her like a boy."[40] Gentle fragile spirits cannot survive in a climate demanding more resilience. The novel ends with the tragic death of both lovers and the triumph of the forces of reaction. In a work equating sex and death in a bourgeois society, Zola clearly anticipated a world described by radical Freudian psychoanalyst Norman O. Brown in *Life Against Death,* a world ruled by the Death Instinct sublimating Eros within the fetishistic domain of filthy lucre. Eugène and Aristide understand the system and use their energies in negative directions by repressing any inclination towards sexual desire, which has now become contaminated in the world Zola depicts.

Eugène is one of Zola's fortunate males. Others are not so lucky and succumb to the forces of sexuality and degradation in various works. Many of Zola's fictional characters such as Silvere of *La Fortune des Rougons* (1871), Florent of *Le Ventre du Paris* and Abbé Mouret of *La Faute de l'Abbé Mouret* are case texts for later twentieth century cinema studies of masculinity in crisis. Finally, in Zola's *Thérèse Raquin,* the gaze becomes the site of a power struggle between the various characters whether they be drowned husband, stroke-ridden mother, or family cat, all of whom eventually drive the guilty couple towards suicide. In 1934, Eisenstein attempted to perform *Thérèse Raquin* on a revolving stage with the paralyzed Madame Raquin haunting the lovers "with her inflexible stare." At the end of the play, she breaks from the circular tableau, her chair moving mysteriously under its own power rolling "straight toward the footlights as she glares malevolently at the audience."[41] As described by Eisenstein, this is the theatrical equivalent to the camera tracking in to a close-up.

The first novel in the Rougon-Macquart series, *La Fortune des Rougons* (1871) not only anticipates a-chronological temporal montage techniques characteristic of *Le Nouveau Roman,* Alain Resnais's *Last Year in Marienbad* (1961), *Je t'aime je t'aime* (1968), and Quentin Tarantino's *Pulp Fiction* (1994) but also reveals particular motifs also utilized by

Sergei Eisenstein. Silent films such as *Strike* (1924) and *Battleship Potemkin* (1925) use a typage technique derived from the French caricaturist Daumier to designate social types. In *Strike*, Eisenstein describes his police spies by animal names often dissolving from human into animal features. In *La Fortune des Rougons*, Zola engages in similar techniques and actually names the source of his ideas. Félicité's face resembles the "snout of a pole cat."⁴² She also buzzes round Pierre in "her grasshopper fashion."⁴³ This insect metaphor uncannily anticipates the montage device used to introduce Fowler's first memory of Alden Pyle in Graham Greene's *The Quiet American*.⁴⁴ While visiting the Rougon salon "yellow room," Pascal occupies himself by drawing Daumier-influenced caricatures of various people present. "He established identities between each of these grotesque creatures and some animal of his acquaintance."⁴⁵ The novel also contains many striking images of metaphorical literary montage metaphors several of which move into the realms of excessive description. Zola describes reactionary Monsieur Isidore Granoux whose "air of mingled satisfaction and astonishment made him resemble a fat goose whose digestion is attended by a wholesome terror of the cook."⁴⁶ Pierre and Félicité's plotting receive Zola's most grotesquely realist description hinting at dark associations between Eros and Thanatos in the service of reactionary politics.

> They kissed each other and went to sleep. On the ceiling the patch of light seemed to be assuming the shape of a terrified eye, that stared wildly and fixedly on those pale slumbering folk, who were reeking with crime beneath their very sheets, and who saw in their dreams a rain of blood falling in the room, when big drops turned into golden pieces as they splashed upon the floor.⁴⁷

This anticipates the metaphorical use of visual montage seen in later Soviet films such as Pudovkin's *Mother* (1926) with the coming of spring melting the ice on the river heralding the revolution and the equation of storm with revolution in the climax of *Storm over Asia* (1928). But in this case, it is as violent as the slaughterhouse sequence in *Strike* depicting the bloody suppression by the authorities.

Perhaps the most excessive of Zola's novels creatively breaching his scientific-naturalist theories and anticipating Eisenstein's Non-Indifferent Nature thesis dealing with the factor of excess is *Le Ventre du Paris* (1873). Hugh Shelley describes this work as an impressionist painting of light and a musical symphony of smells resembling an epic feature film.⁴⁸ The relationship of artistic forms such as painting and music to cinema occurs frequently in Eisenstein's later writings. Furthermore, in adapting to the different demands of a cinema adding both sound and color to its silent visual structure, Eisenstein developed a more sophisticated theory of montage termed vertical montage bringing all the above areas into appropriate consideration.⁴⁹

Again, Zola creatively departs from his naturalist discourse to write a visual and musical symphonic excessive text describing the world of the Parisian market, one having particular political and ideological perspectives. Commerce defines both the system and personal relationships. Returning from exile, Florent recognizes the Halles in terms reminiscent of Fritz Lang's Moloch imagery in *Metropolis*:

> It was like a great central organ furiously pulsing and pumping the blood of life into every vein; sounds of the champing of colossal jaws, the uproar that sprang from stocking and provisioning; at one end the cracking whips of the big buyers departing for the markets in their own districts, at the other the slopping sandals of the poor women who go from door to door offering lettuces from their baskets.⁵⁰

As he proceeds further Florent enters a world of moving images, color, and sound—all of which are inherently cinematic in character:

> Peals of bells sounded overhead, shaking across the murmur of the opening markets. All around him, the sun seemed to set the vegetables afire. He no longer recognized that tender watercolor which had come in the paleness of the dawn. The plump hearts of the lettuces were ablaze, the range of greens burst into wonderful life, the carrots bled, the turnips became incandescent, all in this triumph of fire.⁵¹

As in his other writings, Zola intuitively recognizes the perversion of sexuality into acquisitiveness and violence within capitalist society. His description of Lisa's discovery of Uncle Gradelle's treasure, her intended marriage to Quenu, and the money piled on the bed anticipate the imagery later used by Frank Norris in *McTeague* and Erich von Stroheim in *Greed* (1924). As in *La Fortune des Rougons*, the economic path they choose has indisputable links with perverse sexuality and violence.

> The twilight overtook them, and only then did Lisa blush at finding this boy at her side. They had upset the bed, the sheets were hanging down to the floor and the gold made imprints on the pillow, which separated them, as though two heads, hot with passion, had rolled and twisted there.⁵²

In this world, the Halles becomes a shopkeeper's Gargantua consuming all within its domain, a devouring creature whose relationship to the system Zola intuitively understands. The sensitive Florent recognizes it as "strong and overflowing with food ... a satiated and digesting beast, a well-stuffed Paris brooding on its fatness, heavily supporting the

Empire."⁵³ The young children, Cadine and Marjolin, are soon inducted within this commercial regime by their elders and enjoy the sadistic-voyeuristic pleasures of a slaughterhouse environment.⁵⁴ Unlike the gentle Florent who takes pleasure in the less violent and life-affirming world of the countryside, Lisa follows the ideological perspectives of her more affluent distant relative, Félicité Rougon, in having a particular stake in oppressive mechanisms of social control. Religion is "a kind of police force which helped to keep order and without which no Government could possibly rule."⁵⁵ She sees Florent as being a threat to her property-owning self and schemes at his downfall.

The world of the Halles is as suffocating as that hothouse atmosphere pervading the home of Aristide Saccard in *La Curée* and stimulating the perverse sexual liaison between Maxime and Renée. If the fetishistic ornamentation defines the life-denying environment of the Saccard family, the commercial material gluttony of the Halles and its inhabitants also stifles any attempts at individuality and free expression in *Le Ventre du Paris*. Zola depicts this environment by descriptive mise-en-scène techniques far transcending the literary realm. The world of "the Fats" exhibits an aromatic dimension pervading the environment so that smell, as well as sound and vision, act as montage elements within Zola's scenario. After his excessive description of objects, color, and smell in the opening pages of chapter five, Zola then adds malicious gossip as an additional montage feature in his overall composition.

> The sun was slanting into the market; the cheeses stank even more strongly. At the moment it was particularly the *marolles*, which predominated; it released powerful whiffs into the air, a stink of old stable litter, into the faint odor from the mounds of butter. Then the wind seemed to change; suddenly the deathly presence of the *limbourg* smote the three women, bitter and sour, as though breathed from the throats of dying men.⁵⁶

This leads to the derogatory aspersions against Florent. The imagery finally develops into depicting "a cacophony of foul breaths" moving into a polyphonic montage of "a single explosion of smells" producing "a terrible suffocating power." "It seemed for a moment it was the evil words of Madame Lecaeur and Mademoiselle Saget that had produced such foul and stinking airs."⁵⁷ This entire passage is an excellent example of Eisenstein's recognition of Zola's montage and mise-en-scène techniques working to produce powerful meanings.

Florent's final arrest leads to his recognition of the powerful forces allied against him, both human and environmental. Before he leaves, he releases the chaffinch from its cage. Zola's description lends itself to cinematic metaphorical montage:

> And he watched it perch in the sunlight on the roof of the fish market, as though dazed, and then, again taking flight, disappear above the Halles in the direction of the Square des Innocents. He lingered a moment gazing at the sky, the free and open sky; he thought of the pigeons cooing in the Tuileries, and the pigeons in the storage cellars with their throats slit by Marjolin. Then everything shattered within him and he followed the policemen, who, shrugging their shoulders, had returned the revolvers to their pockets.[58]

The final scenes present Claude Lantier viewing the now-restored, self-satisfied smug world of the Fats in the Halles, "increasing in size, bursting with health, saluting a new day of glorious abandonment to food and drink."[59] It is an ironic depiction as graphic as the caricatures of Daumier satirizing fat capitalist and middle-class reactions, a technique used by Eisenstein in his cinematic work. Bathed in the rosy light of a bright sun, Claude sees the Halles basking in the "pleasure of recovered health, the brisker sounds of people at last relieved of a burden which had for long lain heavily on their stomachs."[60] Seeing former antagonists reunited in a community now erasing Florent's unhappy presence from their memory, Claude's comments end the book. "What swine decent people really are!"[61]

Although no Marxist, Zola has many claims to be considered the sympathetic fellow traveler Eisenstein viewed him as, both politically and artistically. Writing in his era, Zola saw the problems affecting the success of any revolutionary movement, problems both political and personal which still await resolution. Many generations later, Eisenstein personally experienced a revolutionary society that had gone drastically wrong, one whose collapse he would not live to see. However, attempting to keep faith with his revolutionary ideals, he turned towards the works of the past for inspiration in the hope that the arts would provide a possible guarantee for future historical human achievements. In Émile Zola, he found a mentor for the creative thrust of his ideas. If no Marxist, Zola did speak up during the Dreyfus affair. His various works also intuitively hoped for a better world that Eisenstein also believed in. For both men, artistry and humanity were undivided essentials.

Both Eisenstein and Zola treated certain historical events within the societies they belonged to in cinematic and literary terms. Despite his adherence to laws of scientific naturalism, the writings of Émile Zola are at their most dynamic when they break the rules he set for himself. Similarly, although bound by the discourse of Socialist Realism in the thirties and forties, Eisenstein worked out theoretical and cinematic examples both affirming and transcending the narrow parameters defining most films. His *Ivan the Terrible* opus both belongs to the historical great leader films of the era defined by the *Peter the Great* films of Petrov as well as moving towards an articulation of operatic excess, particularly in the second part.[62] Zola's writings also contain their moments of lyrical excess transcending the boundaries of literary naturalism as Eisenstein's later films subtly undermine standard definitions of socialist realism. *La Curée, Le Ventre du Paris, La Faute de l'Abbé Mouret,* and even parts of *Son Excellence* travel far beyond the boundaries of whatever genre may be assigned to them.

Both artists dealt with particular societies and critically analyzed many tendencies. Zola criticized the Second Empire using the family tree as his guiding framework but departing from it whenever necessary. He unveiled the dangerous and often mythic principles governing its oppressive hold over personal, social, and historical events. Similarly, in the hindsight of 2005, we can also look back upon the historical events of the post–1917 era as having more mythical and ideological tendencies than realistic achievements. Both Empires fell suddenly, one with a bang, the other with a whimper. In their excessive descriptions both Eisenstein and Zola often ventured into the realm of mythical rather than realistic interpretations whatever models they may have attempted to follow. As Richard Slotkin notes, humans are essentially myth-making animals who seek to understand their worlds as a means to controlling it. But the first act involves the operation of minds and imaginations, which may leap into other non-rational and cognitive directions. Consummatory myth-makers are often aware of "the need for myth as *myth*—that is, as a construction of symbols and values, derived from real and imaginary experience and ordered by the imagination according to the deepest needs of the psyche."[63]

Consummatory mythmakers often bring a critical awareness and distance to their material often antithetical to those wishing the material to promote credence and belief. Slotkin cites Herman Melville's *Moby Dick* and James Joyce's *Ulysses* as typical examples of works failing to gain recognition among people in the historical time they address. Both Émile Zola and Sergei Eisenstein fall into this category. They engaged in depicting the historical eras they chose using symbolic categories of language less realistic but more mythical and deliberately excessive. These artists were mythographers of their times using carefully chosen formulas to describe societies subject to oppression and wrong directions but not by expressing didactic alternatives. They used a type of excessive depiction aiming at creatively inspiring their various audiences. Both Zola and Eisenstein aimed at a particular emotional excessive dynamism, a *joie de vivre* or *jouissance*, transcending any tendencies of political and personal oppression in the hope of realizing a creative human potential they characteristically could not cognitively define but intuitively felt. Their individual works contained successes and failures. But Eisenstein saw in his literary predecessor who challenged the stifling of human potential a literary and cinematic fellow traveler whom he could adapt to the changed circumstances of his own society.

Although the eras which both Zola and Eisenstein addressed are now gone, the same problems remain. The legacy left by both artists remains to be taken up and reapplied by a new generation understanding mythic tendencies and examining them critically and creatively.

Notes

1. Sergei Eisenstein, "Lessons from Literature," *Film Essays with a Lecture*, ed. Jay Leyda (London: Dennis Dobson, 1968), 79–80.
2. April 1888 letter to Margaret Harkness, *Marx, Engels On Literature and Art* (Moscow: Progress Publishers, 1976), 91–92.
3. June 15, 1887 letter to Laura Lafargue, *Marx, Engels on Literature and Art*, 317.
4. Nadezhda Krupskaya, "Ilyich's Favourite Books," *Lenin On Literature and Art* (Moscow: Progress Publishers, 1978), 256.
5. G.V. Plekhanov, *Art and Social Life* (London: Lawrence & Wishart, undated), 33. My italics.
6. *Leon Trotsky on Literature and Art*, ed. Paul N. Siegel (New York: Pathfinder Press, 1970), 209–210.
7. Plekhanov, *Art and Social Life*, 32; *Leon Trotsky*, 231.
8. Jay Leyda and Zina Voynow, *Eisenstein at Work* (New York: Pantheon Books/Museum of Modern Art, 1982), 3. "This work not only captured my young mind in its tenacious clutches but profoundly and subconsciously influenced the budding artist." Sergei M. Eisenstein, *Immoral Memories: An Autobiography by Sergei M. Eisenstein*, translated by Herbert Marshall (Boston: Houghton Mifflin Company, 1983), 13.
9. Ibid., 8–9.
10. Eisenstein, *Immoral Memories*, 104–109. Eisenstein comments the later film by William Dieterle "didn't interest me or engage me in the least" (108). For an amusing review of Dieterle's *The Life of Émile Zola* (1937), see *The Graham Greene Film Reader*, ed. David Parkinson (New York: Applause, 1995), 234–235.
11. Ibid., 213.
12. "Literature and Cinema. Reply to a Questionnaire," *S.M. Eisenstein. Selected Works Volume 1. Writings, 1922–1934*, Edited and translated by Richard Taylor (Bloomington: Indiana University Press, 1988), 95.
13. "On Imagery" ("Zola i kino"), *Eisenstein 2: A Premature Celebration of Eisenstein's Centenary*, ed. Jay Leyda (London: Methuen, 1988), 12.
14. Ibid., 13.
15. Ibid., 14. In "Lessons from Literature," Eisenstein comments that while Balzac arranges his characters and scenes in a methodological order, his method is less helpful than Zola's who takes the reader into the image (82). By taking the reader into the image, he intends a more emotional effect than Balzac does in his writings.
16. "On Imagery," 15.
17. "Lessons from Literature," 80–81.
18. Ibid., 82. Eisenstein also urged his students to look for particular details of repeated close-ups in Zola such as the occurrence of the erotically-charged throat in *La Bête humaine*, and the changing colors of the streak of paint in *L'Assommoir* from black to red to blue. He also noted "a group of special close-ups of an unusual nature, when we could simply say that Zola suddenly shoots a close-up from an entire angle."

See "On Imagery," 27. For further information concerning the relationship of Impressionism to Zola's writing, see Robert I. Niess, *Zola, Cezanne, and Manet: A Study of L'Oeuvre* (Ann Arbor: The University of Michigan Press, 1968); William J. Berg, *The Visual Novel: Émile Zola and the Art of His Time* (Pennsylvania: Pennsylvania State University Press, 1992).

19. "On Imagery," 15.
20. Ibid., 16.
21. Ibid., 21.
22. Ibid., 25.
23. David Bordwell, "Eisenstein's Epistemological Shift," *Screen* 15.4 (1975): 29–46.
24. Sergei Eisenstein, "Organic Unity and Pathos in the Composition of *Potemkin*," *Notes of A Film Director* (New York: Dover Publications Inc. 1970), 53–61.
25. "Laocoon," *S.M. Eisenstein Selected Works, Vol. II, Towards A Theory of Montage,* eds. Michael Glenny and Richard Taylor (London: BFI Publishing, 1991), 197.
26. David Bordwell, *The Cinema of Eisenstein* (Cambridge, Massachusetts: Harvard University Press, 1993), 123.
27. S.M. Eisenstein, *Non-Indifferent Nature,* trans. Herbert Marshall (New York: Cambridge University Press, 1987), 30.
28. Ibid., 65.
29. Ibid., 69.
30. Ibid., 70–73.
31. Ibid., 73.
32. Ibid., 77–83.
33. Ibid., 395. The disappointing Zola films Eisenstein cites are *Thérèse Raquin* (1928), *L'Argent* (1928), *Nana* (1926), and *La Bête Humaine* (1938).
34. Ibid.
35. Laura Mulvey, "Visual Pleasure and Narrative Cinema," *Film Theory and Criticism,* fourth edition, eds. Gerald Mast, Marshall Cohen, and Leo Braudy (New York: Oxford University Press, 1992), 746–757; "Afterthoughts on 'Visual Pleasure and Narrative Cinema' Inspired by *Duel in the Sun," Framework* 15–17 (1981): 12–15.
36. "Faujas had slowly turned his gaze back to the group directly beneath the window, consisting of his landlord's family." Émile Zola, *A Priest in the House,* trans. Brian Rhys (London: Elek Books, 1957), 31. The upper room is his source of power.
37. "She was standing *on* the center of a table, posing as *Diana the Huntress*. Her thighs were bare, her arms and her bosom were bare, she was all bareness, but perfectly unconcerned. On a sofa, their legs crossed, sat three very solemn gentlemen, smoking fat cigars and looking on with utter impassivity." *His Excellency,* trans. Alec Brown (London: Elek Books), 58.
38. Ibid., 376.
39. Ibid., 191.
40. Ibid., 209.
41. Bordwell, *The Cinema of Eisenstein,* 161.
42. Émile Zola, *The Fortune of the Rougons: A Realistic Novel,* trans. E.A. Viztelly (London: Viztelly, 1886), 75.
43. Ibid., 76.
44. Andrzej Weselinski, *Graham Greene, The Novelist: A Study of the Cinematic Imagination* (Warsaw: University of Warsaw, 1983), 95. In his chapter on montage techniques in *The Quiet American,* Weselinski comments that Greene clearly wishes to draw a parallel between Pyle and an attacking mosquito at their first meeting.
45. Zola, *The Fortune of the Rougons,* 100.
46. Ibid., 82.
47. Ibid., 277.
48. Preface to Émile Zola, *Savage Paris,* trans. David Hughes and Marie-Jacqueline Mason (New York: The Citadel Press, 1955), 6.

49. See the new translation of Vertical Montage which contains the famous analysis of the synchronization of the musical and visual components from a scene in *Alexander Nevsky* in *Eisenstein, Vol. 2,* 327–399.
50. Preface to Émile Zola, *Savage Paris,* 36.
51. Ibid., 38–39.
52. Ibid., 47.
53. Ibid., 138.
54. Ibid., 170–179.
55. Ibid., 210.
56. Ibid., 230.
57. Ibid., 234.
58. Ibid., 289.
59. Ibid., 295.
60. Ibid., 294.
61. Ibid., 296.
62. Kristin Thompson's, *Eisenstein's Ivan the Terrible: A Neo formalist Analysis* (Princeton: Princeton University Press, 1981); Bordwell, *The Cinema of Eisenstein,* 190–195.
63. Richard Slotkin, *Regeneration Through Violence: The Mythology of the American Frontier, 1600–1860* (Middletown, Connecticut: Wesleyan University Press, 1973), 13.

3

Staging the Courtesan: Taking Zola's *Nana* to the Movies

HEATHER HOWARD

> *J'ai appris que les femmes se maquillent en deux occasions, le théâtre et la prostitution. D'ailleurs c'est la même chose.*
> —Jean Renoir[1]

> PROSTITUTE. *A necessary evil. A protection for our daughters and sisters, as long as we have bachelors. Should be harried without pity. It is impossible to go out with one's wife owing to the presence of these women on the boulevards. Are poor girls always seduced by wealthy bourgeois?*
> —Flaubert, *Dictionnaire des idées reçues*[2]

Not unlike the mannequins in the shop windows of the new department stores of nineteenth-century Paris, the streetwalker dresses to advertise her profession, as her business success was dependent upon her ability to be recognized. In contrast, the courtesan plays a much more ambiguous role. As a "high class" prostitute, she dons disguises, which permit her to cross supposedly impermeable class and social barriers. Yet even while mingling with the best of high society on the arm of her current lover, she is somehow capable of generating signs that allow the true nature of her occupation to be read. Her position in society is simultaneously a projection of her lover's wealth, his investment in her as object of desire, and her own personal form of publicity for soliciting future clients. In this way, she becomes simultaneously the focus of male desire and the object of female jealousy. Both mobilizing and mobilized by the male gaze, the courtesan is involved in a constant interplay between presence and absence, visibility and occlusion. It is this mise-en-scène or specular side of prostitution, that I will explore in a comparison of Émile Zola's novel *Nana* and Jean Renoir's 1926 silent film adaptation of the same name.[3]

Whereas for Zola, theater is indistinguishable from the bordello, Renoir problematizes the interrelation of prostitution and theatricality, spectator and object of the gaze. In both works Nana's versatility in role-playing is not merely limited to her profession as a courtesan but is also inseparable from her theatrical performances and aspirations. In Zola's novel, Nana simultaneously attracts wealthy men to her boudoir and becomes a fashion model for the women of the same society. In spite of the powerful position she occupies in society, Nana still longs to discard the sluttish roles she plays so well, and instead become the morally "decent" woman onstage. In contrast, Renoir's Nana, played by Catherine Hessling, fails to exude a similar sensuality onscreen and instead appears as a whirling dervish of mere gesture and facial contortion. Hessling mobilizes and re-deploys the spectator's gaze both onstage and in the courtesan's boudoir. Whereas Zola's Nana captivates the gaze and provokes desires of the flesh, Renoir's Nana incarnates the prostitute's ability to re-create herself, constantly eluding the gaze that attempts to fix her as object of desire. Renoir thus complicates the interplay between spectator and spectacle, beholder of the gaze and object of desire.

Nana: Prostitute and Performance Artist

Movie viewers familiar with Zola's description of Nana as the sexual monster who devoured her lovers and oozed sensuality would have been surprised by Catherine Hessling's portrayal of the prostitute in Renoir's film. Although the film was considered overall to have been a commercial failure, the most interesting range of reactions address Catherine Hessling's interpretation of the central character. The huge divergence in type casting between Hessling's stylized role and Zola's original Nana inevitably drew criticism that the character had not been faithfully represented. Indeed, some critics found that Renoir's Nana, lacking the literary figure's slow-moving sensuality, could have no possible attraction for her lovers: "Sa démarche sautillante, ses yeux aux plafonds et son doigt en l'air n'expliquent nullement l'emprise qu'exerce Nana sur ses adorateurs."[4] Others found Renoir's Nana without interest, as she had been stripped of her mythical powers of destruction: "Nana, à l'écran, devient une sorte de comédie de moeurs, théâtrales et sportives ... elle n'est plus ce 'ferment de décomposition, cet instrument de destruction sociale, cette force de la nature' ... elle n'est plus qu'une poule comme en voit tant aujourd'hui: gaspilleuse, imbécile, sans cervelle et sans coeur."[5]

Hessling (formerly Andrée Heuschling) was Renoir's wife at the time of the filming of the movie (which determined her selection for the role), and had been Auguste Renoir's last model before the painter's death. According to Jean Renoir, Hessling lived out the life of an American silent film star long before she ever was cast in any movie:

Catherine Hessling in a publicity still: *Nana* (1926).

Ajoutons que Dédée appartenait à la même catégorie féminine que les stars dont nous suivions les apparitions sur l'écran. Dédée copiait leurs manières, s'habillait comme elles.... De là à croire que Dédée n'aurait qu'à se montrer pour être acceptée au même titre qu'une Gloria Swanson, une Mae Murray ou une Mary Pickford, il n'y avait qu'un pas.[6]

Already staging herself before she had actually become a star, Hessling easily made the transition to silent film, playing out various roles in the style she herself had already created: a strange mixture of pantomime, dance and exaggerated expressions. It was thus Hessling's performance of Nana as a stage artist that other critics found so intriguing. Renoir played up the side of Nana as mistress of deceit, who, even when caught in a blatant lie, knew how to convince her lovers of her innocence through body language. In one scene from the film, Nana falls back on the role of *la femme honnête* (the respectable woman) in order to convince Count Muffat that nothing immoral has taken place between her and Vandeuvres, asking the Count: "Est-ce qu'une honnête femme n'est pas toujours visible?"[7] It is not simply Nana's appearance that convinces; instead, it is her ability to recreate herself that keeps her lovers interested. Each believes that she cannot be lying to him. It is in this regard that one critic described Renoir's Nana: "Catherine Hessling a fait de Nana une femme vivante, maniérée, toujours portant sur son visage fardé l'expression de sa fausseté et de son inconsciente cruauté. Nana, comédienne de la sincerité."[8]

Hessling's over-stylized acting does not appear pointlessly hyperbolic if it is understood as constant play-acting. Alexand Sesonske notes that Hessling's acting seems ludicrous unless she is seen as a child playing an adult: "her predominant characteristic seems sheer willfulness ... a sort of childishness pervades the character. In Nana's actions one glimpses a little girl playing at being a woman, simultaneously confident of the power of her gesture and yet innocent of any harm because it is only play."[9]

In the film her petulant childishness dominates any sensuality the character might possess. Sesonske remarks that "sexuality seems not at all the key to Hessling's performance; her postures, gestures, movements are feminine, but seldom truly erotic."[10] Nana's character thus defines herself through the orchestration of gesture rather than through a projection of overt sexuality. Renoir explains that it was after seeing Von Stroheim's film *Foolish Wives*, that he had discovered the importance of gesture in the development of his onscreen characters. He remarks that it was after seeing the film that he discovered in society around him:

> ... many things purely French quite capable of transposition to the screen. I begin to ascertain that the gesture of a laundress, of a woman combing her hair before a mirror ... often had an incomparable plastic value. I made again a sort of study of the French gesture across the paintings of my father and the artists of his generation. Then, strengthened by my new acquisitions, I made my first film worth the trouble of discussing, *Nana*, after Zola's novel.[11]

In his focus on gesture, Renoir developed individual characters rather than attempting to portray Zola's entire social milieu. Sesonske points out that "the film presents the portrait of a destructive woman much more than of a degenerate society."[12] Although the sets and costumes were elaborately constructed to recreate the atmosphere of the novel, they are almost entirely indoor spaces that never situate Nana in a real historical time.

Renoir's penchant for the theater is made manifest as early as *Nana*. The director greatly modifies his adaptation of the scene of the Malbille Ball from the novel in order to give Hessling a greater opportunity for "performance." After the deaths of Georges and Vandeuvres, Nana's friends take her dancing to help her recover from her tragic losses. As Bordenave advises her: "Tu es une artiste. Il faut savoir paraître. Viens avec nous au Bal Mabille."[13] Plied with champagne, Nana shakes her melancholy and kicks up her heels to join a crowd of dancing women in a scene that can be seen as precursor to the finale of *French Cancan*. As dance was one of Catherine Hessling's passions, this scene provided an opportunity for her to exercise her talents while once again putting Nana on stage. Nana becomes the center of attention as she nimbly kicks men's hats out of their hands. Sesonske points out that the addition of this scene to the film's plot line illustrates what was to become a major theme in Renoir's work: "a character turns to art, a spectacle, a performance, as a refuge from, and sometimes even a solution to, life's problems."[14] Nana goes onstage to forget Georges' and Vandeuvres' deaths. As the cabaret or dance hall where Nana performed was another natural setting for the prostitute during the nineteenth century, her quick transformation to performance artist was a natural one. In both the novel and its cinematic adaptation, Nana's career at the vaudeville *Théâtre des Variétés* provides another transition between prostitution and theatricality.

Spectator and Voyeur: The Object of the Male Gaze

Renoir's film begins in the theater where the director, Bordenave, is staging "La Blonde Vénus." Nana, in the starring role as Venus, is lowered onto the stage as though she were a puppet caught in her own strings. Rather than making a sensual or impressive entrance, she is ridiculed by the audience. Once having freed herself from the ropes, Nana cavorts about the stage like a drunken ape. If Bordenave's interest is truly to create an attractive mise-en-scène with Nana as the center, one must attest to the immediate failure of this project. Roger Viry-Babel points out that Nana does not control the space in which she is acting but instead follows the choreographing of the director Bordenave, who can be seen to represent Renoir.[15] Bordenave can simultaneously be conceived as the pimp who creates a presentation for the play's actresses. Once presented onstage to the male audience, the women are then available backstage for further seduction, thereby bringing more business to the theater.

In Renoir's theater scene, all eyes do not remain fixed on the stage. Instead, Renoir's *Nana* provides a staged departure point for a series of exchanges of the gaze. Other spectators' reactions to Nana's comic presentation of Venus place the larger stage show *en abyme*. For instance, according to Roger Viry-Babel, Renoir has depicted the traditional space of the "théâtre bourgeois" in this scene, where members of the audience become each other's spectacles in an infinite exchange between bearer of the look and object of the gaze.[16] This scene is crucial to the film's plot, as it introduces Nana to Count Muffat, later to become her lover and principle means of support. It is Count Muffat's wife, Sabine, who initially draws his attention to the stage, as he has been witnessing another drama elsewhere in the audience. This exchange is emphasized by a masked shot replicating the character's use of binoculars. The object of the gaze is thereby isolated within a particular field of vision, limited by the imposition of the "binocular" view, as though s/he were on stage.

Recurrent scenes in the film demonstrate a constant interplay between voyeur and the object of the gaze. According to Christian Metz, the scopic drive "rests on a kind of fiction ... that stipulates that the 'object' agrees, that it is therefore exhibitionist."[17] Since the distance between voyeur and object is never closed, the object is infinitely desirable while never attained. The continuation of the narrative is thus assured. As the courtesan, Nana is actively exhibitionist. She is able to turn the tables on the voyeur by choosing who will look at her and by manipulating their reactions through the tone of her performance. Thus, her onstage performance is calculated to provoke a reaction in Count Muffat, a phenomenon, which is then witnessed by other members of the audience. In this way, Renoir's version of the scene breaks up the exchange between male spectator and object of the gaze, as Hessling's body in motion constantly redeploys and redirects the gaze towards other objects.

A similar scene in the film takes place in Nana's dressing room as the actress gives her own private performance to her male admirers as she performs her toilette. Within the enclosed space of the dressing room, surrounded by Nana's cast-off intimate apparel, Muffat is hopelessly out of his element. When Nana drops her comb, Muffat ends his role as passive observer to retrieve it. Both Nana's widened eyes and the startled reaction of her maid and hairdresser attest to the fact that Muffat has stepped out of his social position in lowering himself to serve Nana. The dropped comb thus establishes the terms of Muffat's and Nana's relationship, while simultaneously refocusing the other characters' attention on Muffat's obvious discomfort.

Throughout Renoir's *Nana*, the woman is seen as image, yet the male gaze seems powerless in completely immobilizing her. Laura Mulvey describes man as "bearer of the look," while the woman connotes "to-be-looked-at-ness," thereby fulfilling her "traditional exhibitionist role" in which she is "simultaneously looked at and displayed."[18] Mulvey also explains that in a dominant or classical narrative film, the spectacle has the effect of "freez[ing] the flow of action in moments of erotic contemplation."[19] The male spectator, as "bearer of the look," is thus empowered with both the ability to slow the narrative while engaged in active contemplation of the object of desire, and the capacity to permit narrative continuity should he choose to divert his gaze from its object. Applying this paradigm to the intradiegetic exchange of the gaze in Renoir's film, one discovers that Nana as spectacle motivates narrative progression. The power usually assumed by the male gaze is undermined as the male spectator himself becomes the object of the gaze of others, both male and female. As a courtesan, Nana is the epitome of infidelity, constantly changing lovers yet assuring herself of continuous male attention. In this way she somehow always dances out of the range of the single male gaze that might threaten to arrest her movement. As François Pouille has pointed out, in Renoir's films "la femme entre dans la vie, dans le monde des hommes; elle est en mouvement; elle intervient, elle envenime, elle attige. On frappe les trois coups, et elles montent en scène, divinement cruelles."[20]

In contrast, Zola's work places Nana at the focal point of a concentrated gaze, which emanates from a large crowd of spectators. Naomi Schor describes this phenomenon as a "dual crowd structure,"[21] wherein the male audience is opposed to the actresses onstage in a client-to-prostitute relationship. As the courtesan becomes the focus of the male attention in society, thereby advertising her availability to a larger group of men, so does the actress onstage in the lower-class vaudeville theater attract future clients. The theater thus presents a microcosm of the polarization of sexual relations in the larger French society. Furthermore, this polarization is undermined as the relationship between spectators and object of the gaze proves to be unstable. While Renoir's Nana constantly redirects the gaze cast upon her, Zola's Nana converts the male gaze of desire to that of lust and corruption. When Nana enters a man's field of vision, his desire to possess her becomes so all-consuming that it eventually destroys him, thereby destabilizing the balance of power between courtesan and client. While Nana continues to increase her wealth and visibility in society, her suitors gradually lose their fortunes and reputations.

It is in the opening scene of "La Blonde Vénus" that Nana's sexual power is first established. Zola initially describes the production of the play as a mockery created in a "fever of irreverence" for the original myth where the characters played out their roles in an Olympus "traîné dans la boue, toute une religion, toute une poésie bafouée ... on cassait les antiques images."[22] At first Nana's presence onstage appears to attest only to a complete lack of grace and sensuality: "elle ne savait même pas se tenir en scène, elle jetait les mains en avant, dans un balancement de tout son corps, qu'on trouva peu convenable et disgracieux."[23] However,

Bordenave has promised his spectators that Nana would reveal a talent that will compensate for her inability to dance and sing: "Nana a autre chose, parbleu! et quelque chose qui remplace tout. Je l'ai flairée, c'est joliment fort chez elle."[24]

Bordenave times the opening of "La Blonde Vénus" with that of the Paris Exposition, linking play and spectacle. Nana's name, printed in bold-face on the theater bills, advertises a promise of her nudity: "Dans la clarté crue du gaz, sur la nudité blafarde de cette salle ... de hautes affiches jaunes s'étalaient violemment, avec le nom de Nana en grosses lettres noires."[25] Bordenave's advertising campaign already "strips" Nana before her onstage exposure, and the men in the audience await her appearance while mechanically chanting her name. Her awkward attempts to imitate Venus soon give way to a bawdy swing of her hips, which solicits an immediate reaction from the audience and causes the heat to rise in the packed theater. When she re-emerges onstage in the second act, the male audience is brought together as a group before the awesome spectacle of Nana unleashing the mythical force of her sexuality:

> Un frisson remua la salle. Nana était nue. Elle était nue avec une tranquille audace, certaine de la tout-puissance de sa sexualité. Une simple gaze l'enveloppait ... tout son corps se devinait, se voyait sous le tissu léger.... Tout d'un coup, dans la bonne enfant, la femme se dressait, inquiétante, apportant le coup de folie de son sexe, ouvrant l'inconnu du désir. Nana souriait toujours, mais d'un sourire aigu de mangeuse d'hommes.[26]

Nana unveils the power of her sexuality, the "something else" which Bordenave had been keeping from the audience. The men within the crowd react physically to a spectacle where only moments before they were laughing in derision. Even Count Muffat, known for his chaste and restrained religious lifestyle, cannot help but be affected: "le comte se haussait, béant, la face marbrée de taches rouges."[27] Kathryn Slott remarks: "The audience focalization intensifies during the description of Nana's voluptuous body, which, in another layer of narrative articulated in the language of the body, returns the energy to the audience, thereby establishing a sub-vocalized dialogue between Nana and her male spectators."[28] As Nana senses the audience's reaction and approval, she increases the bawdiness of her movements, causing the audience's excitement to mount in turn.

Nana's sexuality, originating in her body as object of the male gaze, becomes abstracted as it enters the market of desire. As Kathryn Slott has pointed out: "We are given to understand that the whole dynamic of the narrative in *Nana* derives from, emanates from, her sex.... [T]he *puis-*

sance motrice (driving force) of the text is a *puissance occulte* (hidden power), a hidden source of energy that can be known only in its effects, not in its generative principle."[29] Nana's sexuality, represented by Zola as a corruptive and degenerative force, linked to disease and morbidity, cannot be read on the prostitute's body itself. Nana's naked body not only reveals the marketability of her sexuality but also the danger of its excess. This contagion has taken possession of the crowd just as this "man eater" will later control the men who, ironically, offer to support her financially. The Count will become one of these victims who will ultimately replace his religious devotion with the idolatry of sex, unable to resist the temptations of the flesh.

According to Kathryn Slott's paradigm, it is not the procreative (generative) side of Nana's sexuality that drives the narrative, but rather this unrepresentable nature of the desire she generates—readable only through the reactions of the men around her. The reader gains only rare glimpses into the nature of Nana's own desire—her short idyll with Georges in the countryside and the rediscovery of a more innocent sexual experience: "Nana, entre les bras du petit, retrouvait ses quinze ans.... [U]ne fleur d'amour refleurissant chez elle, dans l'habitude et le dégoût de l'homme."[30] She expresses occasional interest in playing a maternal role towards her illegitimate son, Louiset, but does not appear to connect sexuality and procreation. After her miscarriage, she expresses amazement that she should have become pregnant: "elle avait une continuelle surprise, comme dérangée dans son sexe, ça faisait donc des enfants, même lorsqu'on ne voulait pas et qu'on employait ça à d'autres affaires."[31]

Nana is more than a simple prostitute playing a debauched goddess of Love. While she continually aspires to the role of the virtuous bourgeois society woman, her body betrays its true nature both on and offstage. Even Muffat's frigid temperament warms to the contagious reaction that spreads through the crowd. Nana's body in its incomplete state of nudity reveals the power of female sexuality, while it ultimately prevents complete knowledge of its mysteries, barring total possession of the object of desire. Nana thus controls the male gaze by continuously deferring its satisfaction.

In the dressing room scene in Zola's novel, Nana entertains a roomful of men, including Muffat, as she prepares for her next scene. She remains behind the screen only long enough to don a camisole and underdrawers. As it is another actor's birthday, she serves champagne and attempts to play her coveted role of "la femme honnête": "Ce monde du théâtre prolongeait le monde réel.... Nana, oubliant qu'elle était en pantalon avec son bout de chemise, jouait la grande dame, la reine Vénus, ouvrant ses petits appartements aux personnages de l'Etat."[32] However, her admirers are far from finding Nana's bungling of her role to be ridiculous. It is the proximity to Nana's half-clothed body and the feminine intimacy which reigns in the room—a basin still filled with soapy water, a brush tangled with hair, scattered articles of clothing—that intoxicate and tantalize Muffat. Although Nana occupies the center of Muffat's and the other men's gaze, the effect she has on them is carried by the rising heat and the mélange of odors within the small, enclosed space: female body odor, perfume, and cosmetics. Her body communicates her sexuality without her total nudity.

As on stage, her body remains partially veiled: "Elle se s'était pas couverte du tout, elle venait simplement de boutonner un petit corsage de percale, qui lui cachait à demi la gorge."[33] Explaining that Nana's sex ultimately remains veiled, despite Zola's attempts to reveal it, Peter Brooks in *Bodywork* describes the depiction of Nana as a "strip-tease" rather than a "strip," inviting two disparate readings of the text: Brooks examines what he calls Zola's "zone of hesitation" between wanting to strip bare the prostitute and the desire to cover her with the veil of the respectable woman: "As in the staging of 'La Blonde Vénus,' unveiling ultimately encounters a veil, which is here the ultimate veil: the woman's sex as unknowable and unrepresentable."[34] It is this unrepresentable element of female sexuality—both in terms of her desire and more concretely in the lack of the phallus—that gives impetus to the narrative. It is Nana's concealed sex, which, while remaining shadowed even under the brightest of floodlights, somehow gobbles up men's fortunes and ruins their reputations.

A Choreographed Death: Nana's Final Moments

Following Georges' and Vandeuvres' deaths and her own miscarriage in the novel, Nana, not unlike Gervaise of *L'Assommoir* or Thérèse of *Thérèse Raquin*, becomes obsessed with the idea of death and passes her fears on to Muffat. Late one night, catching sight of herself in a looking glass, Nana is no longer mesmerized by the spectacle of her nudity but instead flees her image in fear. In a conversation with Muffat, she imagines her own death mask: "On est laid, quand on est mort, dit-elle d'une voix lente. Et elle se serrait les joues, elle s'agrandissait les yeux, s'enfonçait la mâchoire pour voir comment elle serait. Puis, se tournant vers le comte, ainsi défigurée: Regarde donc, j'aurai la tête toute petite, moi."[35]

Rather than trying to imagine an aestheticized or "noble" death, Nana's play-acting prefigures the extreme disfigurement of her corpse by smallpox at the end of the novel. Deciding how to read Nana's death within the structure of Zola's novel is difficult. For readers of the nineteenth century, the inclination would have been to understand the courtesan's death as a punishment for her sexual deviancy: a just form of retribution for having ruined countless men and caused the death of others. Smallpox is not unlike syphilis in some of its symptoms, and the French words for the two diseases are also similar: respectively "la petite vérole" (smallpox) and "la grande vérole" (syphilis). However, Zola's ending is more ambiguous, as Nana contracts the disease while ministering to her sick son Louiset, one of the few times in the novel when she remembers her maternal duties. Pushing the argument further, one could insist that therein lies the irony of Nana's demise: she dies because she has failed to fulfill the procreative and childbearing roles of her sex.

Within the framework of Zola's naturalist project, Nana's life and death take their rightful place in the social circulus of natural generation, corruption, and regeneration. In manipulating the dynamics of his controlled experiment, Zola has only given Nana the fate that is documented in her family tree. However, Zola's "scientific experiment" cannot be understood unless it is placed in the context of the Second Empire, the beginning of the Third Republic and the corruption of the society of the time. In this sense Nana is truly a scapegoat, as are Séverine, Catherine, and Gervaise, other heroines of Zola's novels. However, more specifically, Nana incarnates the social reality of so-called "venal woman" and her link to disease.

The ambiguity surrounding a reading of Nana's death in the book results from the fact that, unlike Madame Bovary, she does not die, but is found already dead. Feminist critics have linked the female corpse in nineteenth-century French literature to the voyeuristic desire behind the male scientific or medical gaze to somehow penetrate the unknowable nature of the female sex. Elisabeth Bronfen explains that autopsies of women in the nineteenth century, especially those of prostitutes, express a male desire to understand female sexuality through a reading of the body.[36] Yet Nana's cadaver in no way resembles the romanticized image of the beautiful corpse awaiting dissection by the anatomist's knife. Nana's male conquests stay away from her corpse for fear of contagion. Nana's dead body has lost all its powers of attraction and its final state of corruption inspires only revulsion and fear in its former admirers.

In its decomposing form, Nana's corpse no longer possesses the power to mobilize the gaze. Nana's former female acquaintances express no initial desire to examine the body. Nana's corpse remains covered and only Rose Mignon repeats incessantly: "Ah! Elle est changée."[37] When lighting a candle before leaving the room, Rose inadvertently reveals Nana's face, ravaged by the disease. The women quickly exit the room in horror, and Nana's visage is described as actively decaying flesh with its human features almost entirely obscured: "Nana restait seule, la face en l'air, dans la clarté de la bougie. C'était un charnier, un tas d'humeur et de sang, une pelletée de chair corrompue, jetée là, sur un coussin.... Vénus se décomposait."[38] The candle provides a spotlight that casts light on a final spectacle with no witnesses. All that remains of Nana's sexual glory is the decay and degeneration that it has spawned.

One might read Nana's disfigurement as an effacement of the master text imposed by the male observer, a refusal by the female body in death to continue to play the role of object of desire. The ultimate irony of Nana's demise would be the corpse's self-destruction before it could be textually deciphered: a final veiling of the woman's sex. However, as Janet Beizer so aptly points out, Nana's death puts an end to the narrative conflict, the endless play between presence and absence created by the courtesan's body: "Nana's body, 'stricken with semiotics,' textually afflicted, is the page upon which the narrative conflict is written. Her death in a sense effaces the conflict, for it renders the 'page' illegible."[39] Indeed, the unknowable force of Nana's sexuality, which served to generate the narrative, has lost all its mimetic power. Rose Mignon's account of Nana's final death agony is interrupted by cries of "À Berlin! à Berlin! à Berlin!" from the streets outside, as soldiers mobilize for the beginning of the Franco-Prussian war.[40] The women soon lose all interest in both Rose's tale and Nana's body, as they fall into discussing their own petty affairs and the changes war might bring to their amorous fortunes. Having forgotten why they are assembled in the hotel room, the women could have as easily been trading anecdotes in a café.

In contrast to the novel, Renoir's film features an actual death scene and final spectacle for Nana. Her death was considered to be one of the more redeeming scenes of the film, and critics of the time praised Hessling's acting. In her death, Nana is seen as shedding her numerous veils and discarding her mask of falsity: "Elle revient à la pleine sincérité en face de la mort, quand la petite vérole s'est déclarée."[41] In the movie script, the death scene was altered so that a clearly moral ending could be imposed. Nana was given a chance for redemption from her life of vice, and Muffat also compensated for his earlier weakness and humiliation by asserting himself in a traditionally strong male role as her savior. A summary of the movie in the film journal *L'Ecran* described the scene in the following way:

> Le Comte Muffat ... revient sans crainte de la contagion, auprès de sa triste amante. En lui, le mystique a remplacé l'homme épris, il veut, au suprême moment, sauver cette âme perdue.... [il] pénètre comme le rédempteur au milieu des cauchemars obscurs où elle se débat, prenant les mains de la pécheresse défigurée, [il] supplie le ciel d'éclairer cette agonie.[42]

This new ending leaves the ultimate victory to a man—one of Nana's many victims who is spared and who triumphs over the degradation into which he has fallen. Like the Biblical prostitute, Mary Magdalene, Nana is forgiven; however, the movie audience is also satisfied with the justness of her death.

Renoir's scriptwriter, Pierre Lestringuez, defended the changes he made to the end of Zola's novel, explaining that the rewriting of the death scene allowed the film to depict Muffat's "mystical love" for Nana, something which could not be shown through love scenes in the film:

> D'aucuns nous feront peut-être grief de cette fin qui n'est pas exactement conforme à la lettre du roman de Zola. Cependant nous pensons respecter, en ce faisant, l'esprit même de l'oeuvre. Puisqu'il ne nous était pas possible de montrer comme l'a fait le grand romancier, Muffat éperdument mystique dans l'acte de l'amour, ne pouvons-nous, par transposition, le montrer tel en face de la mort?[43]

Lestringuez's claim that the revised ending nonetheless respects Zola's intentions is more a defense of the necessity of a moral conclusion than an attempt to truly represent what was Muffat's obsession for Nana. In the novel Muffat's continued religious fervor becomes a perverted worship of Nana as the goddess of sexual desire. However, in adapting the novel for the screen, Lestringuez was forced to weigh his desire for a "faithful representation" against what would be morally acceptable and commercially successful in the cinematic world of the 1920's.

In line with Renoir's cinematic philosophy, the death scene can be seen as a final spectacle before the curtain falls on both the movie screen and on Nana's life. Pierre Leprohon points out the dramatic quality of Nana's death, which is set in the luxurious décor of her enormous bedroom, rather than in the novel's hotel room.[44] It is ironic that Nana dies in her own bedroom in the huge bed adorned with cupids—a symbol of her outrageous expenditure and wrongful sexuality. The viewer enters this intimate space to watch Nana die, but never to witness an act of love. Whereas Hessling has previously dominated the screen, in Renoir's film the huge bed dwarfs her, rendering her powerless, and enabling the transition to death. Renoir describes Nana as agitated, fearful, and remorseful before the reality of death. The filmmaker uses intradiegetic inserts to compose the visions Nana has of Georges and Vandeuvres, thereby linking her imminent death with theirs. She is no longer the spectacle and center of attention, but instead the spectator, forced to admit responsibility for two deaths that are replayed before her eyes. The scene evidences the definite religious overtones referred to by Lestringuez, as Nana gazes upward at an unknown portion of offscreen space—"the beyond,"—and Muffat kneels at her bedside like a priest about to perform the last rites. At the same time, he provides her with the spectator necessary for this last performance.

The Curtain Falls: Nana's Final Cinematic Moment

Whether as actress or courtesan, Nana's existence is a constant staging, a game of illusion. For both Zola and Renoir, prostitute and actress are inseparable, since they are constantly involved in role-playing. In the novel and in its cinematic counterpart, Nana fails onstage in her interpretation of the role of "the little duchess," but offstage she plays the role of courtesan so well that she becomes a model for the bourgeois women she longs to equal. As Roger Virey-Babel explains, Renoir's attraction to the figure of the courtesan stems from her proximity to the theatrical: "Renoir ... est séduit par les personnages des prostituées parce qu'elles sont comparables aux comédiennes. Elles feignent l'amour. C'est dans les termes du contrat qui les lie à leurs partenaires. Elles offrent de l'illusion parce que les hommes ont besoin d'illusion."[45] This focus on the performative side of prostitution dominates Renoir's adaptation of Nana.

As the curtain falls on Renoir's mise-en-scène, he rewrites Zola's ending to give Nana one final moment in the limelight. The last camera shot pans back from the bed, showing Nana face-down, like a lifeless puppet whose strings have been cut, tying this scene in with the opening shot of Nana as Venus descending from the heavens on ropes manipulated by the prop-man. The lights are dimmed in the large bedroom, as if the curtain were about to go up, and Muffat stands by Nana's lifeless body as though expecting another show. Hessling will be remembered for having recreated Nana as a unique performer, exercising her power through mobility. Through the manipulation of gesture and the effraction of the gaze, Renoir's Nana plays out her many roles as though in a hall of mirrors, multiplying and complicating the exchanges between spectator and spectacle. In contrast, Zola's Nana, a powerful figure of female sexuality and generator of male desire in the opening scene, has become a decomposing Venus at her deathbed. The link Zola establishes and develops throughout the novel between female sexuality and corruption, disease and death, finds its egress in the reduction of lubricity to rotted flesh. However, Zola's conclusion makes a final concession to the connection between prostitution and theatricality. Before Nana's corpse is abandoned by her former admirers, all remember her in a final glorious role at the "Théâtre des Variétés" where, it is said, she appeared in a production of "Mélusine."

Notes

1. Quoted in Roger Viry-Babel, "Les Images de la femme dans l'oeuvre de Jean Renoir" (Ph.D. diss., University of Nancy, France, 1988), 235. "I learned that women apply make-up on two occasions in theater and as prostitutes. In fact, it's the same thing."
2. Quoted in Martin Seymour-Smith, *Fallen Women* (London: Thomas Nelson & Sons Ltd., 1969), xii.
3. *Nana*, dir. Jean Renoir, Films Jean Renoir, 1926.
4. René Ginet, *Progrès du Nord* (2 May 1926), quoted in *The Renoir Scrapbook* (University of California at Los Angeles Special Collections). "Her bouncy gait, eyes raised to the ceiling and fingers waving in the air, in no way explains the power Nana held over those who adored her."
5. *Paris-Midi Ciné* (30 April 1926), quoted in *The Renoir Scrapbook*. "Onscreen *Nana* becomes a kind of moral, theatrical and athletic comedy ... she is no longer this 'fermenting decomposition, this instrument of social destruction, this force of nature' ... she is now only a 'chick' like so many others we see today: wasteful, stupid, brainless and heartless."
6. Jean Renoir, quoted in Viry-Babel, "Les Images de la femme," 57. "Let's add that Dédée belonged to same category of female stars whose appearances we followed on the big screen. Dédée copied their behavior, dressed like them.... We believed Dédée would only have to become more visible to be accepted as the equivalent of Gloria Swanson, Mae Murray or Mary Pickford."
7. "Isn't a respectable woman always obvious?"
8. L. de St. Vilmer, *La Cinématographie française* (1 May 1926), in *The Renoir Scrapbook*. "Catherine Hessling made Nana into a lively and affected woman whose powdered face always wore an expression of falseness and unconscious cruelty. Nana, the actress of sincerity."
9. Alexander Sesonske, *Jean Renoir: The French Films 1924–1939* (Cambridge & London: Harvard University Press, 1980), 24.
10. Ibid., 23.
11. Ibid., 19–20.
12. Ibid., 21.
13. "You are an artist. You must know how to appear. Come with us to the Mabille Ball."
14. Sesonske, *Jean Renoir*, 34. Later films, such as *La Chienne*, *The Golden Coach*, or *French Cancan*, would attest to the omnipresence of the theater in Renoir's work. In *La Chienne*, a puppet theater presents the framing device for the film, and the film spectator is thus made aware that s/he is entering a theatrical space contained within actual film space. This kind of mise-en-abyme is duplicated in *The Golden Coach*, where the line between reality and theater becomes even more blurred when the curtain goes up on a stage, which becomes the entire space of the unfolding drama. The viewer is again reminded of the theatrical nature of the story in the conclusion of the film when Camilla, the actress in the play and the heroine in her own story, regains her place on the stage and the curtain falls. This kind of complex doubling is very similar to that which takes place in Corneille's *Illusion comique*
15. Viry-Babel, "Les Images de la femme," 306.
16. Ibid., 314.
17. Christian Metz, *Psychoanalysis and Cinema: The Imaginary Signifier* (London: The Macmillan Press, Ltd., 1982), 62.
18. Laura Mulvey, "Visual Pleasure and Narrative Cinema," in *Feminism and Film Theory*, ed. Constance Penley (New York: Routledge, 1988), 62.
19. Ibid.

20. François Pouille, *Renoir 1938 ou Jean Renoir pour rien? Enquête sur un cinéaste* (Paris: Editions du Cerf, 1969), 26. "the woman enters into life, into the world of men; she moves, she intervenes, she inflames, she goes too far. The three knocks are sounded, and they [the actresses] come on stage, divinely cruel."

21. Naomi Schor, *Zola's Crowds* (Baltimore & London: The Johns Hopkins University Press, 1978), 89–90.

22. Émile Zola, *Nana* (Paris: Flammarion, 1968), 47. "this dragging of Olympus in the mud, this mockery of a whole religion, a whole world of poetry ... the ancient images were being shattered." *Nana*, trans. George Holden (London: Penguin Classics, 1972), 38.

23. Zola, *Nana*, 43. "she didn't even know how to deport herself on the stage: she thrust her arms out in front, swaying her whole body in a manner which struck the audience as vulgar and ungraceful" (Holden trans., 34).

24. Ibid., 34. "Nana has something else, dammit, and something that takes the place of everything else. I scented it out, and it smells damnably strong in her..." (Holden trans., 22).

25. Ibid., 33. "In the crude gaslight, on the pale bare walls ... tall yellow posters were boldly displayed with Nana's name in thick black letters" (Holden trans., 21).

26. Ibid., 53. "A shiver went round the house. Nana was naked, flaunting her nakedness with a cold audacity, sure of the sovereign power of her flesh. She was wearing nothing but a veil of gauze ... her whole body, in fact, could be divined, indeed clearly discerned ... beneath the filmy fabric.... All of a sudden, in the good-natured child the woman stood revealed, a disturbing woman with all the impulsive madness of her sex, opening the gates of the unknown world of desire. Nana was still smiling, but with the deadly smile of a man-eater" (Holden trans., 45).

27. Ibid., 54. "The count was sitting bolt upright, his mouth agape and his face mottled with red..." (Holden trans., 46).

28. Kathryn Slott, "Narrative Tension in the Representation of Women in Zola's *L'Assommoir* and *Nana*," *L'Esprit Créateur* 24, no. 4 (1985): 101.

29. Ibid., 102.

30. Zola, *Nana*, 188. "In the boy's arms she became a girl of fifteen once more ... the flower of love blossomed again in a nature jaded and disgusted by experiences of men" (Holden trans., 191).

31. Ibid., 362. "And she felt a perpetual surprise, as if her sexual parts had been deranged; so they still made babies, even when you didn't want them to, and you used them for other purposes?" (Holden trans., 385).

32. Ibid., 153. "The world of the theatre was recreating the real world.... Nana, forgetting that she was dressed only in her drawers, with a bit of her chemise poking out behind, began playing the great lady, Queen Venus, opening her private apartments to the dignitaries of State" (Holden trans., 152).

33. Ibid., 151. "She had not covered herself at all, but simply buttoned on a little cambric bodice which half revealed her breasts" (Holden trans., 149).

34. Peter Brooks, *Body Work: Objects of Desire in Modern Narrative* (Cambridge & London: Harvard University Press, 1993), 141.

35. Zola, *Nana*, 362. "'People are ugly when they're dead,' she said in a solemn tone of voice. And she pressed her cheeks, widening her eyes and dropping her jaw, to see how she would look. Thus disfigured, she turned towards the Count: 'Look—my head will be quite small'" (Holden trans., 384).

36. Elisabeth Bronfen, *Over Her Dead Body: Death, Femininity and the Aesthetic* (New York: Routledge, 1992), 189.

37. Zola, *Nana*, 438. " 'Ah, she's changed...'" (Holden trans., 470).

38. Ibid., 438–39. "Nana was left alone, her face upturned in the light from the candle. What lay on the pillow was a charnel-house, a heap of pus and blood, a shovelful of putrid flesh.... Venus was decomposing"(Holden trans., 470).

39. Janet L. Beizer, "Uncovering *Nana*: The Courtesan's New Clothes," *L'Esprit Créateur* 24, no. 2 (1985): 56.
40. Zola, *Nana*, 433. "To Berlin! to Berlin! to Berlin!" (Holden trans., 458).
41. Lucien Wahl, *Information* (3 May 1926), quoted in *The Renoir Scrapbook*. "When the smallpox broke out and she faced death, she became sincere once again."
42. *L'Ecran* (30 April 1926), quoted in *The Renoir Scrapbook*. "Count Muffat returned to the side of his sad lover without fearing her contagious disease. The mystic had replaced the smitten man in him. At this sublime moment he wanted to save this lost soul ... like a redeemer, he penetrated the midst of the obscure nightmares where she struggled; taking the hands of the disfigured sinner, he begged the heavens to shed light on this suffering."
43. *Mon Film* (21 May 1926), quoted in *The Renoir Scrapbook*. "Some people will perhaps complain to us of the ending, which does not exactly follow Zola's novel. However we believe that we respect the spirit of the [author's] work. Since it wasn't possible for us to show Muffat, as did the great novelist, hopelessly mystical in the act of love, can't we, through adaptation, show him thus when facing death?"
44. Pierre Leprohon, *Jean Renoir*, trans. Brigid Elson (New York: Crown Publishers, 1967), 38.
45. Viry-Babel, "Les Images de la femme," 234. "Renoir ... is seduced by the characters of prostitutes because they can be compared to actresses. They feign love. It's in the terms of the contract that ties them to their partners. They offer illusion because men need illusion."

4

From Theater to Cinema: Jean Renoir's Adaptation of *Nana*

KATHERINE GOLSAN

Spatial dynamics are clearly an important aspect of Émile Zola's novels, particularly as concrete and symbolic manifestations of the interpenetration of classes during the Second Empire. In *Nana*, the failure of class barriers to protect against incursion and contagion occurs in many scenes from theater and racetrack to her deathbed.[1] In Jean Renoir's major silent film adaptation of the novel, *Nana* (1926), the dynamics of space plays an equally critical, although distinctively different role. Its striking use of off-screen space led Noël Burch to claim that it was among the first films to systematically develop the cinematic potential of space above, beyond, and in front of the camera.[2]

Spatial dynamics raise issues of performance and spectatorship, and although situating the spectator in Renoir's films is always a challenge, in this early film the camera shifts constantly between a mid-footlight perspective of the theatergoer and the cinematic eye that punctures the confining surface of a stage or staged performance. The film, like the novel, opens in the theater, but the final scene bears the distinctive signature of cinema in one of the film's rare tracking shots in which the camera sadistically moves in on Nana's anguished, dying face.[3]

The very marked alternation between theatrical and cinematic takes may explain in large part the prevailing critical consensus expressed by Alan Williams that "*Nana* is probably the most interesting, noble failure of all French films of the 1920s."[4] There is no doubt that this film was a major commercial failure that consumed most of Renoir's inheritance and forced him into more mainstream filmmaking. But according to Renoir himself, *Nana* is also his first film worth talking about.[5]

In criticism on the film, two explanations for this failure come up time and again. First is the extremely stylized performance of Renoir's wife, Catherine Hessling, as Nana, in stark contrast to the more natural, muted interpretations of the men around her. Her exaggerated stance and make-up are so excessive that she has been compared to an automaton, an animated doll,[6] a Charlie Chaplin in skirts,[7] with Kabuki theater-like gestures.[8] On the other hand, Werner Krauss and Jean Angelo, as Muffat and Vandeuvres, are far more realistically rendered. These oddly jarring acting styles clearly arise from the juxtaposition in the film between theatrical and cinematic performance. Nana's gestures and body movement seem far more suited to the world of the stage, or even the static world of his father's painting that Renoir studied to make the film,[9] whereas the men fit smoothly into the cinematic realism of Hollywood that Renoir so admired at the time.[10] The failure, in the eyes of critics such as Alexander Sesonske, is due to the fact that rather than complement each other, these radically divergent acting styles tend to undermine and ultimately cancel each other out.[11]

The same type of contrast exists on an aesthetic level in the alternation between cinematic and theatrical shot compositions. Alan Williams believes that "[t]he problem is that the analytic, American-style shooting and editing cuts up the components of the fictional world, so that Nana and the other characters seem to exist in separate spaces with minimal contact."[12] But what Williams sees as unfortunate technical decisions, later resolved by Renoir's development and mastery of the medium and his departure from découpage classique (classical cutting), may be more productively considered as part of this same interest in exploring the different spaces of performance. It is not so much the shooting and editing style that cuts up the film, but the alternation between the Hollywood style of the period and the mid-footlight perspective of the theatergoer.

It is perhaps Sesonske who best discerns Renoir's aim, although he doesn't see the film as successfully achieving it: "Renoir's wish has been to contain, within a film, action of or from the theater and do it in a wholly cinematic way while still not vitiating the air of spectacle that pervades theater."[13] And although this is the first film in which Renoir deals with the theater and the subtleties of performance, it is certainly not the last, as this will become a lifelong fascination. *Nana* is a critical juncture in his work. Performance as filmed theater, an early and unsuccessful option for cinema, as well as performance as plastic gesture, are explored, found wanting, and displaced by a new mode of performance in an art

Catherine Hessling (right) and Jean Angelo dress for an outing in *Nana* (1926).

capable of exploiting what is beyond the space of the stage. Burch's salient comment regarding Renoir's exploration of off-screen space in this film can be understood from a different angle as the stretch beyond the confines of the stage perspective. Renoir is clearly aware of the contrast and pushes the camera, and the spectator, to explore the space beyond doors and windows. On the other hand, in highly theatrical scenes, such as one in which Nana and Muffat inhabit a space of only a table and chair and the camera remains static, there is a tantalizing refusal to access adjacent space. This technique was later employed strategically in his 30s films in which deep focus sometimes promises but refuses to provide the added perspective, forcing the viewer, in films like *La Bête humaine*, to grapple with the implications of spectatorship.[14]

The theatrical theme opens the novel and the film, with Nana's performance of the "Blond Venus." However, while the novel focuses on the insignificance of Nana's appalling lack of acting talent, the film shows—in an ingenious and comic manner—the vulnerability of the theater to mishaps in its rudimentary attempts to create illusion. Nana is seen preparing her descent by rope onto the stage as an airborne goddess. But the rope catches and she is left haplessly suspended in midair wildly swinging her legs in an effort to get her feet on the ground. This crude form of illusion, which has failed, is immediately bested by a highly symbolic cinematic trick. There is a cut to a close-up of Catherine Hessling in the audience enthusiastically applauding her own performance of Nana as the "Blond Venus."[15] This opening is a comment on the self-reflexive nature of Catherine Hessling's stylized rendition of Nana and offers the dizzying perspective of the movie actress as spectator of her own theatrical performance within a film. It draws attention to the theme of performance, and from the outset Renoir invites a comparison between the illusions of theater and those of film.

One of the most interesting aspects of this continual shuttling between theatrical and cinematic takes is that while Catherine Hessling's acting style remains constant, the context changes dramatically as the tragedy of her destructive nature develops. Her theatrical style begins to merge with the cinematic realism of the other characters and the viewer loses the theater spectator's distance and control over the reception of the exaggerated role-playing. When she is haunted by the suicides of Georges and Vandeuvres, her stylized forms perfectly suit the hysteria she now experiences and the spectator is drawn into her nightmarish decline.[16] When she is coerced into going to the *Bal Mabille* to forget her troubles, she drunkenly joins the cancan in a grand finale of spectacle. But the theatrical mode has suddenly shifted from what constitutes her existence into an escape from her own destructiveness.[17] With this change of status and the introduction of the theme of performance as escape, Nana's identity moves to another register. Renoir manages to transform a character, who began as completely inaccessible, and a bit ridiculous in her theatrical prancing and gesticulation, into a convincingly pathetic, terrified victim facing an agonizing death which comes in the form of a tracking camera.

The last four minutes of the film are a critical demonstration of how the theatrical gives way to the cinematic in Muffat's final visit to Nana's deathbed. Muffat enters the elaborate set of Nana's hotel from where he has been sitting on an isolated park bench suspended in darkness like a minimalist stage set in which a single symbolic dead leaf falls on his shoulder. As he mounts the magnificent staircase to Nana's bedroom, her theater friends watch him. They take in this final grandiose scene of his dazed and suicidal ascent toward contagion and then depart as he passes behind the door at the back of the stage. For them, the performance is now over.

One of the four tracking shots of the film occurs in Muffat's ascent, moving the cinema spectator toward seeing what the diegetic spectators do not. We will be allowed to go beyond the confines of the stage. In the next shot, Nana is shown in fixed focus terrified on her deathbed. The viewer is treated to some excellent cinematic illusion of hallucination as her victims revisit her in superimpositions which recall how they died. Vandeuvres' accusatory pointing finger turns into a hand grabbing at the camera lens in such a way that the camera is given over to her delirious visions. Muffat enters and comforts a fearful, clinging Nana, who is now attacked by a tracking camera, which simulates her imminent death. She pleads for mercy as it approaches her face glistening with sweat, the exaggerated make-up resembling a death mask.[18] The camera fades to black, signaling the end of the film. However, in a jolting retake, the entire scene plays itself out again, this time to end in a manner that prefigures Renoir's highly cinematic exploration of both performance and the realities of passion and death, which came to occupy his screen in the thirties. Although the reasons for this strange double take of Nana's death are unclear, it is intriguing to speculate on the difference between these two endings in the context of cinematic and theatrical performance. In the first, the tracking camera signals the moment of death, and the spectator is placed in a position of power and involvement in contrast to many passively witnessed theatrical scenes of her degradation of others, particularly when she makes Muffat jump for chocolate like a dog. But the second take tears the spectator away from this highly subjective perspective and contextualizes the scene within a more complex series of references. It not only focuses on the tragic couple rather than Nana alone, but contains straight cuts to the jewels slipping off the fur coverlet, a stage-like window and a lamp which symbolically blinks off, the grandiose bed with Muffat in profile, then her body, Muffat again in profile at the edge of the screen, his departure, and a final fixed focus shot of the bed before a fade to black.

Although the first take is more mobile than the second, which is constructed through cuts, this second version is far closer to the later

Renoir in tone and content. It is as if the camera does away with Nana/Catherine Hessling in the subjective tracking shot in order to be free to explore broader themes more suited to both the novel and Renoir's later perspective on the relation between space and performance. The jewels falling from the fur are a *vanitas* motif, which comments cryptically on Nana's tragic greed and class aspiration. The lamp and window add an ironic touch marking the end of a staged performance, much like the puppet show prologue and epilogue of *La Chienne*, and Muffat in profile over Nana's inverted, sprawled body looks forward to later dramatic sound film scenes of passion and violence both in *La Chienne* and Renoir's next Zola adaptation, *La Bête humaine*. In those two films, this same type of death scene will be shot as a long take and diegetic music will play a critical role. But Renoir is extremely close to his mature rendering of Zola in this second take of Nana's death.

Nana is a pivotal film in Renoir's repertoire because, as these last four minutes reveal, he seems to work through questions of how he wished to render performance in cinematic space, going beyond the plasticity of gesture found in painting, theater, and even silent film, as well the expressionist and avant-garde subjective camera of his time. This shift is reflected in Renoir's comment that in his personal development *Nana* was a move from cinema as a plastic art to one of action and drama.[19] In the wide sweep of this final version of Nana's death, Renoir takes in the potential of cinema to integrate and surpass not only the plasticity of painting, but theater-bound notions of performance and spectatorship. In doing so, he creates a new spatial dynamic in which the spectator can no longer just sit back and enjoy the show.

Notes

1. Chantal Jennings, "La Symbolique de l'espace dans *Nana*," *MLN* 88 (1973): 64–74.
2. Noël Burch, "Nana ou les deux espaces," in *Praxis du cinéma* (Paris: Gallimard, 1986), 39–58.
3. Noël Burch and Geneviève Sellier have remarked on Renoir's strangely sadistic directing of his wife in this film, although unfortunately not in reference to any particular scene. See Noël Burch and Geneviève Sellier, *La Drôle de guerre des sexes dans le cinéma français: 1930–56* (Paris: Nathan, 1996), 52.
4. Alan Williams, *Republic of Images* (Cambridge: Harvard University Press, 1992), 136.
5. Jean Renoir, *Ecrits: 1926–1971* (Paris: Belfont, 1974), 52.
6. Pierre Leprohon, *Jean Renoir*, trans. Brigid Elson (New York: Crown, 1971), 37.
7. Barthélemy Amengual, "Renoir, Chaplin, Stroheim, Griffith," in *Réalisme au cinema* (Paris: Nathan, 1997), 655–677.
8. Williams, *Republic of Images*, 137.
9. "Je refis une espèce d'étude du geste français à travers les tableaux de mon père et des peintres de sa génération. Puis, fort de mes nouvelles acquisitions, je tournai

mon permier film qui vaille la peine qu'on en parle, Nana, d'après le roman d'Émile Zola." Quoted in André Bazin, *Jean Renoir* (Paris: Gérard Lebovici, 1989), 146–47. ("I redid a kind of study of French gesture through my father's paintings and those of painters from his generation. Then, wiser for my new acquisitions, I was shooting my first film worth talking about, *Nana*, based on the novel by Émile Zola").

10. On the wish to "faire américain," see Roger Viry-Babel, *Jean Renoir: le jeu et la règle* (Paris: Denoël, 1986), 34–37.

11. Alexander Sesonske, *Jean Renoir: The French Films 1924–1939* (Cambridge: Harvard University Press, 1980), 29.

12. Williams, *Republic of Images*, 137.

13. Sesonske, *Jean Renoir*, 35.

14. I discuss this use of deep focus in detail in "'Vous allez vous user les yeux': Renoir's Framing of *La Bête humaine*," *The French Review* 73.1 (Oct. 1999): 110–122.

15. "L'Oeuvre de Jean Renoir," in *Cinéma d'aujourd'hui: Jean Renoir: le spectacle, la vie* 2 (mai-juin 1975): 105. This doubling is mentioned only as an element of Renoir's fascination with the contrast between appearance and reality.

16. It is perhaps this type of effect that Renoir was speaking of when he said he felt he had respected the nightmarish atmosphere of Zola's novel: "J'ai respecté la pensée de Zola...... Je me suis surtout attaché à conserver au film l'atmosphère naturaliste du livre, ainsi cette lueur blafarde du gaz qui le traverse d'un bout à l'autre et lui donne par intermittences son air de cauchemar, vous le retrouverez dans mon film." Quoted in "L'Oeuvre de Jean Renoir," 105. ("I followed Zola's thinking.... I was especially fond of preserving in the film the naturalist atmosphere of the book, thus the pale glimmer of gas that runs throughout it and intermittently gives it its nightmarish air, you will find it in my film").

17. Sesonske notes this as a recurrent theme in Renoir's later works: "a character turns to art, a spectacle, a performance, as a refuge from, and sometimes even a solution to, life's problems" (*Jean Renoir*, 35).

18. Although Burch and Sellier (*La Drôle de guerre des sexes*) do not explain in what way Renoir's directing of his wife was sadistic, this scene certainly supports such a remark.

19. Renoir, *Écrits*, 306.

5

The Eye Behind the Writing Hand: Surveillance and Adaptation in *La Bête humaine*

MONICA FILIMON

The second half of the nineteenth century brought about the change that would redefine human experience in terms of its newly-emphasized attribute: visibility. The rapid evolution of the printed word and image, the increased speed of communication, the shrinking of distances and, above all, the limelight appearance of photography and later film finally resulted in an enhanced awareness of the other's intrusive eye into one's former private space. Furthermore, the similarly fast development of technology, coupled with the empowering sense of eventual mastery of the universe, turned man's attention to scientific methods and tools as the prime facilitators of knowledge and truth. It is, therefore, no wonder that visibility and science would ultimately group under the piercing power of inevitable surveillance and find their way into literature, more exactly into naturalist writings with their "under-the-microscope" display of human life and character.

The postmodern obsession with surveillance is usually traced back to Jeremy Bentham's *Panopticon* penitentiary and it has resurfaced in Michel Foucault's definition of power relations and space. The utopian function of the prison described by Bentham was that of social discipline and it basically derived from the nature of the relation between the guards as seers and the prisoners as the seen. While the former exerted control over the space and time they supervised, the latter had access only to a unilateral restricted view of their own space and no notion of the exact time they were being watched. As a result, the simple impression of being under the controlling gaze could produce the necessary disciplined behavior in the prison. The internalization of the other's seemingly permanent gaze is not limited to prisoners, but can be extended to every single individual born into a culture of "do's" and "don'ts."

Film theorist Laura Mulvey has taken up the idea of a regulatory gaze. She redefined it in terms of visual pleasure and its relation to gender and the spectator's process of identification with an alter ego on the screen.[1] Thus, the woman becomes the object of male desire in film and her figure is displayed for the pleasure of a male protagonist. The male spectator identifies with the male protagonist's active gaze which dominates and disciplines the passive female image, while the female spectator may identify either with the woman as an object of the male gaze, or with the same active gaze of the male protagonist. However, the female image proves not only a source of erotic contemplation, but also one of castration anxiety for the male spectator because it functions as a reminder of a fundamental lack. As a result, the protagonist either subjects the woman to a sadistic voyeuristic gaze aimed at punishing her for her difference, or denies her the difference and assumes a fetishistic look which compensates for the lack by transforming parts of the female body into symbolic "penis substitutes" whose display and spectacle produce captivation and not fear. The spectator who has identified with the male protagonist makes the same choices. Consequently, in a Panopticon structure, the woman's look-at-ness renders her the most supervised inmate, the object of constant reconstruction in terms of the masculine regulating gaze.

The organization of space and its allocation to different individuals also regulates the interchange of power between or among them. Foucault clearly emphasizes the role played by the architecture of prisons in the way the individual perceives and appropriates the controlling eye of the system.[2] Other buildings such as city halls, hospitals, and schools may very well function similarly to prisons in that they strictly define the interactions among the occupants. There is usually only one door into the building, which makes it easier to record each person's entrances and exits, and there are especially restricted areas preventing one category—the regular citizen, the patient, or the student—from trespassing and ensuring the other group's autonomy and control. Moreover, rules and regulations are to be observed when the two sides meet; these empower the clerks, doctors and teachers in our institutions (although the power relations between the two sides remain always subject to change). The notion of disciplining institutions may be further fluidized and broadened to include small communities and means of public transport such as trains, coaches or planes.³

Although small communities cannot be defined as material geographical spaces, they are nevertheless constituted in reference to a particular time—the lifespan of one generation, usually—and to the limited network of relations in which everybody knows everybody. They may incorporate one's family, neighbors, friends, or mere acquaintances, and they may group around a social function—such as small congregations, whose function is religious, for example—or they may be defined by a particular way of communication—such as all the members of a chat room on the internet. They may be real or imaginary, such as the community of the characters in a literary work. In all cases, a disciplining space plays a significant role in defining the power relations among all members, the manner in which these can change and what constitutes a punishable trespassing. In such communities, the gaze of the other functions as the main regulator of the intricate relation web. It may be direct, external and subject to time or indirect, internal and everlasting. It is, therefore, challenging to observe these small communities in the nineteenth century, especially in its latter half when the community became more elusive and power relations started to change.

Means of transport, on the other hand, fall under the classic definition of disciplining spaces. From the rear mirror of a small coach to the perception of the conductor or the flight attendants as ubiquitous, and even to the more sophisticated surveillance system of digital cameras in the more expensive planes, everything functions as the embodiment of the empowered gaze of that who may be physically absent, but always present in the minds of those it watches. Furthermore, the material space is always very well defined and people "buy" their "business" or "economic" class way into the network. However, unlike other classic regulating spaces, power relations within such means of transport are also preserved by the constant element of fear of a possible future accident, which obviates major dislocations within the network.⁴ In addition, the occupants of trains and coaches, for example, partake in another type of power: they can gaze outside the windows at the panoramic picture unfolding before them as they move. Thus, they become multiplied "eyes" spying on the people and situations they meet along the road. The very mobility of the vehicle ensures their anonymity and ultimately their power over those they spot and who go about their lives unaware of this penetrating surveillance. Therefore, it would be captivating to study spaces such as trains, for example, exactly at the moment when, due to unexpectedly fast scientific and technological progress, they become the battleground of different power relations not only within the confined space of the engine and carriages, but also in the larger picture of society.

As a result, one interesting center of interest for the study of small communities and trains as Panopticon devices may be furnished by the nineteenth-century society so permeated by change and reform that its members found it compulsory to *remap* the territory of the self. Of course, there are various ways in which one can proceed about this task, but one of the most efficient is to reconsider the literary production and currents of the age. And where can one find a better example of the imperceptible rise in the degree of surveillance incorporated in the self than in the experimental method of Émile Zola's naturalism?

If we stop and reflect on the well-known definition one associates with this influential literary trend of the late nineteenth-century France, we should not be surprised at all to discover the very grounds for the future exposure of the permeating disciplinary forces at work in society:

> Et c'est là ce qui constitue le roman expérimental: posséder le mécanisme des phénomènes chez l'homme, montrer les rouages des manifestations intellectuelles et sensuelles telles que la physiologie nous les expliquera, sous les influences de l'hérédité et des circonstances ambiantes, puis montrer l'homme vivant dans le milieu social qu'il a produit lui-même, qu'il modifie tous les jours, et au sein duquel il éprouve à son tour une transformation continue.[5]

The naturalist *modus operandi* was nothing else but the placing of the subject under the microscopic lens which is practically synonymous with placing it in a Panopticon environment in order to observe the desired effect of such corrective 'guardians' as heredity and environment. The derangement—or the catalytic agent that sets the experiment a-going—is not a chance occurrence, but the result of the perfect combination of biological and social forces.[6] With the advent of the naturalist film, the Panopticon structure has found its perfect embodiment: through the "eye" of the camera, viewers are encouraged to "dissect" the "reality" on screen and intrude upon the life of the characters. The derangement acquires new values and becomes the source of spectacle: every time the narrative is interrupted, viewers are encouraged to go beneath the veneer of the captivating image into its intricate symbolism upon whose understanding lies the foundation of the very narrative. Furthermore, the director takes up the role initially played by the naturalist writer and provides the spectator with the exact details of the characters' downfall and the reasons behind it. In the novel, the reader is presented with a multiplicity of diverse surveillance cameras embodied in all the characters spying on their neighbors, friends, enemies, or circumstantial acquaintances.

The availability of the real camera makes the naturalist film differ from the novel: the viewer does not need "witnesses" to see because the "magical eye" is always there. As a result, the film usually operates a radical change in the number of characters and secondary plots whose sole function was to provide the reader with the opportunity to spy into the main story. An illuminating example in this sense is Jean Renoir's adaptation (1938) of Émile Zola's *La Bête humaine* (1890). While the text may be interpreted as a sex-and-murder thriller whose characters cannot escape the entanglements of their nature and of the milieu they are cast into, one may certainly read it as the expression of the fluidity of power relations and the role played by seeing and being seen in the development of the events.

Let us, then, start with the novel and its first and probably most influential corrective space: the small community which can be subdivided into the "public" characters who belong to the upper classes, and whose names and faces allegedly appear in the press of the day, and the "private" characters, or the anonymous lower classes whose lives, though complex and intricate, are rarely news headlines. The latter are the only ones who can see and remain unseen: because they had little or no access to the public space, the disenfranchised enjoyed the privilege of an anonymous life. It is characters such as Mme Lebleu, Flore, Cabuche, Pecqueux, and Aunt Phasie who can read about Grandmorin's tragic death and the trial that follows, while Mme Bonnehon, Berthe de Lachesnaye, and even Denizet and M. Camy-Lamotte can never peek into the lives of the former group (in fact, Inspector's Denizet's lack of vision eventually leads to the condemnation of the only character who is innocent, Cabuche). Paradoxically, however, because Zola makes them the center of the experiment, the diegetic "private" characters become extra-diegetically "public": the reader follows each and every one's whereabouts and possesses the omnipotence to invade their inner life as well.

In order to achieve ubiquity for his reader, Zola makes sure that the primary focus of interest for the "private" characters is not the upper class, but their own lower class fellows. Mme Lebleu always spies on her neighbors with a morbid curiosity and the stories she knows about them empower her. It is not for the view outside that she wants that particular apartment, but because it gives her access to the hall of the building, the space that controls the mobility of all the tenants. Nobody can enter or exit without her knowing it. The readers, in their turn, can thus spy into the lives of the dwellers through the character of Mme Lebleu who functions as the author's little camera. When she is forced to move because she knows too much, she perceives the moment as her final incarceration and is crushed by her new inability to see. It is also her death as a character in the novel. Similarly, another female character, Aunt Phasie, closely watches her own husband, Misard, for fear that he will eventually poison her to death. However, her incapacity to move prevents her from total coverage of the domestic space and finally she dies because she could not see the poison in the salt. Her eyes remain open in death, always watching because she still functions as the authorial camera, which enables the reader to see Misard's fruitless efforts to find the money. In fact, the latter can never get his hands on it because he has been trying all along to avoid his wife's surveying eye and this effort has rendered him blind to her other activities.

Although the private characters' scope of vision may be wide enough to include both the upper, public classes and their own peers, it can never be broad enough to allow them the privileged position of the author. It is the latter who is the ultimate seer and who, therefore, exercises the ultimate discipline by grinding down the characters for their most punishable sin: to imagine they are godlike in vision. The whole novel, therefore, may be read as a Panopticon device, with the author/reader in the center, the disenfranchised as the first row of "inmates," functioning *heteroglossically* as both the author's eyes and as the powerful, unseen eyes of the small community in the novel, and the second row of "inmates," the public characters who are the most watched and, paradoxically, the least powerful in the book. Although the distribution of power in this small community may seem to favor the private characters, it only makes them the subject under the microscope and, therefore, most likely to prove the ill-fated influence of heredity and environment, the author's disciplining instruments.

Renoir's adaptation resorts to the power of the visual motif to convey the same idea of punishable trespassing on the part of the characters. Renoir abandons the multiple "eyes" Zola employed in the form of secondary characters in favor of a more persuasive device: the window with its frame, shutters and shadow. The viewer is constantly reminded of its position at the center of the Panopticon by means of a window frame which, either directly or through its shadow projected on the characters' faces, identifies them as objects to be looked at and disciplined. The mise-en-scène for the most important actions includes the presence of a frame, whether the window or the door, in order to make viewers aware of spying into a box and enhance their apprehension of witnessing an experiment: there is the window of the engine through which Jacques watches the tracks divide and merge in a perfect dance, then the window of Séverine and Roubaud's apartment through which Roubaud sees the solution to his jealousy, but which is just an opportunity to enjoy the spectacle of the perfect geometry of trains and tracks for Séverine; next we have the huge window that separates the kitchen from the dining room at the motormen's quarters and through which we witness Jacques and Pecqueux debating their problems as part of a male-bonding ritual; and finally there are the train's multiple windows with their corresponding bars and symmetry suggestive of the disciplined geometry of the prison.

The three most watched characters in the text, Roubaud, Jacques, and Séverine, are thus the most "imprisoned" ones, because they fall not only under the scrutiny of the private class, but also under that of the public class and, above all, under the author's/the viewer's. They are trespassers who do not belong to any clear category: although they seem to be members of the private network of characters, they are also connected to the public ones (especially Séverine, Grandmorin's adoptee) and their lives sometimes become the topic of the news. Most of all, they are *the* subject under scrutiny. They are constructed in the most traditionally naturalistic manner as "bêtes humaines," whose actions are ground within the constraints of their genes and social milieu.

Probably the most disputed identity is that of Séverine who is differently constructed in the two texts. In the novel, she is the very victim of environment: perverted by the lust and corruption of Grandmorin, she submissively allows him to marry her off to a man with the drives and tenderness of a beast, only to find her true love in another one built on the same pattern. She is the perfect example of the socially constructed identity, which cannot escape the wolf's claws.[7] As the novel opens, Zola introduces her as the child-woman who loves to be petted and makes no display of profound passion towards her husband.[8]

Moreover, Séverine is also the most coveted "merchandise." A maid's daughter, she really belongs with the lower class, but her appropriation by Grandmorin—due, probably, to the fact that she has inherited certain appealing features from her ancestors—allows her to partake in the advantages and disadvantages of another life station, that of the upper class. She is the "private" turned "public" and all the men associated with her can also make this leap. She is Roubaud's ticket to power and protection, and Jacques' opportunity to bring his inherited instincts out in the open (in his case, this is not the public space of the upper class, but rather that of any social encounter). With Séverine, Jacques can, eventually, become the beast inside. Her inability to see beyond her "cell" and her more and more confined private space make her the perfect victim. She is Roubaud's victim because what he sees gives him power over her and she is Jacques' victim for the very same reason. It is through their regulating gazes that the author himself disciplines her. Séverine's gender status bears a major influence on her tragic fate. She is the only main character who never "sees" anything: neither Grandmorin's perversity, nor Roubaud's rapacity, nor Jacques' bestiality. Her innocence has rendered her blind and her fate becomes illustrative of the women's condition and inability to transcend it in a male-dominated nineteenth-century France.

Renoir makes her retain the same blindness, despite the semi-awareness she proves when she declares to Jacques as they first get on the train together: "Nous faisons un voyage et quand on regarde ça par la portière, alors on voit rien, tu sais?"[9] When she is introduced to the viewer, she is sitting down on the sill of a window that opens wide to a long shot of the train station. Her round curves contrast with the straight geometry of the frame, rail tracks and the trains, but are in perfect harmony with the slender figure of the white cat she is gently stroking. The pose fetishizes her image as a beautiful and fragile object of gaze and, at the same time, gives us the first hint to her identity: she is the cat-woman.[10] Her discussion with Roubaud, her husband, further underplays the same idea: she tells him about her coming of age in Grandmorin's house where she had everything she wanted. Her quick look at the cat then makes the viewer aware of the similarity between the cat's and Séverine's own status: raised up as a pet, she is a captive within the four walls of the powerless domestic sphere of life. Roubaud's promises that, if she conforms to his wishes, she will have everything she desires, confirm the viewer's suspicion that she is entrapped and is additionally supported by a left pan on the framed photo of Séverine and Grandmorin. The cat imagery is later strengthened by Pecqueux's remark that, "Cette femme-là, c'est comme les chats,"[11] which also adds a new shade of meaning: cats are not only household pets, but also dangerous predators who threaten man's integrity. Séverine herself identifies with the cat in another shot when, before kissing Jacques, she imitates a cat's purr. A fourth reference to the feline woman is her white, claw-like hand grabbing Jacques as he attempts to kill Roubaud in the train yard at night. If film is a fantasy to master castration anxiety, then Simone Simon's ambivalent image as both the compensatory charismatic "object" and the troubling reminder of the lacking "Other" satisfies both fetishistic scopophilia and sadistic voyeurism: she is both the beautiful cat to be looked at and the dangerous cat to be punished.

The other two trespassers, Roubaud and Jacques, are also brutish human beings but, unlike Séverine, they have the power to see what others cannot. The reader may not be offered a wide picture of Roubaud's genealogy in the novel, but, from the very beginning, we perceive in him the simmering bestiality that only needs the smallest outlet to boil over.[12] We could not be offered a better "derangement" than Séverine's confession of her affair with Grandmorin. Roubaud could see through her lies about the ring because he becomes the authorial eye and functions to satisfy Zola's intention of bringing in the rupture and setting the experiment on its way. However, as a character, Roubaud is now bound to self-destruct precisely because he has seen too much. In the Panopticon system, the inmates cannot peek into each other's cell,[13] so the fact that

Roubaud trespasses and peeks into Séverine's secrets transforms him into a godlike watcher. The real "god," the author, will punish him.

Renoir suggests Roubaud's bestiality and capacity to see using another window frame as a motif shot. Having just discovered Séverine's secret, he blindly attacks her in a fit of jealousy, frustration and anger. As she slowly comes out of the corner with an animal's precaution not to be seen, a cut immediately makes the transition to a medium shot of Roubaud whose paw-like hands cover two fragile bird cages in the lower half of the frame as he is looking out of the window at the train station below. His sense of mastery over the situation comes from his ability to see the train as the perfect setting for a murder. However, the viewer is aware of Roubaud's own entrapment: the window frame on both sides limits his freedom just as much as his sudden impulses, jealousy and later greed, will bring him to self-destruction. For him, as for Séverine, there is no way out. He may be the master of Séverine's cage, but he is, nevertheless, a prisoner of fate and of the Panopticon experiment. Furthermore, the viewer is twice reminded of Roubaud's status as an inmate by means of window shadows projected on his face: once as he is leaving Grandmorin, immediately after killing him, and a second time as he and Jacques are discussing the murder outside the judge's chambers.

Jacques, on the other hand, is a brute with a reason: he has to pay for the misdeeds and alcoholism of a long line of Lantiers, so, no matter how hard he may struggle to keep it bottled inside, he can never succeed. His is an already inscribed destiny, which, again, needs only a little push to tragically unfold and lead him to his deserved end.[14] By starting with the titles that sum up Jacques' family history, Renoir introduces him as the object of the experiment and, hence, the most important prisoner to be supervised. Zola's penetrating eye creates the perfect cell for this "inmate": the main "guard" watching over Jacques is his tainted blood. However, as long as the other "sentinel"—the network of social power relations and its constant change—does not intervene, and as long as there is no sudden rupture, Jacques can enjoy the relative freedom of his cell. But that is not Zola's intention and so he will eventually introduce the negative catalyst: Jacques is involuntarily the witness of the murder.

Renoir also endows Jacques with an extraordinary power to see. He represents the eyes of the train, as the opening point-of-view shots suggest, and has an extraordinary power to realize his own condition as bound by fate to a tragic legacy of foul blood for which he feels he will be made to pay, as he declares to Flore: "J'ai fini par croire que je paye pour les autres, toutes les générations des générations d'ivrognes qui m'ont pourri le sang; c'est eux qui m'ont allaité cette sauvagerie."[15] But his major power is to see into Séverine's secret without having been a direct witness to the murder. He can see unseen. As in the case of Roubaud, this is an attribute belonging only to the author and, just like Roubaud, Jacques is a trespasser who is doomed to be disciplined and punished. His bestiality is blamed on his tainted heredity, which is presented in the film as a terrible disease, the source of concern for his closest relative, Aunt Phasie. The self-possessed demeanor he displays, his competence as a motorman and his affection for her lay the grounds for the viewer's identification with Jacques as the positive, active hero. But this is short-lived. He meets Flore and she, the object of his and other men's hungry looks, wakes up the beast inside; he chases her as if she were his prey and, if initially his lust appeared sexual, it soon becomes clear that it is more. As Jacques' bear-like hands caress Flore's fragile neck, the camera moves to a medium close up of the two; as soon as his blank look remains motionless, we understand it as a symptom of his terrible disease: the drive to kill as part of an atavistic regression to the animal inside. The same empty, out-of-focus look characterizes Roubaud as he is about to kill Grandmorin, and then reappears as Jacques is killing Séverine.

It is necessary now that we turn our attention to the way in which the characters perceive the external eyes set on them. In order to do that, we must first look at the conditions that facilitate the gaze and, implicitly, at the very notion of space and the role it plays in the events. The essential observation one may make is that, whenever characters are spotted, they are always within an enclosed space that gives them the impression of being protected and hidden. This space is either the train or part of a building: in the novel, Jacques witnesses Séverine and Roubaud's murder while they are on the train; Mme Lebleu spies on her neighbors in the building; Flore looks out for Jacques and Séverine on the Friday train; Aunt Phasie supervises Misard's every move in the house, and all the people's eyes are on Jacques in the court. The film preserves the same symbolism: Grandmorin is killed on the train, while Séverine finds her death inside the house, in the bedroom. This private, *intra muros* space is not only the restrictive space of the Panopticon cell, but also that of the characters' own subconscious. The outside "eye" is an intruder and characters are never aware that they are being watched. The film further amplifies this value by preventing even the viewer from seeing the murders: Grandmorin pulls down the shade just before being murdered, while Séverine fights Jacques behind the opaque bedroom wall. Therefore, one may say that the regulating gaze of society is not welcomed in and, thus, not internalized by any of the protagonists, hence their lack of self-surveillance and their ultimate reduction to beasts. As a result of the combination between foul genes and lack of self-surveillance, Jacques eventually has no need for a reason that might humanize his murderous nature.[16]

Renoir, however, draws a clear connection between Jacques' murderous impulses and Séverine's feline behavior. After her refusal to see him because he has proven unable to kill Roubaud, they eventually meet again at the ball. Instantly attracted to each other, they share in the sexual intensity of a dance under the close scrutiny of another male, Séverine's married neighbor. Jacques follows her home and promises to kill Roubaud that same night only to have her back. When they hear footsteps approaching, he takes the gun and waits with excitement. In an uninspired move, suggestive of a feline desire to control the situation by sexual appeal, Séverine asks him to kiss her. The projection of a window frame shadow on their faces in the medium close up of the kiss is Renoir's direct comment on their state as prisoners in an experimental Panopticon. As the camera tracks to the left, the keylight focuses on Jacques' suddenly immobile eyes and we immediately understand: he is ready to kill. A cut to a neighbor coming home solves the mystery of the footsteps and increases the tension; it is not Roubaud that Jacques can kill to satisfy his crave. A close up on his face coupled with an intensified keylight on his eyes and Séverine's nearness to him are all the necessary clues; he is going to kill her. The window frame shadow, the enclosed space of the room, the fixed look become representative of a dangerously one-sided subconscious from which there is no way out. Renoir strengthens our belief that it is his "madness" that has conquered him by using a medium close up of Jacques' hand grabbing a knife from between two bottles—one empty and one half full—on the table. His gloomy inheritance has finally caught up with him and now, in spite of his bottle being empty, Jacques has to pay for his ancestors' thirst: he will kill Séverine.

On the other hand, we may argue that all characters take precautions not to be seen when they decide to take action or after they have done it. This may, therefore, seem a clear proof that they realize their deeds are morally wrong. However, there is no fragment or replica in the novel or the film to sustain this statement. On the contrary, the characters feel the need to hide from society in order to protect their own selves and not because they are troubled by remorse. In Renoir's adaptation, Séverine tries to prevent Jacques from killing Roubaud, not because she considers it morally wrong, but because she is afraid he may go to jail and she will be left alone. It is the self-preservation instinct that one may find in animals hiding their prey from the others so as not to be attacked by them, and not the self-awareness of the evil nature of the deed, which is associated with human beings. Séverine's eyes in death may remain open and haunt Jacques from time to time, but they are no more than Zola's own watchful gaze upon his inmate and a reminder to the reader that, within the Panopticon-novel/film, he cannot escape punishment. The film preserves Séverine's immobile death gaze and adds Jacques'

Jean Gabin and Simone Simon (left) pause to contemplate their dilemma in *La Bête Humaine* (1938).

own open eyes and the authoritarian replica of the railroad supervisor, the man of the Law: "Il faut songer à dégager la voie."¹⁷

Jacques, however, enjoys a serious advantage over all the other characters and this is the reason why he can elude the disciplinary gaze of society for so long: he is motorman. It is the mobility of the engine that gives him his freedom, but his love for this "woman" (Lison) protects him only as long as it is not replaced by another love. The perfect harmony between man and machine is one of the first images in Renoir's adaptation: as the train rides through tunnels and past towns, the point-of-view shots alternate between Jacques' and the engine's, which not only enhances the spectacle in the tradition of the cinema of attractions, but also animates the train in an attempt to make it a viable partner for the man. In the novel, Jacques has the capacity to witness a murder on the train not only because he is the authorial gaze, but also because he knows where to look and what to look for. The film preserves the same idea of Jacques' mastery over the machine and repeatedly emphasizes it by means of close-ups on his hands as they operate the brakes or feed the fire, and by placing him in a medium shot against the huge wheels of the train as he is checking them upon arrival. When he seems to lose control of his life, he also loses control of the engine, which plunges in a mad ride for death as the accelerated speed and the shorter and shorter cuts suggest in the last minutes of the film.

The metaphorical function of the train is supplemented by its Panopticon nature. While the conductor's presence may discipline the passengers, the motorman's ability to steer the machine gives him the absolute power over the whole system. It is, therefore, no surprise that, in the novel, Henri's desire for Séverine cannot materialize as long as Jacques is alive. The latter is the master of the machine and his powerful vision extends over the conductor. Paradoxically, in his magnanimity as the seer, he cannot realize his own vulnerability: the train, especially at low speed, becomes itself the subject of the outsider's gaze represented by the characters in the novel or the spectator of the film. Thus, Zola has Flore dispose of her knowledge of trains in order to spy on the two lovers. She therefore gains power over Jacques and this almost kills him. However, while acting as the authorial gaze, Flore as a character is guilty of trespassing and assuming the invincible position of the author. In consequence, the only disciplining power in the novel, Zola, has to punish her, too. She commits suicide not because she felt remorseful, but because Jacques and Séverine had managed to escape her control. The train is, thus, not only the facilitator of vision, but also a vulnerable space where power relations cannot always remain stable. It is also a handy device to punish the characters.

The Panopticon value of the train is more naturally perceived in the film. After Roubaud's decision to kill Grandmorin, the viewer is transported inside the train, to a medium shot of Séverine sitting down, head leaning against the back of the train couch, in visible relation to the word "État" inscribed on the white head cover: she is a prisoner in the public sphere of the State. The tracking movement of the camera further strengthens the same impression of peeking into prison cells; it follows Jacques as he is boarding the train and lets spectators witness Grandmorin pulling down the window shade and Jacques' search for a proper seat in a preferable empty compartment/cell. A supplementary point-of-view shot in a linear perspective, slightly off-center, displays the orderly geometry of the train aisle which reminds viewers of the order and silence inside a prison and, at the same time, produces a feeling of impotence and futility for any act that might be taken to escape the system. The train is, thus, a metonymical representation of the powerful authority of the State. The spectators are placed, once more, at the center of the Panopticon structure when they can watch, through the train windows, the murder of Grandmorin, Séverine's failed attempts to determine whether Jacques has noticed her, Roubaud's return to their compartment after the murder, or the discovery of Grandmorin's body by a train conductor. When Jacques has eventually killed Séverine and steers the engine for one last time, the long shot in linear perspective of the train leaving the station, with the word "État" inscribed on each coach and with its opaque windows, suggests the imminence of bad times ahead, not only for nineteenth century France, but also for twentieth century Europe on the brink of war.

Throughout the novel, as the reader can notice, power relations are dominated by one's capacity to see without being seen. While this may seem an advantage, especially if we consider the abstract Panopticon model, for the characters in the book this can only lead to destruction. All those who watch others become victims of their own vision. There is a difference, though, in point of gender. Women such as Flore, Mme Lebleu or Aunt Phasie mainly try to preserve their status quo and cannot produce a change in the ones they observe. However, because they see too much, they are doomed to disappear and the author disposes of them once their 'mission' is accomplished.

The film re-emphasizes the woman's status as the object of fetishistic or voyeuristic vision. Simone Simon's appealing features and her famous pout are thoroughly exploited in the many close-ups, which construct her as an object of erotic contemplation. Her reflected image in the mirror at three important moments in the film—when the possibility that Grandmorin could be her father looms menacing, or when she is a passive passenger of the train before the murder, or, finally, when, after the ball, Jacques has followed her home—is Renoir's own comment on the Panopticon: she can realize her status as an object of admiration while, at the same time, being incapable of escaping her fate as the entrapped beautiful pet. Although men closely supervise her and can "see" into her secrets, she has the power to reciprocate the look when she catches Roubaud taking the hidden money from under the floorboards, and she can sense Jacques' potential as a murderer. But her vision is very limited and, for the little she can see, she becomes a threatening, castrating presence, as the viewer can deduce from Roubaud's transformation after the murder. As a result, she has to be "punished" so that the viewer's voyeuristic pleasure can be satisfied.

Flore makes another important statement on woman's look-at-ness. She is introduced via a vertical pan, which is a statement on the opposition between the masculine and the feminine, nature and technology. From the racing speed of the mighty engine crossing the bridge, the camera moves down to reveal the silhouette of a woman enjoying the smooth freshness of the lake on a hot summer day. She appears as the modern version of Venus; her distance from the train and proximity to the water construct her as the daughter of the wild. It is this spectacle that the two men enjoy until she becomes aware of being watched. Her protest and the impossibility of reversing their gaze further enhance the idea of woman as the objectified "Other." The fetishist value of the initial image of her wiping her feet is re-emphasized with Jacques' own look, which she perceives to be as invasive and depersonalizing.

Men, on the other hand, are different because theirs is an active look; while women can only see surfaces, men can look deeper. In the novel, Flore only sees Jacques and Séverine traveling on the same train; Mme Lebleu only sees people coming in and out of the hall, while Aunt Phasie only sees her husband's moves, and not all of them, either. In the film, both Séverine and Flore realize their fate as objects of the male gaze, but have different reactions to it: Flore openly confronts her voyeurs, while Séverine assumes the mask of femininity in an attempt to distract men's attention from what she has understood. Nevertheless, Flore's transvestism and Séverine's masquerade come to no avail eventually because they are both victims of Jacques' violent strength and controlling mania. It is the same man who decides the women's fate, despite their capacity to "see" through the power mechanism. The film further strengthens the power of male vision by encouraging spectators' identification with Jacques, Roubaud or Pecqueux through frequent point-of-view shots from their perspective. Thus, both spectator and Roubaud can go beyond the surface of polite relations between patron and protégée, while Jacques and we can always penetrate Séverine's soul because we have witnessed the murder in the novel, or because we can easily read her eyes in the film. For both Roubaud and Jacques, this capacity allows for identification with the assailant. After his discovery, Roubaud can only regard his wife as "an old man's leavings,"[18] while Jacques perceives her as both Grandmorin's and Roubaud's source of power, and it makes her all the more desirable to him. Their fascination with this "Other"—Roubaud's with Grandmorin and Jacques' with Roubaud and Grandmorin—urges

Jean Gabin sees his murderous reflection in *La Bête humaine* (1938)

them to attempt and incorporate it through the act of supreme consumption: murder. Roubaud kills Grandmorin precisely because he perceives the old man as his rival predator, while Jacques "consumes" Séverine because, through her, he controls the others. This comes completely in agreement with Zola's notion of the bestiality in men: Jacques does nothing more than take unquestionable possession of the most coveted "prey" and this makes him the ultimate leader of beasts.[19]

His terrible instincts die with him when he commits suicide after attempting to kill Pecqueux, who functions as the director's close eye and major commentator in the film. In a way, the suicide redeems part of Jacques' guilt and partially restores his initially appealing image as the active hero at odds with fate. Nevertheless, it is with Pecqueux that the spectator ultimately identifies, not only because, throughout the film, he has proven to have the clearest insight into events, but also because he ends up as the ultimate winner, the new motorman, thus gratifying the spectator's desire for power and dominance. If Zola eventually punishes Pecqueux, too, and has him killed in the final confrontation with Jacques, it is because he did not need to satisfy the reader's visual pleasure of identification with an alter ego on the screen. The novel better preserves its value as an experiment, while the film operates more within a Panopticon structure of discipline and punish.

Jacques, Séverine and Roubaud are, thus, at the center of the reader's/viewer's attention. They are always spied on, followed or just unintentionally caught in the act. The multiple eyes set on them are nothing else but the diverse microscope lenses installed by the master puppeteer, the author/director, with the explicit intention of observing their reaction to a particular destabilizing agent and within a specific milieu. The variety of these external little cameras compensates for their absence from the internal world of the characters and works to meet the reader's/viewer's demands to witness the involution of the subject under scrutiny. *To see unseen*. It may seem Zola's or Renoir's ultimate power, but, in fact, it is eventually we, the readers and viewers, who have the most encompassing view: we can watch both the characters and the maestros, and there is nothing they can do to discipline us.[20]

Notes

1. Laura Mulvey subsequently revised her thesis to include a discussion of the female spectator and her visual pleasure. Her 1981 article, "Afterthoughts on 'Visual Pleasure and Narrative Cinema' inspired by King Vidor's *Duel in the Sun*" resorts to Freud's theory of the unique libido. This accounts for the times in a woman's life when she oscillates between femininity and masculinity. As a result, Mulvey suggests that the female spectator may either identify with the woman as the object of the male gaze, or adopt a more "masculine" point of view and find pleasure in identifying with the active hero on the screen, thus reverting to the pre–Oedipal phase of sexual identity.

In a later article, "Changes: Thoughts on Myth, Narrative and Historical Experience" (1985), Mulvey admits to the either/or trap of the binary pattern of masculine/feminine positions which allows for little change afterwards and seems to block further development. Drawing on Bakhtin's notion of the carnival as an intermediate space between two states of equilibrium, she reconsiders the role of the narrative as the carnival which engenders a re-evaluation of the symbolic order. Consequently, the mythic stages of separation, transformation and reincorporation are perceived to be in accordance with the linear narrative of the Oedipus complex: the pre-Oedipal dyadic relationship between mother and child, the Oedipus phase of desire and contradiction, and finally the third stage of closure around the symbolic order. To avoid the blockage of a bipolar pattern of the masculine vs. the feminine, Mulvey suggests that the future of the feminist theory lies in the study of a "change without closure" (175), which does not force woman into masquerade and inversion as the means to find a place in a man's world.

The present article is centered on Mulvey's first two articles on visual pleasure and the binary opposition between the masculine and the feminine because, in the context of the naturalist experiment and the Panopticon structure, her arguments concerning the castration anxiety and fetishism still hold true. The naturalist narrative follows the three stages of separation, transformation and reintegration with a clear emphasis on the last one as reinstating the law of the father by means of the punishment to which the carnivalesque figures of the trespassers are subjected. Furthermore, my intentions were to assess the role of the diegetic female spectator—exemplified by characters such as Séverine or Flore—in relation to the narrative closure and the rebalance of the patriarchal order, and not to discuss the way in which the regular female reader or spectator may approach Zola's novel or Renoir's film.

2. "In the 1830s, the Panopticon became the architectural program of most prison projects. It was the most direct way of expressing 'the intelligence of discipline in stone'; of making architecture transparent to the administration of power; of making it possible to substitute for force or other violent constraints the gentle efficiency of total surveillance; of ordering space according to the recent humanization of the codes and the new penitentiary theory.... In short, its task was to constitute a prison-machine with a cell of visibility in which the inmate will find himself caught as 'in the glass house of the Greek philosopher' and a central point from which a permanent gaze may control prisoners and staff." Michel Foucault, "Complete and Austere Institutions," in *The Foucault Reader*, ed. Paul Rabinow (New York: Pantheon Books, 1984), 217.

3. Of course the list may include other social institutions (for example, the family) or public spaces (such as hotels, theater halls, etc.). I have chosen to restrict my analysis to small communities and means of public transport (trains in particular) because these are representative to the topic of this paper.

4. In most cases, passengers find themselves not only under the scrutinizing control of the other as the representative of authority, but also under the more surreptitious curb of their own instinct for self-preservation. Neither of these, however, is relevant in other cases. For instance, the terrorist hijackers in the 9-11 tragedy used planes as means to an end, which proves that notions of authority and even apparently "natural" feelings such as fear are ultimately culturally constructed.

5. Émile Zola, "Le roman expérimental," in Herbert S. Gershman, ed., *Anthologie des préfaces de romans français du XIXe siècle* (Paris: Union Générale d'Éditions, 1971), 326. "This is what constitutes the experimental novel: to possess a knowledge of the mechanism of the phenomena inherent in man, to show the machinery of his intellectual and sensory manifestations, under the influences of heredity and environment, such as physiology shall give them to us, and then finally to exhibit man living in social conditions produced by himself, which he modifies daily, and in the heart of which he himself experiences a continual transformation." Émile Zola, "The Experimental Novel," *The Experimental Novel and Other Essays*, trans. Belle M. Sherman (New York: Haskell House, 1964), 20.

6. One essential difference between the naturalist "microscope" and the Foucaultian Panopticon structure ought to be made here: if Zola and the naturalists believed in

the body-like structure of the state and in its role as the unique ultimate power, Foucault's postmodernist discourse refutes this idea and considers power to be dispersed into a network of relations and forces. When a trespasser disrupts the power equilibrium, it is the local power agents who have been directly involved that work to restore a certain balance, and not a supreme authority. To Zola, Pecqueux and Jacques fall victims of the state machine impersonated in the engine; it is because of Lison that they are endowed with the power to see and it is also, paradoxically, Lison that drives them to their death. To Foucault, the engine is just one of the possible agents; the two men die because they have upset each other's equilibrium and the balance of power between themselves and the others around them.

7. "This passive and docile woman, who as a young girl had lent herself to the desires of an old man and later had accepted her marriage solely because she wanted to regularize her life, simply could not comprehend such an outburst of jealousy over some misconduct long past and that she repented of. She had no vice in her, her flesh had scarcely yet been aroused, and being only half able to grasp the real values of things, still virginal despite everything, she watched her husband going up and down and turning in fury just as she might have watched a wolf or some creature of another species." Émile Zola, *La Bête humaine*, trans. Leonard Tancock (London: Penguin Books, 1977), 41.

8. "He smothered her with kisses, which she did not return, and that was what made him vaguely uneasy—she was a big, passive child with a filial affection in which no passion was ever aroused." Émile Zola, *La Bête humaine*, Tancock trans., 24.

9. "When I look out of the window I see nothing."

10. Quite interestingly, this image was to follow French actress Simone Simon in two later films, "Cat People" (1942) and "The Curse of the Cat People" (1944).

11. "women are like cats..."

12. "He never had any suspicions at Le Havre, but in Paris he thought of all kinds of dangers, deceptions and misdeeds. The blood rushed up into his head and his fists, the fists of an ex-laborer, clenched themselves as they used to when he pushed trucks along. He became once again the brute unaware of his own strength, capable of pulverizing her in a fit of blind rage." Zola, *La Bête humaine*, Tancock trans., 23.

13. "The crowd is replaced by a 'collection of separated individualities.'" David Lyon, *The Electronic Eye: The Rise of Surveillance Society* (Minneapolis: University of Minnesota Press, 1994), 66.

14. "At certain times he could clearly feel this hereditary taint, not that his health was bad, for it was only nervousness and shame about his attacks that had made him lose weight in his early days But there were sudden attacks of instability in his being, like cracks or holes through which his personality seemed to leak away, amid a sort of thick vapor that deformed everything. At such times he lost all control of himself and just obeyed his muscles, the wild beast inside him. Yet, he did not drink, not even allowing himself a single tot of spirits, having seen that the least drop of alcohol drove him out of his mind. He was coming to think that he was paying for others, fathers, grandfathers who had drunk, generations of drunkards, that he had their blood, tainted with a slow poison and a bestiality that dragged him back to the woman-devouring savages in the forests." Zola, *La Bête humaine*, Tancock trans., 66.

15. "I'm beginning to think I'm paying for all my ancestors who drank. Generations of drunkards who rotted my blood and gave me this madness."

16. "And now, against his own interests, he had been carried away by inherited violence, the instinct for murder that in the primeval forests hurled one beast on to another. Does anyone kill as the result of reasoning? No, men only kill when driven on by their blood and nerves as a legacy of ancient struggles for survival and the joy of being strong." Zola, *La Bête humaine*, Tancock trans., 332–333.

17. "We must clear the line."

18. Zola, *La Bête humaine*, Tancock trans., 35.

19. "But Jacques was astounded. He could hear the sniffing of an animal, the snorting of a wild boar, the roaring of a lion, but then he was reassured—it was only his own heavy breathing. At last, at last! He had satisfied himself, he had killed! Yes, he had done it. Boundless joy and an awful exultation bore him aloft in the complete contentment of his eternal desire. He felt a surprising pride, an enhanced sense of his male sovereignty. Woman—he had killed her, and now, as he had so long desired, he possessed her completely to the point of destroying her. She was no more and never would be anybody else's." Ibid., 331–332.

20. The following texts were instrumental in the production of this article: Barbara Creed, "Film and Psychoanalysis," *Film Studies: Critical Approaches,* eds. John Hill and Pamela Church Gibson (Oxford: Oxford University Press, 2000), 75–89; Michel Foucault, "Space, Knowledge and Power," *The Foucault Reader,* ed. Paul Rabinow (New York: Pantheon Books, 1984), 239–256; Michel Foucault, "Panopticism," *The Foucault Reader,* ed. Paul Rabinow (New York: Pantheon Books, 1984), 206–213; Anne Friedberg, "The Mobilized and Virtual Gaze in Modernity: Flaneur/Flaneuse," *The Visual Culture Reader,* ed. Nicholas Mirzoeff (London: Routledge, 1998), 253–262; June Howard, "Preface and Casting out the Brute," *Documents of American Realism and Naturalism,* ed. Donald Pizer (Carbondale: University Press, 1998), 386–403; David Lyon, *The Electronic Eye: The Rise of Surveillance Society* (Minneapolis: University of Minnesota Press), 1994; Paul P. Reuben, "Chapter 6: Late Nineteenth Century: Naturalism—A Brief Introduction," *PAL: Perspectives in American Literature—A Research and Reference Guide,* http:// www. Csustan.edu/English/ reuben/pal/chap6/ 6intro.html (accessed Oct. 20, 2003).

6

"La Rançon du progrès"[1]: Naturalistic Discourse and Two Adaptations of Zola's *Au Bonheur des Dames*

KLAUS PETER WALTER

The prose production of naturalism and in particular of naturalist novels by Émile Zola has supplied film with a substantial number of topics for adaptation as a survey of the history of the *septième* art shows, for example, starting with Albert Capellani (*Germinal*, 1913); and Jean Renoir (*Nana*, 1926, *La Bête humaine*, 1938); to René Clément in the fifties (*Gervaise*, 1956) and Claude Berri's *Germinal* from 1993.

Even Zola's department store novel *Au Bonheur des Dames*, which David Baguley has after all called the "pivotal text in Zola's development,"[2] has not been rejected as an attractive subject because of its metaphorical possibilities and the problems it treats. The following article intends to closely examine both film adaptations of the eleventh volume of *Rougon-Macquart*, which was published in 1883. Such an undertaking seems to be especially worthwhile since the individual technical conditions under which the films were made have led to the emergence of two different discourses. Julien Duvivier's *Au Bonheur des Dames* from 1930 is a silent film whose effects are derived from the power of visual impressions, while the 1943 version of the same title, directed by André Cayatte, can fall back on the blessings of a soundtrack and the voluptuous mise-en-scène of the so-called "qualité française." Of course, it cannot be the aim to balance the sum of correspondences with or divergences from Zola's model in an encyclopedic approach. It should instead be the aim to work out the significant characteristics of both filmic department store discourses with regard to their medial, authorial and time specific factors.

In order to assess on a fundamental basis what both films really achieve or neglect, it is above all necessary to arrive at terms of reference for a comparative approach and to name the central concerns of Zola's *Au Bonheur des Dame* discourse with regard to both the content and the techniques of representation.

With regard to the novel's configuration of meaning, on several occasions the author has extensively formulated what he is interested in representing within the framework of his extensive preparatory work. It is therefore written in a "Sommaire": "Le petit commerce écrasé par les grands magasins. Ceux-ci de véritables machines à vapeur en fonction. *La lutte pour la vie.* Gaie."[3] The novel tries to illustrate the principle of the existence of Darwinism, the struggle for life, with the paradigm of the competition between trade and commercial enterprise. As the supplement "gaie" signals, the novel intends to give proof of the fact that the struggle of historical necessity of modern times results in the meaningful realization of the mentality of activity and achievement. Let us quote Zola in his "*Ébauche*" (preface) in order to illustrate this:

> Je veux dans *Au Bonheur des Dames* faire le poème de l'activité moderne. Donc, changement complet de philosophie: plus de pessimisme d'abord, ne pas conclure la bêtise et à la mélancolie de la vie, conclure au contraire son continuel labeur, à la puissance et à la gaieté de son enfantement. En un mot, aller avec le siècle, exprimer le siècle, qui est un siècle d'action et de conquête, d'efforts dans tous les sens.[4]

If the department store magnate Octave Mouret now hands over the totality of small traders, who live in the shade of the more and more gigantic department store, to a merciless process of execution, he can in his defense refer to the fact that he has realized the "spirit of time" and helped it to full realization.

An important feature of the construction of Zola's fiction in *Au Bonheur des Dames* consists of the depiction of what may be called the detailed "microscope" of the milieu, which in this case could be called the department store universe, including the "lutte sans trêve ni pitié"[5] that rages among the employed over the maintenance of the workplace or promotion and the detailed explanation of the "renouvellement incessant du capital qui faisait la force invincible du nouveau commerce."[6] Above all, the text insists on the explanation of the fundamental method of marketing with which Octave Mouret operates so successfully, namely, "la continuelle exploitation de la femme,"[7] which is a strategy of marketing that consists of directing the female libido into the act of buying. The text of the novel is overloaded with references to the "triomphe de Vénus,"[8] which leaves nothing to be desired with regard to ambiguity. This is the case, for instance, when the novel talks about the "tentation aigüe, le coup de la folie du désir qui détraquaient toutes les femmes,"[9] and the clients are described as "créatures en folies"[10] who disappear ashamed immediately after the act of buying: "la clientèle, dépouillée, violée, s'en allait à moitié défaite, avec la volonté assouvie et la sourde honte d'un désir contenté au fond d'un hôtel louche."[11]

It is exactly at this point that the outstanding function of the character Denise becomes clear. Her behavior is in two respects responsible for the intended happy ending of the novel. In this way it offers the regulating agent, which permits us to understand the novel as an optimistic document of the beginning of the modern age.

On the one hand, Denise is the avenger of her sex against Octave and the exploitation of women as he commits it.[12] But the revenge of the girl is not exclusively restricted to the Christian image of the Virgin Mary: "[L"] image fière et vengeresse de Denise, dont [Octave] sentait sur sa gorge le talon victorieux."[13] Neither is it restricted to leading him to the loss of soundness of mind through her categorical resistance to becoming his mistress. Furthermore, she treats the man successfully according to the "invincible logique des faits"[14] due to his "superstition selon laquelle le directeur d'une grande maison de nouveautés devrait être célibataire, s'il voulait garder sa royauté de mâle sur les désirs épandus de son peuple de clientes."[15] She also persuades Octave of the necessity of marriage and in this way gives the enterprise its necessary moral concrete form.

Above all, thanks to her final triumph, Denise is a guarantee of the positive evaluation of the commercial "struggle for life." It is exactly in this respect that the text never tires of awarding the quality of "logic" to Denise's way of thinking and pragmatic behavior. The incarnate executor of this logic—"Denise se sentait choisie par la logique des faits"[16]—comprehends the necessity of the economic-social program as a genius of the historical moment as it is pursued by *Au Bonheur des Dames*. This she does because of her own traumatic experiences.

In this way it is only consistent that it is she who takes the initiative to carry out social work. With this work, the Darwinian conditions of the department store existence are moderated (protection of workplaces, social welfare, care of pregnant women, and legal protection of nursing mothers as well as leisure activity).[17]

In order to erase the therapeutically relieving function of Denise, Zola adapts a narrative structure known as the *dispositif romanesque* (dispositif romanesque), which is, above all, used in the contemporary popular novel to mark the destiny of female protagonists. After the exposition the heroine has to suffer a temporal social and existential decline in order to demonstrate "sa bonne grace à souffrir,"[18] to prove her moral steadfastness, and to perfect "sa sérénité dans la souffrance."[19] This she needs to do before she can enjoy the well-deserved, "success final de son long courage,"[20] which she owes to her key quality of "douceur invincible"[21] as a veritable overcompensation for what she has suffered. It is obvious that this sketch of a female gentleness, which though physically non-violent is all the more "redoubtable dans sa douceur"[22] in its "force de volonté douce et inexorable,"[23] pays tribute to the self-confidence of the *deuxième sexe*.[24] In the logic of this development, to use once again the term which has been used so recurrently in *Au Bonheur des Dames*, it is no mere coincidence that the novel ends with the adjective "toute-puissante,"[25] which was tailored to fit the character of Denise, as the last word of the text.[26]

After the construction of the terms of reference, let us move on to the comparative analysis of the two film adaptations of *Au Bonheur des Dames*. Here the two versions by Duvivier (1930) and Cayatte (1943) can be treated together with regard to the individual results from a wider perspective. Only with the evaluation of the individual film endings, to which a lot of importance is attached, will a separate consideration be essential. Compared to Zola's model, the mimetic method of both films can be designated as a process of a general reduction of the novelistic complexity on the level of narration and representation of reality. With this principle of reduction the two versions definitely do not differ from virtually all efforts at adapting important novels for two important reasons. Firstly, from a receptional-aesthetic point of view the filmic work of art needs to be based on a relatively easily understandable narrative and the accentuation of emotionalizing reading-experiences. It has to do this, as it is limited to a unique length of 80 to 100 minutes while reading a printed text can be stretched out for days and weeks and allows for recapitulations at any time. Secondly, only in a rare case can film reproduce the employment of metaphorical expressions and symbols (for instance, the department store as a Moloch) typical of Zola's naturalistic aesthetic. There are many medial difficulties of the cinema here to find visually convincing equivalents of such mentally constructed symbols of the printed word.

For this reason both directors must simply do without copying the detailed perspective Zola uses in his novel. Neither do the cameras work on the intrigues between the employed in the professional struggle for life nor is the viewer's attention directed in an equally detailed manner to the economic functioning of the capitalist commercial enterprises as is the case with Zola. Above all, the erotic exploitation of female clients without any sexual inhibitions cannot come to fruition as a fundamental concept of the novel's content for censorship reasons.

On the basis of narration both films no longer comply with the very important narrative strategy (*romanesque dispositive*) of the deep fall of Denise as *conditio sine qua non* for the final triumph of a woman who is powerful in her *douceur* (gentleness). Instead, Denise's ascent is virtually straight with Duvivier and Cayatte; delaying factors which threaten the alliance between Denise and Octave, are subjected to what is typical of another genre, namely the necessity to fulfill the modes of melodramatic effect. For this reason in both versions Octave needs to believe that he is dealing with a rival when conquering Denise, Denise's brother Pierre in Cayatte's film and Colomban, the *premier commis* (first clerk) Baudu in Duvivier's film, so that a sentimental effect can be derived from the touching clearing up of the misunderstanding with the short-lived complications and the trembling reconciliation.

On the basis of the construction of meaning it will have to be shown that both film versions demonstrate Zola's optimistic version of economic development on screen with certain reservations. But it is significant that the films therefore shy away from Zola's opinion of the evolutionary *fait-accompli* of the novel and conduct again a very thoughtful debate on the conditions under which this progress can be realized and the doubtfulness of its price.

The re-problematization of "Rançon du progrès"—such is the quotation from Cayatte—finds its real-life expression in the increase in status of the character of Baudu on the screen. The novel also tries to symbolize the defeat of small commerce passively in the character of the ailing Geneviève Baudu; the funeral procession of the unhappy girl becomes the final defeat of the retail trade as Denise observes appropriately: "il lui semblait entendre le piétinement d'un troupeau conduit à l'abattoir, toute la déconfiture des boutiques d'un quartier, le petit commerce traînant sa ruine, avec un bruit mouillé de savates, dans la boue noire de Paris."[27]

Under the direction of Zola, a fatal and irreversible moment is now attached to the decadence of this class, which is even emphasized by the stubborn bigotry with the help of which Baudu and his fellow-sufferers rise up against the evidence of progress. Duvivier and Cayatte, on the other hand, give Baudu more realism in his military uprising against the monopolistic power of the department store. At the same time they give him an almost martyr-like tragic greatness in the face of the historically necessary struggle for survival. In both films it is explicitly shown—here, the symbolism of film can work as well—how Baudu is run over by Octave. While in the novel Baudu spends his last days in an old people's home as an old, broken man, in the two film versions, after a vain protest, the same character is run over and killed immediately by the driver of an *Au Bonheur* delivery truck.

Even if both film endings need to be considered individually, they nevertheless have some things in common. In a kind of final line of argumentation both films condense what Zola presents as a delicate process of development which covers the more than four years of the narrative time (1864–1869), namely the final triumph of *femme vierge* (virgin woman) and her incarnate "logic" of the social-economic process of monopolization. Because of the lack of the erotic dimension on the screen, Denise is not, of course, a "female-avenger" of her sex but is reduced solely to her therapeutic effect by Duvivier and Cayatte. This effect has no other meaning than in terms of civilization.

Let us begin with Cayatte's "more advanced" version, more advanced because it has the expressive means of a soundtrack at its disposal and because it makes full use of its qualitative extension, presenting at the end an emotional dispute in the course of which the controversial debate about the price of progress takes place and is solved. Baudu shows up at Mouret's party, which is given on the occasion of the success of the "grande exposition du blanc" (great exhibition of white). Baudu comes not only in order to pay back with contempt the 100,000 francs to his adversary, who wanted to offer him the money as compensation, but also in order to hurl his forecast of the future development of trade at Mouret. In this shot sequence, Baudu stands on the stairs of the department store, breathing heavily, addressing Octave, who stands above him:

> BAUDU: Vous m'avez ruiné, jeté à la rue. Mais vous ne triompherez pas longtemps. Vous avez créé une machine monstrueuse que rien n'arrêtera désormais. Vous aussi, vous rencontrerez un jour votre Mouret, un forban plus puissant que vous, qui vous écrasera comme vous avez écrasé les autres et qui sera écrasé à son tour. Dans vingt ans, le commerce ne sera plus qu'une bataille affreuse où la qualité, la probité et la confiance seront piétinées, assassinées comme le Vieil Elbeuf. Prenez garde, Mouret, vous instaurez le règne de la camelote et du tape-à-l'œil. Mais patience, tout se paie. Vous aussi, vous connaîtrez un jour le chômage et la même honte. Vous deviendrez l'esclave des financiers, et vos cathédrales de pacotille s'écrouleront dans un chaos de ruine, de scandale et de sang. Moi, je suis trop vieux, j'aurai la chance de crever avant d'avoir vu tout ça.[28] *He turns away and directs himself towards the exit.*

Considered on its own, this tirade could be taken seriously as an extremely pessimistic view of the future and it would severely qualify Octave's present triumph. However, one has to realize that Cayatte conceived his film as a historicizing work, which seeks to imitate and understand the epoch of rapid industrial expansion as presented in Zola's *Au bonheur des Dames*. This is signaled to us in the film's opening credits where, with a vibrant waltz in the background, an engraving on a department store building dating from the 19th century is shown. However, with this pointed location in an epoch in which the industrialization of trade had just begun, Baudu's horrid scenario of monocapitalism's murderous future loses its prognostic obligation for the spectator of 1943, and its edge is taken off even further since it is articulated as a mere *possibility*. But that is also why in his immediate reply, Octave can gratefully take up Baudu's words as a "warning" (that is how he interprets them). Moreover, in one breath, and as the director of the enterprise, literally condescendingly, he can announce improvements, which will refute the harsh pessimism of the ruined retailer and guarantee the realization of "capitalism with a human face." In this shot sequence, Mouret takes a step forward on the stairs and begins to speak:

> MOURET. Oui, mes amis, M. Baudu a raison. Une entreprise comme la mienne n'a pu s'édifier qu'en ruinant, hélas, de braves gens comme lui. C'est la rançon du progrès. Mais le succès impose aussi des devoirs. Et si, involontairement, j'ai fait du mal, je veux consciemment faire du bien. Et c'est à vous, mes collaborateurs que j'ai pensé. Voici mon programme: Réintégration du personnel licencié sans motif, *[Applause. Octave asks for silence]* création d'une caisse de prêt aux mariages, *[Applause. During the following speech, Mouret is not seen; the camera follows Baudu, who forces his way to the exit, passing the assembly of employees, who do not notice him at all since they are concentrating on Octave's speech coming from the opposite direction]* aide aux jeunes mères, construction d'une maternité, d'un hospice, garantie d'une retraite honorable à ceux qui toute leur vie, auront peiné ici.*[Passionate applause]*[29]

And that is why despite Baudu's fatal accident, which takes place immediately after the dispute, the film can end with pictures and sounds of a festive ball. To put it in exaggerated terms, Cayatte's work offers a sort of sound film documentary about the debate on progress as it was conducted in the early stage of the "industrialization" of trade, and exactly because of the historical distance it outlines an optimistic picture of the status achieved 60 years later which, imposed from above, set in thanks to the acceptance of the necessity of social improvement.

What does this configuration have to do with a woman's therapeutic functions? Octave himself answers this question.

> OCTAVE: Ne me remerciez pas. Si j'ai été amené à me pencher sur votre sort, c'était parce que l'une d'entre vous m'a fait comprendre votre misère et vos espoirs. *[Denise is brought in by Jouve, and Octave seizes her hand]*. Remerciez donc Mlle Baudu qui, j'espère, sera bientôt Mme Mouret.[30]

Similar to the novel, yet here explicitly acknowledged by the industrialist, the inspiration for the announced reforms, which aim at the improvement of working conditions, goes back to Denise's healing influence. On the other hand, it is Octave, as a man, who proclaims the incisive improvements and whose generosity is consequently celebrated. And there is also another respect in which Cayatte's female role model falls back behind that of Zola. This is due to the patriarchal gesture of the film's conclusion. At the end of the plot, we do not encounter an omnipotent Denise, but an obedient woman, who, through a decree issued by her dominating and triumphant husband, is first made to come and then freed from her heartbreak. It is Octave who decides upon the forthcoming marriage without having consulted the woman in advance. There is absolutely no trace of refusal on the part of Denise, a refusal that is found in the novel.

The silent film created by Duvivier in 1930 carries out the step towards the future delineated by Cayatte's Baudu. The plot of the film takes place at the time of its shooting, that is around 1930, a time, which, because of the introduction of talking pictures, constitutes a turning point in the history of media. It is indeed clearly discernible how the claim of absoluteness displayed until now by the visual strategy of representation comes to its limits, even though the work still relies primarily on the expressive force of pictures.

The opening of Duvivier's film is considerably more reflective than Cayatte's gay and buoyant *entrée*. Duvivier begins his film with a verbal leader, in the form of a programmatic sign, which emphasizes the relevance of the problems treated in the plot, and shifts the nature of these problems towards the question of development of progress: "Le grand magasin contre la petite boutique. Problème toujours d'actualité. Lutte cruelle, inégale, qui engender les deuils et les ruines, et dont seul est responsible celui qui règle la marche du monde: le progrès."[31]

The fundamental question raised here is whether progress and happiness are really compatible. The film discusses and solves this problem by the means of a remarkable three-step procedure of a technique, which eventually became known as "*caméra stylo.*" The beginning of the film, with the scene of Denise's arrival, translates the skepticism articulated in the leader into suggestive pictures. Denise arrives in a world visibly and totally impregnated by the presence of *Au Bonheur des Dames* and hence by its merchandise ideology. The camera records breathlessly the sheer mass of advertisements on kiosks and delivery cars, of food handlers, of flyers thrown down from a plane, and of *Au Bonheur* balloons for children. At the same time, the film makes use of a creative device typical of French silent film, namely that of cross-fading (much used by Abel Gance, for instance). Through this means, and according to the skeptical connotation of the film's leader, the film points out that the girl, living in an urban world dominated by department stores, is in danger of being destroyed as an individual being. Through the technique of fading from various pictures of the big city, Denise is thus pictorially run over by a tramway speeding by or, in another scene, she gets squeezed between the buffers of two locomotives.

In the further course of the plot, this destructive and menacing perception gives way to a more hopeful effect of reality. Duvivier now employs a framing technique in order to make clear that the department store is not exclusively determined by the uncomfortable reality of menace, exploitation and enslavement. It is remarkable that the camera repeatedly peeps through the opening doors and windows of the "sombre Vieil Elbeuf" ("somber Old Elbeuf") shop. This happens in a manner that makes the observer see only the framed particles "Bonheur" or "Au Bonheur" from the neon light advertising sign of the department store on the opposite side of the street. What is suggested here, as far as metonymy is concerned, is that beyond the old, extinct world of the Baudus, the department store harbors a promise of happiness. The fact that this focusing technique of specific framing is not to be interpreted as a cynical derision of the true reality, but that it actually anticipates a notion of happiness inherent in the department store, is proven by the end of the film. The final confrontation between Denise and Octave and their subsequent embrace is constructed as an alternating play of dialogue and interspersed pictures, which foster a visionary meaningfulness. Let us first look at the dialogue separately. It is presented, according to the necessities of silent film, through the so-called "intertitres" (intertitles). The amount of information attributed to the reading of these signs is so enormous that it becomes clear how here, at the very end of the epoch of silent film, the sound track in a way is urgently needed in order to replace the makeshift and to guarantee an authentic reproduction of the verbally coded message.

As far as the content of the dialogue is concerned, Duvivier wholly approaches Zola's discourse. In contrast to Cayatte's "patriarchal" solution to the relationship's main problem, it is Denise who plays the role of the savior, just as is the case in the novel. In view of the human disaster brought about by the modern enterprise (Geneviève dies; Baudu goes mad and dies under the crushing wheels of an *Au Bonheur* delivery car, after shooting several people in the department store and causing a general state of panic), Octave has come to the resigned conclusion that progress, as it is practiced by him, is murderous, and he thus wants to give up his business. At this point Denise joins him and, through sudden inspiration, creates an astonishing *peripety*. She declares to Octave that the power of love has in general the ability to reconcile progress and the pursuit of happiness.

OCTAVE: Je croyais faire œuvre utile.... Je n'ai créé qu'un peu plus de douleur et de ruines! J'abandonne.[32]

DENISE: [embittered] Vous avez servi le Progrès.... Lui seul est responsable. C'est nous qui avions tort.... Je le comprends maintenant.[33]

Paris during sundown. The illuminated department store. A neon-light advertising sign "Au Bonheur des Dames" pulsates.

DENISE: [now enthusiastic, visionary] Soyez fier de votre œuvre.... Soyez fort pour la continuer.[34]

During the following takes, Denise and Octave, each in the pulsating light-and-dark of the advertising sign.

OCTAVE: Denise ... j'avais été fort.... Si vous m'aviez aimé.[35]

DENISE: [with a tender glance] Je vous ai toujours aimé.... Je n'ai aimé que vous.[36]

Mlle Desforges triumphs at first seeing Octave's looming defeat. Then she notices Denise and Octave and their loving togetherness. Shattered at this view, she drives away.

DENISE: [pointing to the "Bonheur des Dames"] Ruines, misères ... tout cela demain sera le passé. [Special effect: a curtain is drawn back, the new "Bonheur" portal is unveiled.] Votre rêve s'accomplira. [A gigantic, illuminated "Au Bonheur des Dames" building, constructed in the style of a Greek temple. A little spot of light coming from a plane moving away from the department store. In the background, a tiny *Eiffel Tour*.[37]

OCTAVE: Pour le réaliser, nous serons deux.[38]

Despite the fact that the frequently inserted dialogue signs must be regarded as disturbing alien elements, one shouldn't fail to realize that Duvivier supports this level of content through several cinematic techniques with the effect that the form of the film is once again brought closer to that of the novel. We're talking here about the interspersed pictures of the illuminated department store. Zola, in a remarkable pictorial creation, had already used the white color as an expression of the local atmosphere. In the big exhibition of white merchandise, "la débauche du blanc,"[39] Zola arranges the white color in a way which magnifies it to light: "Rien que du blanc, et jamais le même blanc, tous les blancs, s'enlevant les uns sur les autres, s'opposant, se complétant, arrivant à l'éclat même de la lumière."[40] Such an apotheosis of light symbolizes unequivocally the triumph of modern times. For the cinematic version of the novel it is not difficult to translate onto screen the result of Zola's verbally ingenious technique of description. Following the already noticeable semantic framing technique of the neon-light advertising sign, the film now definitely confirms the grandiose illuminated department store as the visionary epitome of redeeming progress.[41]

Moreover, the new building's optical affinity with a Greek temple is certainly not coincidental. This sort of architecture is chosen in order to refer to the *sacral* character of the modern department store business, which actually achieves the status of a cult through the provision of a new "redeeming offer" in the shape of merchandise and a desire for consumption, a condition already extensively recorded by Zola. But this verbal and optic conclusion of the film and hence the cinematic debate on principles is not everything. It is topped by the film's emblematic summary of the redeeming vision. A plane writes "Au Bonheur" in the sky with the trails of smoke from its engines, and thus produces a verbal realization of the term "happy ending." In the game of an advertising campaign, the *signifier* of the department store advertising becomes a new *signified* which does justice to the positive myth of progress as it is realized by Denise and Octave. Not only does the modern temple of merchandise now conquer the sky and thus seem to determine reality in a truly totalitarian way (think about the takes from the film's beginning mentioned earlier), the conclusion recapitulates once more the equation formulated by the film. The plane, as a technical apparatus and as a vehicle of advertising, unites progress and the department store in one. It furthermore adds an additional equals sign through the deliberately abbreviated writing, "Au Bonheur": department store = progress = happiness.

On the level of configuration of sense, both adaptations, Duvivier's work dating from the end of the era of silent film as well as Cayatte's talking version, deal with the same essential problem formulated in Émile Zola's novel: the historical necessity of commercial and industrial progress under modern mono-capitalist conditions and the consequences of this process for human conditions of existence. Fifty or sixty years after Zola's example, the discussion about the price of "modern times" is obviously still virulent in the collective consciousness. Yet, we can find a fundamental difference within this generally congruent discussion about the "tribute of progress." In Zola's naturalistic optics the possibility of realizing "l'activité moderne"[42] was a compelling matter of his time: "[Octave] répéta qu'il était de son temps";[43] "aller avec le siècle, exprimer le siècle."[44] He also considered the conflict arising after the labor dispute definitely solved at the end of his novel.[45] In contrast, both cinematic discourses display a much more skeptical approach, even though they ultimately merge into a happy ending. In this manner, both films proceed to a certain extent from a *teleological* concept which claims that one has to work in order to achieve a state in which economic progress and human conditions of existence become compatible. The realization of this harmony will first be possible in a *future* historical moment. In return, one can observe an almost hymnal celebration of the hope for this happy future in Cayatte's film, and of the vision of its completion in Duvivier's work.

One could speculate whether in our postmodern times a contemporary filmmaker, call him Claude Chabrol, Bertrand Tavernier or Robert Altman, would take an equally positive view on screen if he tackled Zola's material. In view of the *event*-culture of our supermarkets and shopping malls, the attempt at a new film adaptation seems to me more tempting than ever.

Notes

1. "The price of progress."
2. David Baguley, "From Man's Misfortune to *Au Bonheur des Dames*," *Excavatio* 3 (1993): 112.
3. "Summary": "Small commerce crushed by the big stores. Those true steam engines at work. *A fight for life*. Cheerful." The page numbers refer to the Pléiade edition of *Au Bonheur des Dames* and of the "Dossier préparatoire." Émile Zola, *Au Bonheur des Dames, Les Rougon-Macquart, Histoire naturelle et sociale d'une famille sous le second Empire*, eds. Armand Lanoux and Henri Mitterrand, Vol. III (Paris: Bibliothèque de la Pléiade, 1964), 1696. Italics in the original.
4. Ibid., 1680. "I want in *Au Bonheur des Dames* to create a poem of modern activity. Therefore, it's a complete change of philosophy: first, more pessimism, but rather than leading to a conclusion emphasizing stupidity and the melancholy of life, on the contrary, the conclusion will emphasize continual labor, the power and the cheerfulness of its birth. In a word, go with the century; express the century, which is a century of action and of conquest, of efforts in all directions."
5. Ibid., 479. "Struggle without truce or pity."
6. Ibid., 598. "Continuous renewal of the capital which was the invincible force of the new commerce."
7. Ibid., 748. "The continuous exploitation of woman."
8. Ibid., 1648. "Triumph of Venus."
9. Ibid., 790. "Acute temptation, a blow of mad desire that disconcerts all women."
10. Ibid., 632. "Mad creatures."
11. Ibid., 797. "The clientele, stripped, violated, was leaving partially undone, with a fulfilled will and a silent shame about a desire satisfied in a shady hotel." The reader should refer to Hannah Thompson's "Une perversion du désir, une névrose nouvelle': Female Sexuality in Zola's *Au Bonheur des Dames*," *Romance Studies* 32 (1998).
12. "Octave exploitant la femme, puis vaincu par la femme. Mais cela très gai" ("Octave exploiting woman, then defeated by woman. Yet very cheerful." Ibid., 1682.
13. Ibid., 796. "Proud and vindictive image of Denise, whose victorious heel [Octave] felt on his throat."
14. Ibid., 773. "Invincible logic of facts."
15. Ibid. "Superstition according to which the director of a big house of novelties should be single if he wanted to keep his male superiority over the extended desires of his group of female customers."
16. Ibid., 761. "Denise felt chosen by the logic of the facts."
17. Cf. the detailed description of this social work (727–731) and the motivation of Denise: "Et elle plaidait la cause des rouages de la machine, non par des raisons

sentimentales, mais par des arguments tirés de l'intérêt même des patrons. Quand on veut une machine solide, on emploie du bon fer; si le fer casse ou si on le casse, il y a un arrêt du travail, des frais répétés de mise en train, toute une déperdition de force." ("And she pled the cause of the gearwheels of the machine, not for sentimental reasons, but because of arguments drawn from the employers' interests. When one wants a solid machine, one uses good iron; if the iron breaks or if one breaks it, the work is stopped, repetitive expenses of activation, a great loss of energy."). Ibid., 728.

18. Ibid., 504. "Her good grace about suffering."
19. Ibid., 634. "Her serenity in the suffering."
20. Ibid., 726. "Final success of her long courage."
21. Ibid., 504. "Invincible gentleness."
22. Ibid., 701. "Redoubtable in her gentleness."
23. Ibid., 657. "Gentle and inexorable strength of will."
24. Cf. for this configuration the fundamental study of Jean Borie, *Le tyran timide: Le naturalisme de la femme au XIXe siècle* (Paris: Klincksieck, 1973).
25. Ibid., 803. "Almighty."
26. J.D. Kaminskas notes the subversion of the structure of the fairytale employed in *Au bonheur des Dames* in order to deconstruct the patriarchal definition of the woman: "Si, à la fin du roman la femme a une voix, c'est parce qu'elle n'est plus *l'objet* mais le sujet du discours" ("If, at the end of the novel the woman has a voice, it is because she is no longer the object but the subject of the discourse"). "Itinéraires de la femme seule à Paris, pour une lecture renouvelée de *Au bonheur des dames*," *Excavatio* 6/7 (1995): 141. See also the much more skeptical analysis of N. Schorr who explains the femininity conquered by Denise as a "pure construction, un effet produit par son entrée dans le grand magasin, la plus belle réussite de Mouret" ("pure construction, an effect produced by her entrance into the big store, Mouret's greatest success"). "Devant le château femmes, marchandises et modernité dans *Au Bonheur des Dames*," in Philippe Hamon and Jean-Pierre Leduc-Adine, eds., *Mimesis et semiosis: Littérature et représentation. Miscellanées offertes à Henri Mitterrand* (Paris: Nathan, 1992): 186.
27. Ibid., 743. "It seemed to him that he was hearing the stamping of a herd on its way to the slaughterhouse, all the disintegration of shops in a neighborhood, small commerce dragging its ruin, with the wet noise of a worn-out shoe, in the black mud of Paris."
28. Baudu: "You have ruined me, thrown me out on the street. But you won't be triumphant for long. You have created a monstrous machine that nothing will stop from now on. You too will meet your Mouret one day, a crook more powerful than you, who will crush you like you crushed the others and who will in turn be crushed. In twenty years commerce will only be a hideous battle where quality, integrity and trust will be trampled on, killed like the Old Elbeuf. Be careful Mouret, you impose the rule of rubbish and of the showy. Be patient, there is a price for everything. You too will know unemployment and a similar shame. You will become the slave of your financiers and your cathedrals of rubbish will fall down with echoes of ruins, of scandals and blood. Me, I am too old, I will have the good fortune to die before witnessing all that."
29. Mouret: "Yes, friends, M. Baudu is right. A company like mine could only be built by ruining, unfortunately, brave people like him. It is the price of progress. But success also imposes duties. And if, unwillingly, I have caused pain, consciously I want to do well. And it is about you, my collaborators, that I am thinking. Here is my program: reintegration of personnel fired without motives *[Applause. Octave asks for silence]*, creation of a marriage allowance office *[Applause. During the following speech, Mouret is not seen; the camera follows Baudu, who forces his way to the exit, passing the assembly of employees, who do not notice him at all since they are concentrating on Octave's speech coming from the opposite direction]*, assistance for young mothers, construction

of a maternity home, of an old people's home, guarantees of a respectable retirement for all those who have suffered here all their life *[Passionate applause]*."

30. Octave: "Don't thank me. If I have been brought to consider your case, it is because one of you made me understand your misery and your hopes *[Denise is brought in by Jouve, and Octave seizes her hand]*. Thank Miss Baudu, who, I hope will soon be Mrs. Mouret."

31. "The big shop against the small boutique. An always current problem. A cruel, unequal battle that generates grievances and ruins and the responsibility for which lies solely with that which regulates the march of the world: progress."

32. Octave: "I thought I was doing a good deed.... And I only created more pain and ruins. I am quitting."

33. Denise: "You have done well for progress.... It alone is responsible. We were the ones who were wrong.... I know that now."

34. Denise: "Be proud of your work.... Be strong to continue it."

35. Octave: "Denise ... I would have been strong.... If you had loved me."

36. Denise: "I have always loved you.... You were the only one I loved."

37. Denise: "*[pointing to the "Bonheur des Dames"]* Ruins, misery.... Tomorrow, all this will belong to the past. [Special effect: a curtain is drawn back, the new "Bonheur" portal is unveiled.] Your dream will become true. [*A gigantic, illuminated "Au Bonheur des Dames" building, constructed in the style of a Greek temple. A little spot of light coming from a plane moving away from the department store. In the background, a tiny Eiffel Tower]*."

38. Octave: "To fulfill it, there will be two of us."

39. Ibid., 768. "The profusion of white."

40. Ibid., 769. "Of white only, and never the same white, all whites taking away from each other, opposing, and completing each other, attaining the brightness of light."

41. This is achieved, by the way, through a special effect in which an artificial curtain is slowly drawn back by an invisible hand, in order to reveal the splendid illuminated new building of *Bonheur des Dames*.

42. Ibid., 1681. "Modern activity."

43. Ibid., 751. "[Octave] repeated that was in tune with his times."

44. Ibid., 1680. "To progress with the century, to convey the century."

45. Cf. Denise's perspective: "ces maux irrémédiables, qui sont l'enfantement douloureux de chaque génération" ("these incurable sorrows that are the painful beginnings of every generation"). Ibid., 747. For further analysis of the "naturalisation" of the capitalist competition in the sense of a compelling necessity of progress, compare Habiba B. Deming, "Naturalisme ou 'naturalisation' dans *Au Bonheur des Dames*," *Excavatio* 1 (1992): 45–51.

7

Viewing *Au Bonheur des Dames* in the Context of Occupied France

JENNIFER WOLTER

André Cayatte's 1943 film adaptation of *Au Bonheur des Dames*,[1] though largely overlooked by critics and the public alike, is a worthy subject for study on two levels. First, the film stands on its own as an example of the success of French cinema under German Occupation during World War II. Cayatte's biography adds to the intrigue surrounding this film, which contains subtle hints of anti–Nazi sentiment as well as more overt signs of French national pride. A second level of study is the comparison of the film with its literary source. Cayatte's film revisits many of the issues first brought to light in the 1883 novel by Émile Zola, including the life-or-death struggle of the *petit commerce* (small business) with the *grand magasin* (department store). The significance of this conflict in the film takes on a new symbolic meaning in the context of World War II as the French are made to succumb to the German occupiers. Cayatte's intentions in making *Au Bonheur des Dames* were indeed more profound than the love story, which appears most dominant in the film. Cayatte's own words, along with other historical and critical studies, support the interpretation of this film as a commentary on the war situation at the time of the film's release. Furthermore, an analysis of Zola's novel in relation to the film provides insight into some of Cayatte's choices as a filmmaker. Overall, Cayatte's film does remain true to Zola's novel, which not only upholds the integrity of the work, but also helps to ensure the author's presence in the minds of viewers.[2]

Before undertaking a comparison of the film with the novel, it is essential to establish first the status of filmmaking during the war period and to proceed with a presentation of André Cayatte and his adaptation of *Au Bonheur des Dames*. Although the production side of the industry suffered from limited resources during the Occupation, the viewing public looked to the cinema as a diversion from reality.[3] In addition to providing a sort of physical haven from the outside world, theaters offered the chance to escape mentally into fantasy worlds or to reminisce about happier times. Adaptations of literary works were a particularly good source for films. Audiences were familiar with many of the great novels of nineteenth-century authors and would flock to see their cinematographic adaptations. Moreover, the realist style of nineteenth-century literature was well-suited to this visual medium. In fact, films adapted from literary works were already quite popular by 1943 when Continental Films, a German-controlled production company operating in occupied France, decided to make Zola's *Au Bonheur des Dames*.

André Cayatte's employment as a director for Continental came about in the absence of many of the great directors who had been working up to that point. If not for the German Occupation, Cayatte might never have achieved success as a director. Born in 1909, Cayatte's prewar existence included careers as a lawyer and journalist before he made his way into the world of cinema as a scriptwriter and, eventually, director. His big break came amid the initial "disarray" of the French cinema during the war, according to Jean-Pierre Bertin-Maghit: "Artistes, techniciens, metteurs en scène qui avaient fait les beaux jours des années 30 étaient portés 'disparus' (exil, mobilisation générale, mort)."[4] Cayatte himself was engaged in the war for a time before joining Continental Films. Yet, his involvement with the German production company would later come under scrutiny by the Comité de libération du cinéma français (CLCF).[5] In a hearing before the commission on October 17, 1944, Cayatte explained his early participation in the war and how he came to be associated with Continental Films:

> J'ai fait la guerre comme soldat sur la ligne Maginot. Fait prisonnier en juin 1940, je m'évade quelques semaines plus tard et arrive à Paris le 3 octobre sans papiers d'identité, avec 800 francs en poche et ma femme venant d'avoir un enfant.... On est fin décembre 1940, début 1941. Je suis donc engagé à la Continental comme scénariste et metteur en scène. En mars ou avril 1942, [Alfred] Greven me convoque et m'apprend qu'il a découvert ma condition de prisonnier évadé et m'interdit de travailler pour une autre maison de production sous peine d'être envoyé dans un camp.... J'ai donc réalisé quatre films pour Continental: *La Fausse Maîtresse*, 1942; *Au Bonheur des Dames, Pierre et Jean* et *Le Dernier Sou*, 1943.[6]

Cayatte continued to plead his case by demonstrating his support of the Resistance movement: "Pendant toute l'Occupation j'ai écrit régulièrement, sous le pseudonyme d'Abel Cartier, des nouvelles violemment antinazies sur la Résistance en France que je faisais passer à l'étranger par l'intermédiaire de M. d'Aguiar. J'ai rejoint dès sa création le groupe Ceux de la Résistance."[7] This statement, taken into consideration with the experience of being an escaped prisoner, his family situation, and the circumstances of his work under Alfred Greven at Continental, eventually led the CLCF to dismiss charges against Cayatte.

If we accept Cayatte's testimony of his strong anti–Nazi position, as well as take into account that he wrote under the pseudonym of Abel Cartier, it is not unreasonable to expect some latent references to the war situation in his films. *Au Bonheur des Dames* contains in fact several commentaries on the Occupation. The decor and costumes required to recreate the luxurious department store setting suggest an escape from the dreary atmosphere of occupied France. Add to that the rags-to-riches story of the main character, Denise Baudu, which Dominique Jullien likens to the fairy tale of Cinderella: "À l'intrigue réaliste (le triomphe du grand magasin sur la petite boutique) est tissée une intrigue de conte, encore plus satisfaisante pour l'imagination du lecteur et peut-être, surtout, de la lectrice, la victoire de l'innocente jeune fille sur l'homme à bonnes fortunes, du faible sur le fort."[8] While the triumph of Denise over Mouret may remind readers and moviegoers of a fairy tale ending, the struggle between the two male characters, Mouret and Baudu, culminates in the very real defeat of the weak by the strong. Thus, the story itself presents a juxtaposition of realist and fairy tale qualities, a juxtaposition which also applies to the conditions of shooting the film.

Continental Films enjoyed many benefits that were not readily available to other production companies.[9] Yet, even the filming of *Au Bonheur des Dames* suffered from the effects of the Occupation. In an interview with Guy Braucourt, Cayatte spoke of the difficult circumstances the team endured while shooting the film:

> On ne travaillait que la nuit au studio de Billancourt, car il n'y avait pas d'électricité dans la journée; or pratiquement toutes les nuits il y avait des alertes, et toute l'équipe allait se réfugier dans le cimetière voisin, passant par une brèche du mur et plongeant dans les tranchées creusées pour la prochaine fournée de morts! Et à cinq heures du matin, au sortir du cimetière, il fallait faire danser tout ce beau monde en grande toilette.... Le paradoxe, c'était que, pour décrire l'abondance, pour raconter la tentation des femmes pour les richesses des grands magasins, je ne disposais pour ainsi dire de rien en raison des restrictions.... Les conditions suggéraient en somme le climat du

> roman de Zola une vie insouciante, des bals, des toilettes, mais en
> même temps, l'inquiétude d'une société qui marche vers ce gigan-
> tesque abattoir de 70.[10]

In this detailed account, Cayatte reveals the dichotomy between the film and its actual production. The lack of electricity and the necessity of filming at night contrast with the brightness in the lighting of the film's set. Another paradox to note is the experience of hiding in a real cemetery, then returning to the set of the "pretend" department store, which actually should be a safe haven since it is described in the novel as a place of refuge and comfort for women.[11]

The irony of having to film such a lavish production among the restrictions of the period points to the underlying turmoil of Zola's time, as Cayatte suggested in the passage above. Without going too far into the meaning of Cayatte's statement on the conditions leading up to the conflict of 1870, it is still possible to see the correlation between the social atmosphere depicted in Zola's novel and that of the film. The achievement of making *Au Bonheur des Dames* under the conditions described above is comparable to the victories won in the story itself. Out of misery and hardship can come individual happiness and social progress. These two end results may be representative of the hope that Cayatte wished to suggest, whether overtly or subconsciously, to his French audience in the face of German Occupation. First, the audience can appreciate the rise of Denise from salesgirl to *première*, ultimately becoming Mouret's wife and partner, thanks to her decent character. Denise could even be a symbol of a virtuous France that must strive to overcome the oppression of an unjust German Occupation. Second, the fact that Mouret's department store is transformed into a more humane, egalitarian environment signals a movement of social progress, which leads to an optimistic ending of the film and possibly indicates an optimistic outcome for France also.

Surely there are different implications to explore in the interpretation of both the film and the novel, but it is important to take as a point of departure Zola's attitude toward social progress, which he reveals in the *ébauche* (introduction) of the novel:

> Je veux dans Au Bonheur des Dames faire le poème de l'activité moderne. Donc, changement complet de philosophie, plus de pessimisme d'abord, ne pas conclure à la bêtise et à la mélancolie de la vie, conclure au contraire à son continuel labeur, à la puissance et à la gaieté de son enfantement. En un mot, aller avec le siècle, exprimer le siècle, qui est un siècle d'action et de conquêtes.[12]

Zola's "poem of modern activity" revolves around the *grand magasin* and the revolution it brings to the world of commerce. The triumph of the *grand magasin* over the *petit commerce* is contingent upon the strength of the "dictator" Mouret and his "army" of employees, especially the young saleswomen who come from modest backgrounds to work in the new department store, "Au Bonheur des Dames." In fact, the contrast of milieu these women experience can be likened to that experienced by the personnel while making the film, as Cayatte reported, and can even be compared to the situation of moviegoers who left the somber atmosphere of occupied France to escape into the theater and into the story presented on-screen. But, the story of Denise Baudu is not too far from reality. Zola's basis for this juxtaposition of the salesgirls and the high-society ladies who make up their clientele is founded on his research of the major Parisian department stores, including Au Bon Marché.[13] Zola's naming of his fictional store epitomizes the irony of the *grand magasin:* Au Bonheur des Dames is a welcoming place for the *grandes dames* of Parisian bourgeois society, while the women who actually work in the store find little happiness there.

The idea that the salesgirls are caught between two different socioeconomic worlds is evident in the film's realistic depiction of their cramped living quarters above the spacious store in which they must serve the upper-class women. The management treats the young saleswomen almost like prisoners, rushing them off to work early in the morning and depriving them of electricity at night. Cutting the electricity in the girls' rooms was sure to remind French viewers of the very limitations they experienced. In addition, one scene in Denise's room opens with a close-up of a sign that forbids washing laundry in the sink; the camera then pulls back to show Denise and her friend Pauline doing their laundry. This act of defiance suggests that the young women refuse to obey unpractical rules. Pauline's advice to Denise seems to condone breaking the rules because the management does not understand their needs and denies them such simple privileges, while expecting them to be impeccably dressed for work. Likewise, viewers could interpret this scene as a justification to question the authority of the German occupiers who imposed their rules on the French.

Another character who challenges authority and breaks the rules is Denise's brother Jean. His secret meetings with her imply a kind of danger. Then, when he is caught, he infuriates the manager by refusing to reveal his identity, joking that it is a "secret d'état." The relationship between Denise and her brothers firmly establishes her wholesome role as "petite mère." Also, her innocence and modesty distinguish her from the other women characters. Zola's novel insists even more than the film on the contrast between Denise and the clientele of the department store as well as between Denise and the more sophisticated saleswomen. Furthermore, Denise's provincial origins set her apart from the Parisian women from the very start. When we first encounter Denise, both in the novel and in the film, she is just arriving in Paris with her two younger brothers. The opening scene of the film shows the difference in her clothing as she descends from the omnibus in comparison to the well-dressed woman being helped aboard. The awkward appearance of the three siblings is further emphasized by the way in which the camera looks down on them from a high-angle view. This camera position has the effect of reducing them to marginalized characters, overwhelmed by these unfamiliar city surroundings, including the luminous department store.

As we follow Denise's ascent in the *grand magasin*, we observe her swift transformation from a beginning salesgirl with an ill-fitting uniform into a confident woman who becomes the object of Mouret's desire. This development happens much faster in the film than in the novel and omits a great deal of the hardships that Denise must face. For example, Zola includes many instances where the taunts and harassment by her co-workers and her superiors reduce Denise to tears. Additionally, most of the financial difficulties she experiences in the novel are left out of Cayatte's film. Of course, one explanation for this choice is the time constraint of condensing an entire novel into a standard-length film. But perhaps a deeper motive is that the filmmaker did not want to focus on such misery, which might remind viewers of their own troubles during the Occupation. It seems, however, that the most significant reason for downplaying Denise's suffering in the film is to stress her triumph as a positive force within the *grand magasin*. The contrast between Denise and Henriette Desforges also serves to highlight Denise's virtue. Mouret's involvement with Henriette in the novel is driven primarily by his desire to mingle with the upper class of Paris. He exploits his relationship with Henriette to gain access to prominent businessmen, such as the Baron Hartmann, who share his aspiration to modernize the city of Paris. However, while Mouret uses Henriette to advance his business with the Baron Hartmann in the novel, Mouret's interests in the film are centered on directly buying out the small shopkeepers of the area. Therefore, Henriette's role as a go-between shifts focus in the film as she swindles Baudu on behalf of Mouret.

According to Cayatte's film, Henriette Desforges is comparable to a secret negotiator who works with both enemy camps. On the one hand, we witness her smooth, flirtatious conversations with Mouret, whether in his office or in her home, while playing the piano or shot against the unusual background of performing acrobats. All of these scenes clearly demonstrate the mixing of pleasure and business between Henriette and Mouret. But on the other hand, she works her charms on Baudu, leading him to sign away his shop for a loan by pretending that she is on his side, not Mouret's. Her hypocrisy may have had a special significance in the eyes of French viewers at the time of World War II, as it brings to mind the treachery of some collaborators. Moreover, Denise and Henriette are pitted as rivals in a battle of good versus evil, with Denise gaining the upper hand as Mouret falls for her. Henriette's judgment of Denise ranges from harsh criticism to bitter jealousy as she observes Denise's growing relationship with Mouret. For instance, in one of their first encounters, Denise and Mouret dress a mannequin while Henriette and Mouret's associate Bourdoncle look on from a distance. The fact that the camera reveals a mirror reflection of the backs of Denise and Mouret with Henriette and Bourdoncle spying on them indicates an act of surveillance.

The inspector Bourdoncle is a cunning figure of surveillance in the film as in the novel. He is always lurking about with his clipboard, waiting to catch someone making a mistake, and then pouncing on them with his infamous lines: "Premier et dernier avertissement!"("First and last warning") and "Passez à la caisse!" ("Proceed to the cashier [for your final wages]!"). These threats are taken very seriously by the employees, but their repetition throughout the film and the way in which actor Jean Tissier delivers the lines produce a comical effect. In contrast, Zola's description of Bourdoncle in the novel is much more vicious than Cayatte's. The language Zola uses to tell of the lay-offs is quite violent: "Bourdoncle se chargeait des exécutions. Il avait, de ses lèvres minces, un terrible 'Passez à la caisse!' qui tombait comme un coup de hache. Tout lui devenait prétexte pour déblayer le plancher. Il inventait des méfaits, il spéculait sur les plus légères negligences.... Et les braves eux-mêmes tremblaient, devant le massacre qu'il laissait derrière lui."[14] Despite the differences in how punishment is dealt, both the novel and the film make it clear that management has the right to decide what is right and what is wrong. The punishment does not necessarily fit the crime, but rather is handed out according to social status: while shoppers are treated with respect and are even excused for stealing, sales clerks are subject to much stricter standards of conduct.

Mouret's surveillance of women extends to the clientele in addition to his own employees. In the novel, the narrator often portrays him towering over his "peuple de clients"("nation of female clients"). The film conveys this image with the camera showing Mouret looking from his office window down on the women shoppers below. Yet, Zola's novel delicately balances this position of domination with Mouret's submission to women: "Mouret avait l'unique passion de vaincre la femme. Il la voulait reine dans sa maison, il lui avait bâti ce temple, pour l'y tenir à sa merci."[15] According to the narrator, Mouret seduces the women of Paris, salesgirls and customers alike, for his own financial benefit: "L'énorme succès du magasin venait de cette séduction galante."[16]

Mouret's attitude toward women reveals an attempt to control female sexuality. However, Denise overcomes Mouret by controlling his sexuality, though unintentionally. Her presence affects him to the point that he no longer desires other women and she becomes the ruler of the store: "Le règne de Denise commençait."[17] Brian Nelson even calls Denise's conquest of Mouret a "counter-revolution" which breaks the mold of male domination because "Denise is the only one of the salesgirls who refuses to play the game, refuses to be commodified. The price of her hand in marriage is the introduction of humanitarian reforms in the running of the store."[18]

The improvements that Denise convinces Mouret to make represent for Zola the announcement of a future society: "C'était l'embryon des vastes sociétés ouvrières du vingtième siècle."[19] It is clear, however, that the community remains a work-in-progress as Zola closes the story before the marriage takes place. Despite the sudden ending, it is implied that Denise's rise to the top will instill an atmosphere of family values among the store community, as indicated by her ability to revise Mouret's formal policies and his personal feelings toward marriage and maternity. However, the film seems to insist more on Mouret, not Denise, as the instigator of change. One reason why Cayatte shifted the main focus to Mouret at this point may simply be because Albert Préjean, in the role of Mouret, was the major star of the film along with Michel Simon playing Baudu. The film plays up the rivalry between the two male actors and their characters' engagement in a price war that grows to encompass the much larger battle of a struggling *petit commerce* against the powerful *grand magasin*. As Barbara Vinken notes, this conflict becomes an allegory, "a fight for life against death": "The department store represents life, whereas the specialized trades represent death. What life finally kills are the already dead.... Mouret does not bring death, he forces it into the open and thereby exorcises it."[20] Indeed, the decisive encounter between Mouret and Baudu is perhaps the most significant scene of the film, considering the social commentary it carries.

Before analyzing this final scene, which did not occur in the novel, it is important to understand Baudu's situation as the demise of his shop signals the death of the *petit commerce*. Like his niece Denise, Baudu is very headstrong and serves as a symbol of a resistant France under German Occupation in the film. The passionate performance given by Michel Simon stirs the French people to rally behind Baudu's character. In his first appearance of the film, Baudu bursts upon the scene, ranting and raving about his enemy Mouret. His determination to fight Mouret is contagious as he becomes the leader of the resistance movement in the neighborhood. The small shopkeepers all gather around Baudu's table to plan their strategy against Mouret in a scene which seems to recreate an actual resistance meeting from the time of World War II. Regardless of whether that was Cayatte's intention or whether the audience made that association, this scene presents a united front against the giant modern commerce.

Along with Baudu, several other characters lose their business to Mouret, such as old Bourras whose display of umbrellas looks pitiful next to the abundance of items in the windows of the department store. Families are destroyed because of the *grand magasin*. Baudu's daughter dies, presumably of a broken heart, at the precise moment when her fiancé declares that he is abandoning her and the shop. His betrayal and alliance with the enemy may be yet another reference to the war, as he rejects the Baudu family and collaborates with Mouret. Zola's novel follows the death of Baudu's daughter with the death of her mother and the attempted suicide of another shopkeeper. Cayatte communicates this effect in the film through the representation of the "death" of Baudu's store, made final when its sign crashes to the ground. Although Denise is there to support her uncle in the film, the novel takes us a step further by allowing us to read her thoughts, which reflect the conflicting emotions of the narrator, and perhaps of Zola himself:

> Mon Dieu! que de tortures! des familles qui pleurent, des vieillards jetés au pavé, tous les drames poignants de la ruine! Et elle ne pouvait sauver personne, et elle avait conscience que cela était bon, qu'il fallait ce fumier de misères à la santé du Paris de demain.... Oui, c'était la part du sang, toute révolution voulait des martyrs, on ne marchait en avant que sur des morts.[21]

Denise understands that it is necessary to suffer in order to advance toward the future. She accepts that the *petit commerce* must be sacrificed to the prosperity of the *grand magasin*. Vinken sums up Denise's point of view: "The misery of today is a precondition of the health of tomorrow's Paris.... The victims suffer for some public happiness to come."[22]

Unlike Denise, Baudu is determined to hold on to the past. His fight for survival culminates in a public confrontation with Mouret in the film. Looking at the way Cayatte staged this scene, one cannot help but notice Baudu's position of inferiority as the camera looks down on him from a high-angle view. The fact that he is ostracized as he leaves the store adds to the notion that he does not belong in this palace of modern commerce. And although Baudu dies, ironically from being run over by a carriage of *nouveautés* (novelty items) from the department store, he has upheld the dignity of his people. Thus, the audience must decide whether Baudu's death is a sheer tragedy, perhaps in the same way France was victimized by the Nazi regime, or as an honorable but obligatory submission which will bring progress toward the future. Many critics would choose the latter interpretation. In *Le Cinéma sous l'occupation,* Bertin-Maghit sees Baudu's death as necessary to the success of the union between Denise and Mouret: "Cette union finale lie à tout jamais le passé et le présent dans le progrès—c'est dans ce sens qu'il faut analyser la mort de Boudu (sic), renversé par un fiacre, il doit disparaître pour rendre l'association possible."[23] Thus, progress comes from the linking of the past with the present in the form of Denise and Mouret's marriage, whereas Baudu denied progress by choosing the stagnation of the past.

The final and lasting image of the film centers on Mouret and Denise, as symbols of the France of the future. They are united at the top of the staircase, but the key is that they descend to take their place among their employees, renamed associates. The ending embraces the vision of an ideal community in which all are treated as equals. Cayatte's film communicates a similar message to French viewers. Rather than accepting the Occupation and submitting to the Germans, Cayatte points toward a solution where good overcomes evil and hierarchy is abolished. The film encourages the French to leave behind that which is past and to concentrate instead on improving the future of their nation. Mouret comes to incarnate this notion of French national pride both in the novel and in Cayatte's film. He is always looking toward the future, planning a season ahead, and he eventually accepts the suggestions made by Denise, whose compassion and sense of innovation both humanize and modernize the department store. Bertin-Maghit classifies *Au Bonheur des Dames* among those films which call for workers to unite for the sake of productivity: "Tous ces films se regroupent derrière la charte du travail qui appelle à l'union de tous: 'patrons, artisans, techniciens, employés, ouvriers, oubliez vos origines, oubliez vos divisions du passé.'"[24] Although Bertin-Maghit takes these words from Philippe Pétain, it sounds as though they could have come from Mouret's speech in the final scene of the film. The success of the *grand magasin* hinges upon the resolution of conflict between the sales clerks and management in order to prioritize the business itself, which Bertin-Maghit also sees in the French economy during the war: "[D]ès la fin 1942-43, efficacité, productivité, planification deviennent les mots d'ordre de l'économie française."[25]

Trying to define what the French people saw in Cayatte's film is feasible only if we consider the audience as a group that shared the common experience of living under German Occupation. While the concepts of resistance and progress discussed here may seem contradictory, they can also work together in the context of occupied France. Denise and her uncle Baudu are both characters of resistance. Although Baudu's efforts fail, Denise succeeds because her motivation is different from his. Denise embraces the *grand magasin* and the ways of the future; she works to create a more humane social environment. By resisting the manipulation and degradation of salesgirls at the hands of Mouret and his associates, Denise's actions result in a complete transformation of the department store and its personnel. Mouret's improvements, both of his own character and of his store, would not have been possible without the positive influence of Denise. The happy ending, therefore, signifies a step toward a better future for the protagonists and provides a welcome message to the French people at the time of occupied France. The fairy tale quality of this story comes across very strongly at the film's conclusion, leaving viewers with a sense of contentment and hope for the future, even though they cannot help but recognize the artificiality of the drama. One could easily add the French equivalent of the phrase "and they lived happily ever after" at the end of the film, dismissing it all as a fairy tale. In fact, at the time of its release, a critic writing for *Comœdia* issued this rather reductive analysis of the film:

> [Le film] nous montre les marionnettes d'une sorte, non pas de dessin animé, mais de modelage animé.... Ils [les acteurs] nous apparaissent comme des figurines de cire tournant au bout des doigts agiles de leur plasmateur.... On dirait une rétrospective du costume. Devant nous, pour une pavane absurde, une vitrine de Carnavalet s'est animée quelques instants.... De ce point de vue féerique, l'ours de Cayatte mérite peut-être qu'on le considère.... Mais faire un film pour faire un film n'est pas une bonne formule.[26]

Although this review treats the film as not much more than a puppet show, it does contain some truth, which Cayatte acknowledged along with his critics. However, his estimation of *Au Bonheur des Dames,* along with his other early films, affirms his voice as a cinematic *auteur* who never compromised his vision: "J'ai appris mon métier à travers quelques films qui sont peut-être ridicules, mais dont je n'ai pas à avoir honte parce que je n'y ai jamais soutenu ou exprimé des sentiments contraires à mes convictions."[27] *Au Bonheur des Dames* prevails as a film made under the Occupation, yet refuses to submit entirely to its doctrine. Cayatte maintains and even promotes his system of beliefs in the production of this film, bringing social issues to the fore as he would continue to do throughout his career in cinema, according to Braucourt:

> Pamphlétaire, témoin de son (de notre) temps, Cayatte va donner pour le meilleur de son œuvre des films de combat, débattant non seulement de thèmes, de préoccupations philosophiques ou morales élevées comme la justice, la responsabilité, la solidarité, les droits de l'individu, etc., mais encore posant ces problèmes dans une perspective sociale qui va permettre à ses films de cerner une réalité française rarement étudiée de si près et si en profondeur à l'écran.[28]

Indeed, André Cayatte's career reveals a commitment to making films of substance, both in dealing with social and moral themes and in their truthful representation of French society. Rather than disregard *Au Bonheur des Dames* for its idealism and superficiality, viewers must be aware of the deeper significance of this film. *Au Bonheur des Dames* surpasses the usual expectations for a film that is adapted directly from a literary work. Ultimately, Cayatte's film proves to be much more complex than one would imagine and, therefore, calls for closer examination in terms of its place in the cinema of the Occupation as well as its relation to Zola's novel.

Notes

1. *Au Bonheur des Dames*, screenplay by André Cayatte and André Legrand, dir. André Cayatte, perfs. Michel Simon, Albert Préjean, and Blanchette Brunoy, Tobis Film, 1943.

2. Although beyond the scope of this study, one could argue that Zola's authorial presence in the film adaptation might have had special significance because of his involvement in the Dreyfus Affair. Viewers of Cayatte's film may or may not have considered that connection, but even the basic knowledge that the film was adapted from Zola was likely to stir the memory of the Dreyfus Affair and the issue of anti-Semitism.

3. Jacques Siclier, for instance, recalls going to the movie theater as a way to forget about the reality of the Occupation despite the intrusion of propaganda both in the films and in the newsreels which often preceded them: "On n'allait pas au cinéma pour retrouver la vie réelle, arrangée ou non à la sauce propagandiste, on y allait pour l'oublier." ("We did not go to the cinema to find 'real' life, served up, or not, in a propagandist sauce; we went there to forget it.") Jacques Siclier, *La France de Pétain et son cinéma* (Paris: Henri Veyrier, 1981), 37.

4. Jean-Pierre Bertin-Maghit, *Le Cinéma français sous Vichy: les films français de 1940 à 1944* (Paris: Revue du Cinéma and Editions Albatros, 1980), 9. "Artists, technicians, film directors who had experienced the flourishing of film in the 30's were reported 'missing' (i.e. exiled, mobilized, dead)."

5. The acts of the CLCF are documented in Jean-Pierre Bertin-Maghit's thorough study, *Le Cinéma sous l'occupation: le monde du cinéma français de 1940 à 1946* (Paris: Olivier Orban, 1989). Along with André Cayatte, seven others were on the list of suspended filmmakers issued by the CLCF on September 4, 1944. Henri-Georges Clouzot and Marcel Carné were among those cited. Within days, the list grew significantly, including technicians, stagehands, even make-up artists (194).

6. Quoted in Bertin-Maghit, *Le Cinéma français sous l'occupation*, 195. "I fought as a soldier on the Maginot line. Taken prisoner in June 1940, I escaped a few weeks later and arrived in Paris on October 3 with no identity papers, 800 francs in my pocket, and my wife just having given birth. It was the end of December 1940, beginning of 1941. I was therefore hired at Continental Films as a scriptwriter and director. In March or April of 1943 [Alfred] Greven called me in and revealed to me that he had discovered my status as an escaped prisoner and forbade me to work for another film production company, with the threat that I would be sent to a prison camp.... For this reason, I directed four films for Continental: *La Fausse Maîtresse*, 1942; *Au Bonheur des Dames*, *Pierre et Jean* and *Le Dernier Sou*, 1943."

7. Ibid., 196. "During the entire Occupation I wrote regularly, under the pseudonym of Abel Cartier, violently anti-Nazi short stories about the Resistance in France that I was able to get through to the outside world with the help of M. D'Aguiar. At its inception, I joined the group *Ceux de la Résistance*."

8. Dominique Jullien, "Cendrillon au grand magasin: *Au Bonheur des Dames* et *Le Rêve*," *Les Cahiers naturalistes* 67 (1993): 97. "Woven into the realist plot (the triumph of the department store over the family-owned and operated shop) is a story line that is even more satisfying for the reader and, perhaps, especially the female reader: the victory of the innocent young girl over the wealthy man, of weakness over strength."

9. According to Evelyn Ehrlich, Continental Films was able to flourish because it "not only had more money than French production companies, it also had first call on all raw materials, including film stock, material for set construction, and the increasingly scarce electricity." *Cinema of Paradox: French Filmmaking under the German Occupation* (New York: Columbia University Press, 1985), 44. Additionally, its films were not subject to review by Vichy censors, which meant that films made for a German company actually enjoyed more artistic freedom than French productions (46).

10. Guy Braucourt, *André Cayatte* (Paris: Seghers, 1969), 63–64. "We only worked nights at the Billancourt studio, since there was no electricity during the day; yet almost every night there were alerts and the entire team would take refuge in the nearby cemetery, going through a gap in the wall and diving into the trenches dug for the next batch of corpses! And, at five in the morning, upon leaving the cemetery, we had to force the lot of them to perform on the set in nineteenth-century finery.... The paradox was that to represent abundance, in order to tell the story of women's temptation for the wealth of the department stores, I had basically nothing, as a result of the restrictions [imposed by the Occupation].... These conditions in fact suggested the very climate of Zola's novel: a careless life, fancy-dress balls, but at the same time the discomfort felt in a society that was progressing towards the gigantic slaughter of 1870."

11. Sylvie Collot develops Zola's image of the department store in terms of being a womb because of its warm, enveloping nature as well as the fact that it serves as a dormitory for the young women who work there. Sylvie Collot, *Les Lieux du désir: topologie amoureuse de Zola* (Paris: Hachette, 1992), 179–80.

12. Émile Zola, *Au Bonheur des Dames* (Paris: Fasquelle, 1967), 708. "In *Au Bonheur des Dames* I want to create the poetry of modern activity. Therefore a complex change in philosophy [took place]: first of all, no pessimism; no conclusion involving the inhumanity and sadness of life; a conclusion drawn instead about life's continual labor, the power and joy of a continual coming into existence. In a word [I want to] move along with the century, express an era of action and conquest."

13. The situation of the young saleswomen places them in a unique social category, as Zola demonstrates through his characters' discussion of the phenomenon of raising daughters specifically for a career in a *grand magasin:* "[E]lles n'étaient pas, comme les ouvrières du pavé parisien, obligées de se nourrir et de se loger: elles avaient la table et le lit, leur existence se trouvait assurée, une existence très dure sans doute. Le pis était leur situation neutre, mal déterminée, entre la boutiquière et la dame. Ainsi jetées dans le luxe, souvent sans instruction première, elles formaient une classe à part, innommée. Leurs misères et leurs vices venaient de là" (948). ("They were not obliged, as were the working women of the Parisian sidewalks, to find room and board for themselves: they had meals and a bed provided; their existence was assured, although a difficult one. The worst was that their neutral situation was not clearly delineated, since they were situated somewhere between shop worker and woman. Thus thrown into a world of luxury, often without basic instruction, they formed a separate class, unnamed. Their miseries and their vices came from that.")

14. Zola, *Au Bonheur des Dames*, 826–827. "Bourdoncle was in charge of the executions. With his thin lips he pronounced a terrible "Go collect your [final] wages from the cashier!" that fell like an executioner's ax. Everything became a pretext for him to sweep the floor clean. He invented misdeeds and speculations about the slightest omissions.... Even the most courageous trembled at the massacre he left behind.

Zola did not completely invent this scene for his novel. As Michael B. Miller points out, it was common practice to employ inspectors, "a corps of internal police," at the Bon Marché. Michael B. Miller, *The Bon Marché: Bourgeois Culture and the Department Store, 1869–1920* (Princeton: Princeton University Press, 1981), 96.

15. Zola, *Au Bonheur des Dames*, 889. "Mouret had the unique passion of gaining a victory over woman. He wanted her to be queen in his store and he had built this temple for her, in order to keep her at his mercy."

16. Ibid., 960. "The enormous success of the store was the result of this gallant seduction."

17. Ibid., 963. "Denise's reign was beginning."

18. Brian Nelson, "Zola and the Counter Revolution: *Au Bonheur des Dames*," *Australian Journal of French Studies* 30.2 (1993): 238.

19. Ibid., 982. "It was the embryo of the vast nation of female workers of the twentieth century."

20. Barbara Vinken, "Temples of Delight: Consuming Consumption in Émile Zola's *Au Bonheur des Dames*," in Margaret Cohen and Christopher Prendergast, eds., *Spectacles of Realism* (Minneapolis: University of Minnesota Press, 1995), 249–50.

21. Zola, *Au Bonheur des Dames*, 997–98. "My God! What torture! Families who weep; old men throw themselves onto the pavement; all are on the verge of a drama of ruin! And she could rescue no one, and yet she was aware that it was good, that this manure heap of misfortune was necessary for the health of a future Paris.... Yes, it was the portion of blood: every revolution required martyrs; movement forward would be made over dead bodies."

22. Vinken, "Temples of Delight," 249.

23. "This ultimate union will link forever the past and the present in progress—Boudu's [sic] death must be seen in this light: [he is] run over by a carriage; he must disappear in order to make this connection possible...." Bertin-Maghit, *Le Cinéma sous l'occupation*, 149.

24. Bertin-Maghit, *Le Cinéma français sous Vichy*, 121. "All these films can be grouped under the banner of labor that calls for all workers to unite: 'employers, craftspeople, technicians, employees, workers, forget your origins, forget your divisions of the past.'" Bertin-Maghit quotes Philippe Pétain's speech at the inaugural session of the Comité d'organisation professionnelle on June 4, 1941.

25. "By the end of 1942-43, efficiency, productivity, planning become the watchwords of the French economy." Ibid.

26. Audiberti, Rev. of *Au Bonheur des Dames*, *Comœdia* 109 (31 July 1943), quoted in Braucourt, *André Cayatte*, 151–52. "[The film] shows us marionettes of one kind, not like a cartoon, but like animated clay figures.... They [the actors] seem to us like wax figures moving at the end of the nimble fingers of the one who shaped them.... One could say, it was like a retrospective of the costume. In front of our eyes, for an absurd pavane, Carnavalet's display window came alive for a few instants.... From this fairy tale perspective, Cayatte—as a bear—perhaps deserves our attention.... But, to make a film just to be making a film is not a good formula." The full review of the film, written by Audiberti, is available in Braucourt.

27. Quoted in Braucourt, *André Cayatte*, 26. "I learned my profession from several films that are perhaps ridiculous, yet I need not be ashamed, since I never supported or expressed sentiments that contradicted my convictions."

28. Ibid., 7. "As pamphleteer, witness of his [our] times, Cayatte turned out his best films as arguments that debate not only themes, high caliber philosophical or moral questions, such as justice, responsibility, solidarity, individual rights, etc., but put these issues forward from a social perspective that will allow his films to define a French reality rarely examined in such detail and depth on screen."

Thérèse Raquin in a Fog-Covered Corner

ALICJA HELMAN

Émile Zola's novel *Thérèse Raquin* (1867) and Marcel Carné's film (1953) of the same title lend themselves to comparative analysis and interpretation. The film is not a classic, literal case of adaptation, and the filmmaker Carné and his screenwriter Charles Spaak have created a work that is difficult to assess according to traditional categories of adaptation.

Although numerous books dedicated to the subject of adaptation have appeared in the last decade, the term itself has begun to raise debate and doubts, has undergone interpretations, or has simply been called into question. Here I tend to agree with Carlo Testa, who claims that confusing the notion of interpretation with the complex issues connected to the faithfulness of the film to the literary original makes this term rather problematic.[1] Fidelity is generally not the goal of a director who deals with his or her own independent creation; and furthermore, the incomparability of the media makes such fidelity something unattainable in practice. Moreover, faithfulness is not a measurable category; it is dependent on the collective and individual reception of the audience. There is also no need to claim that the fidelity of an adaptation to an original prejudges the outstanding value of a film. Testa substitutes the notion of adaptation for the notion of recreation based on a cultural-historical homology. The author distinguishes between several types of recreation, all of which are a result of the filmmaker's relationship to the literary material. However, the case of *Thérèse Raquin* is difficult to classify. It has certain traits of the first two models, that is, homological and epigraphic recreation. In the first model, recreation is based on an intellectual link connected to the original and manifested through allusion. As far as narration is concerned, such films are independent of their prototypes, which they transform in a manner characteristic of twentieth-century culture. However, the epigraphic recreations are more entangled in diegetic material despite the fact that the original is not directly evoked and the director uses visually selected fragments.

In screenwriting practice, such situations have been noted as films "based on" or "inspired by" (as in the case of *Thérèse Raquin*). This practice is not only simpler but it reveals the essence of the creation more effectively. Carné's film certainly alludes to the original and transforms it in the context of twentieth-century culture (homological recreation). The film also uses diegetic material (epigraphic recreation), although it subjects the recreation to the types of transformations that have not been adequately presented in any of Testa's models.

These types of transformation are conditioned in a characteristic way by the movement from which Carné's production arose: poetic realism. Carné's particular approach to literary material, and the "elegance" of the French cinema, has been referred to as *papa's cinema*.

The last prestigious success of Marcel Carné for which he was awarded the Silver Lion at the Venice Film Festival, *Thérèse Raquin*, is generally placed in the decadent period of the director's filmmaking career, even though Carné was an active filmmaker for many more years, having made a handful of films. The high point of his career was the 1940s when he directed his masterpieces: *Les Visiteurs du Soir* and *Les Enfants du Paradis*. The rest of his life was marked by little success, the failure of *Les Portes de la Nuit*, the interrupted production of *La Fleur de l'Age*, and the departure of his closest collaborators with whom he developed a unique style. *Les Portes de la Nuit* was the last film produced with Jacques Prévert, and *Juliette ou la Clef des Songes* was the last film for which Joseph Kosma's composed a soundtrack. During the filming of *Thérèse Raquin* the two were replaced with Charles Spaak and Maurice Thiriet.

Carné drew inspiration for his work from various literary sources, but rarely from Prévert's original screenplays. Prévert adapted for Carné such authors as Pierre Rocher, Storer-Clouston, Pierre MacOrlan, and Eugéne Dabit. Whatever the novels' characters or the authors' individual styles were, "the Prévert-Carné" touch dominated their cinematic versions. This "touch" made all films of Carné and Prévert immediately recognizable. Carné's choice to adapt Émile Zola's novel was not supposed to be a threshold in his career, nor was it a turn towards a different poetics from the one that defined his work in the 1930s and had resulted in a string of successes. Carné filmed *Thérèse Raquin* in a similar manner to *Le Quai des brumes*. In the latter, however, he changed the place of action, sequence of events, fate and qualities of the characters, "and marked the story with a stigma of sadness and despair."[2] He created a story about the strength of destiny and doom in the lives of the unfortunate. Carné took a similar approach to *Thérèse Raquin*. In order to interpret his adaptation, we must go back to the original text.

It is evident that Zola assigned great importance to the conception of the plot, characters, and conflict in *Thérèse Raquin* since he reproduced the story in three different works: in the novella *Un Mariage d'amour* (1866), in the novel *Thérèse Raquin* (1867), and in a theatrical play that was published under the same title six years later. The play was not an altogether new work dealing with the same theme but an auto-adaptation, a practice that was very popular amongst French authors such as Dumas *fils*, Octave Feuillet, George Sand, Alphonse Daudet, Jules Renard and Guy de Maupassant, all of whom often adapted their prose works for the theatre.

Thérèse Raquin is generally considered Zola's first realist novel. The action, which includes motifs of adultery, murder and remorse leading to a double suicide appeared perfectly suited for communicating a world vision characteristic of naturalism, as well as for communicating a motivation for human actions and reactions shaped by biological and social conditions. Zola himself characterized his work "as a great psychological and physiological study" and, in the preface to the second edition, he expressed a thought inspired by the novel:

> J'ai choisi des personnages souverainement dominés par leurs nerfs et leur sang, dépourvus de libre arbitre, entraînés à chaque acte de leur vie par les fatalités de leur chair. Thérèse et Laurent sont des brutes humaines, rien de plus. J'ai cherché à suivre pas à pas dans ces brutes le travail sourd des passions, les poussés de l'instinct, les détraquements cérébraux survenus à la suite d'une crise nerveuse.[3]

This quotation distinguishes Zola's intentions from those of Marcel Carné despite the fact that Carné followed in the author's footsteps in presenting treachery, murder and qualms of the conscience.

The novella has only three characters: a married couple—Michel and Suzanne—and their friend Jacques. Suzanne and Jacques are having an affair, while Michel is completely unaware of what is going on. The two lovers eventually decide to get rid of the husband and legalize their union. This objective requires that they carefully orchestrate a murder. They invite Michel for a boat ride, then drown him and make it look like an accident. The marriage is then postponed for one and a half and during that time they see each other rarely and only in the company of witnesses in order to avoid arousing suspicion. After the wedding, instead of experiencing marital bliss, they suffer. The lovers have lost their passion. They are paralyzed with fear and tortured by the memory of the murdered husband. The two begin to hate each other, blaming one another for the crime and fearing that the other will confess everything to the police. They both want to get rid of their partner-in-crime. When their feelings surface, both decide to commit suicide by drinking poison that one prepared for the other.

The novel did not change the sequence of events. Zola gave his characters new names: Thérèse, Camille and Laurent. He also introduced new characters: Camille's mother, who plays a very important role not only in the prequel to the actual story but also in the course of events, and a number of close friends and acquaintances. However, in the theatrical play Zola shortened the action, retained three characters and concentrated on the turning point, which he strongly dramatized.

What is significant in Zola's three works is that he does not emphasize the time before the murder but rather what happens afterwards: the anxiety and pain are intensified in the description of the wedding night, an event that resembles a night of fear, repulsion and fright. These are feelings that will forever be present in the characters' lives. This period is exhibited most intensely in the play after the first act, when the murder takes place and the other three acts are simply filled thereafter with gruesome dénouement. The lovers commit what crime literature calls "a perfect murder." Because their act is never discovered, no one suspects them, and the paralyzed mother is helpless against the two. It is the lovers themselves who become their own enemies, unable to cope with what they have done or even to tolerate the other's presence. Death is the only solution.

Without going into detail about the difference between Zola's various works, one point must be acknowledged, the common thread in all of the texts: the lovers' complete lack of scruples at the beginning and in the continuation of their affair, their premeditation in ridding themselves of the husband, the carrying out of the murder, the lack of immediate punishment, the ease they experience attaining their goal of marriage, the inability to emotionally deal with the situation, the increasing animosity and hatred that metamorphoses into open hostility, the decision to get rid of one another, and finally the suicide. Rather than employ these commonalities, Carné would later work against them.

The motivational base for the story is also extremely significant, since its basis is the previously mentioned biologically and socially conditioned actions, choices and decisions of the characters. Zola emphasizes that his characters are not free. They are doubly enslaved by their own instincts that push them towards "satisfying the need" and getting rid of obstacles on the road to that satisfaction. They are enslaved by the social pressures of an environment in which any straying from the norm is threatened by a scandal that can ruin the life of the individuals. There is also materialistically conditioned pressure since only the maintenance of the status quo can guarantee the characters' positions and well-being. The characters do not want to consider running away since they would lose their means to survive. Completely unscrupulous, Laurent takes advantage of the relationship with the Raquin family. Camille is his friend, Thérèse his lover, and Madame Raquin takes care of him in a motherly fashion by offering culinary pleasures while their friends provide him a social life. While nothing threatens his intimate meetings with Thérèse, he only wants to maintain his status quo. When this becomes impossible, he tries to get rid of Camille, to take his place, marry his wife, take up residence in his home, inherit his money and allow Madame Raquin to be a mother to him. However, when he finally reaches his goal, the goal is not the one he aimed at, that is, a good and wealthy middle-class life where he could quit his job, soak up the passion of a chosen woman and lose himself in life's small pleasures. When the lovers can no longer find their passion that joined them in the first place, there begins a slow process of the destruction of their relationship, all of which Zola describes in great detail.

The downfall begins in stages, from desensitization and apathy, the period when the lovers wait for a while before getting married, through desperate trials of rekindling the old relationship which fear has made impossible, to growing dislike and recurring visions that bring on insomnia and crisis. All of these feelings intensify the hatred between the partners who are unfaithful to one another in order to escape their present situation and who, more and more frequently, think about getting rid of one another and finally become determined to commit another crime. Zola studies the subsequent phases of this process with clinical indifference. Not for one moment does he persuade his readers to feel sympathy for his characters who are capable of murder but incapable of accepting its consequences. Laurent is not Raskolnikov, and ethical-moral murder is not what troubles his conscience. He wants to completely cut himself off from the past. In fact, he would rather not marry Thérèse, but he cannot accept the thought that he killed Camille for nothing; neither can he forgo all the material rewards. Because of poverty and lack of personal prospects, his actions are governed by cynical calculation.

The story of *Thérèse Raquin* is of an *ex definitione* nature, similar to other novels by Zola that were frequently adapted by film directors. Carné was neither the first nor the last filmmaker to adapt *Thérèse Raquin* for the cinema. However, his predecessors, Nino Mortoglio (1915, Italy) and Jacques Feyder (1928, Germany, entitled *Du sollst nicht ehebrechen*, and surviving in parts) are closer to the poetics of the original than Carné.

According to some critics, Mortoglio, who directed only a few films, was the predecessor of the so-called 'south style' and of the critical poetic realism of Italian cinematography. His other films, not only *Thérèse Raquin*, convincingly portray social conflicts and marginal heroes in an urban environment.[4] Similarly, Feyder, who refers to the tradition of German realism and the poetics of "Kammerspiel," created a piece of work close to the spirit of the original. He "emphasizes the details in a natural way, the overwhelming atmosphere and the numbness of city life which dominates the instincts of the roles."[5] As for Carné's literary inspiration, this filmmaker seems to be closer not to Zola but to James M. Cain, the author of the frequently adapted novel *The Postman Always Rings Twice*. Carné was probably familiar with three adaptations of the Cain novel: *Le Dernier Tournanat* (1939, France) by Pierre Chenal, *Ossessione* (1942, Italy) by Luchino Visconti and *The Postman Always Rings Twice* (1946, USA) by Tay Garnett. The climate and the poetics of the film noir, mainly from the American cinema, were more inspirational than Zola. Moreover, we should remember that the American film noir had much in common with French poetic realism: Carné's school. I do not claim that Marcel Carné borrowed anything from the American cinema but rather that he took the same route by making the adaptation contemporary and emphasizing the universal traits of the drama that can be played out independently of the time and place of the source material.

Carné's adaptation of *Thérèse Raquin* is set in a more contemporary era than the Zola novel. There is no clear indication of a particular time frame; however, based on one of the characters' memories, the action takes place probably after the Second World War, once life has returned to normal. The director moved the setting from Paris to Lyon, although the location does not seem to play any significant role. Almost the entire film takes place indoors, mainly at the Raquin residence, above their fabric store. The outline of the action corresponds to that of Zola's novel but the same events are experienced by different people who in no way can be referred to as human animals or wolves governed by blind instincts, as Zola would have it in his novel. Let us make this clear: the contemporarization of the action and the transformation of some of the characters make certain parts of the script unconvincing because it is difficult not to notice that where Zola's characters had no other choice in order to fulfill their dreams, Carné's characters most often have freedom to determine the course of their lives. In Zola's novella, novel and theatrical play, Thérèse and her lover, amateur artist Laurent, hide their romance for a long time and Laurent pretends to be her husband's best friend, and in fact, he is. Deceitful middle-class morality aids this arrangement. As long as no one suspects anything and neighbors have no reason to gossip, it can last without any obstacles.

The film is very different. Laurent is not Camille's friend nor is he a civil servant and an artist. He is also not from the same social class as the Raquins. He is an Italian man, an outsider, not used to living in one place for long. He is a taxi driver whose only possession is his vehicle. He moves freely. When he is bored with one city, he moves to the next. He meets Camille Raquin by chance. An accidental argument ends with a glass of wine, and if it were not for fate, that is where the acquaintance would have ended. However, Laurent and Thérèse come face-to-face and look into each other's eyes. It becomes evident from the start that they have experienced a *coup de foudre* (falling in love head over heels) and fall in love at first sight.

The novel is entirely different. In the beginning Laurent does not even like Thérèse. She becomes his lover as a result of premeditation since he cannot afford to pay for sex. It is only after the satisfaction of his routine sexual needs is threatened that he begins to feel a desperate passion. Zola emphasizes that Laurent, who comes from a rural area, is a strong man with an enormous appetite and a need for a regular union with a woman. Raf Vallone, who plays the role of Laurent, is handsome and very masculine but not primitive. Simone Signoret is beautiful, full of feminine charm. These two appear as if made for one another. Scrawny and sickly, Camille, played by Jacques Duby, reminds one of a rat.

In this film adaptation, Laurent departs from his literary prototype. He makes it very clear that he has no desire to become a friend of the family and wait for a fortunate occasion. He is direct and honest. Already after the second meeting he suggests to Thérèse that they should go away together—anywhere—as long as they do it immediately. Although he is unable to obtain the woman's permission, he nevertheless tries to persuade her. They become lovers but Laurent does not want to continue their affair in secret. He forces Thérèse to let him tell Camille the truth so that the two can leave him. However, fate intervenes yet another time, and the sequence of events of the screenplay becomes tangled and unconvincing. Submissive and timid, Thérèse wants to obtain Camille's permission and even his understanding for her choice. She accepts his proposal to go to Paris, unsuspecting of any ill will on her husband's behalf. She assumes that once Camille is away from his mother, who exercises great influence over him, he will be easily persuaded to grant her a divorce.

It should be stressed that the lovers do not contemplate murder for even one moment; on the contrary, they appear to be far removed from such an act and unable to commit a crime. Carné convinces us of it, although he creates a crucial moment during which audience members who are familiar with the original become confused. When Thérèse and

Simone Signoret seduces her lover in *Thérèse Raquin* (1953) (courtesy *bfi*, film stills).

Laurent meet outside her home for the very first time, they explain to one another that they have no chance at an intimate relationship. Thérèse, who never leaves the house by herself, would need to fake a toothache in order to go out. Such motivation, which is convincing in the nineteenth-century novel, is a complete miss with regards to a woman living in the middle of the twentieth-century. When Laurent mentions his plan to escape, she refuses and utters an ambiguous phrase: "perhaps there is a way." But our suspicion that she may be thinking of getting rid of Camille evaporates. What Thérèse has in mind is a meeting in her own home. The shame and repulsion that arise as a result of this attempt (in the novel the lovers find this solution ideal) bring up the long dreaded suggestion; they will tell Camille everything and will move in together. When the planned trip to Paris takes place, a very nervous Laurent follows the husband and wife. He finds them in a dark compartment of a train where Camille and an unknown passenger are sleeping. Laurent calls Thérèse into a corridor and once again brings up the old argument. He manages to convince Thérèse to get off the train in Chalons from where they could disappear to Italy. But fate crosses their path once again. If Camille had only awakened a few minutes later, they would have been able to realize their dream. Instead, the husband finds them in a corridor and an argument breaks out that turns into a physical struggle. Laurent, who becomes angry at Camille's stubbornness and his threats, opens the door and throws him off the train.

When molding the character of Laurent, Carné stressed on numerous occasions that he is an impulsive Italian who easily becomes irritable and angry, although generally his outbursts do not result in harm towards others. Let us recall that his first argument with Camille ends in a glass of wine. Although this situation is different, it is not a premeditated crime. Laurent does not realize that he kills Camille by throwing him off the train. He yells, "I will silence you," and not "I will kill you." Therefore, it is a crime of passion. Laurent's first thought is to give himself up to the police. He wants to take responsibility for what has happened. It is Thérèse who convinces him that no one witnessed the crime, and if they were careful no one would suspect them. The instinct of self-preservation wins out.

Just like Zola's characters, Carné's also try not to accept the responsibility and get away without punishment. But the situation in this adap-

Raf Vallone (right) will kill his former friend, Jacques Duby, in *Thérèse Raquin* (1953) (courtesy *bfi*, film stills).

tation is entirely different. Thérèse and Laurent are threatened from the very beginning. The police are suspicious; there is an ongoing investigation, and the expression in the paralyzed Madame Raquin's eyes seems to attest to the fact that she suspects something. After some time, a blackmailer appears. He is the unknown passenger from the train, a low-ranking sailor who saw enough to be dangerous. He finds Thérèse and demands a sum of money in exchange for his silence.

In the adaptation, it is not a question of a simply straying from the story but rather of consequential changes of the entire structure of the plot. The nature of the murder is different, and so is the behavior of the characters and the psychological motivation for their further actions.

In both the novel and the film subsequent action has nothing to do with a troubled conscience. Zola talks about "the reaction of the organism" and about the fact that the nervous system of the characters cannot deal with the stress, rather than morality or remorse. The writer describes his characters as persons with no regrets; thus, the fact of their villainous behavior is reason enough for their lack of trust and solidarity. They blame one another and each one waits for the day when the other will confess to the authorities. According to the mechanism of the criminal psyche, confessing the crime allows freedom from it.

In fact, Carné's Thérèse turns against Laurent for just a moment. She is the one who must identify the massacred remains of her husband, and she cannot deal with the shock. She blames Laurent for Camille's death and, by pushing him away, tries to free herself from the responsibility for his death. She talks about admitting to the murder since an admission is the only thing that can free her from nightmares. However, Laurent thinks only about the woman he loves and takes the weight of the guilt onto his shoulders, suffering not from what he had done but over the loss of Thérèse. The entrance of the blackmailer will reunite the lovers again, who now desire to save their love and hope for a future together. The thought of escaping together returns since it might present a solution to the problem, but the blackmailer is able to outsmart them. And it is fate that thwarts their chance to escape from their imprisonment. When a solution finally arrives, it is somewhat on the order of a *deus ex machina*; an insurance claim from the train company makes it possible to satisfy the blackmailer's demands and for the lovers to protect themselves against his further threats. Fate comes into the picture for the last time. The blackmailer fears Laurent's temper and suspects that desperate Laurent could kill him. He protects himself with a letter to a prosecutor, which he leaves with a maid with instructions to send it if he were not to return to his room at a designated time. He perishes in a car accident.

This series of events, or providence, is a repeated model of Carné's earlier films and not the scheme of Zola's novel. Fate sends the lost lovers a chance to be reborn through love, but it does not allow for a happy ending. Everything needs to happen that will ultimately lead them to disaster, whether they are guilty or not. Just like the hero of Cain's novel who is punished not for the crime he committed (the murder of his lover's husband), but for that which he did not commit (the accidental death of the heroine), Carné's film is similar in nature. The lovers could have gotten away with murdering Camille, but its consequences and a death that they are not guilty of will threaten their existence.

Unlike Zola, Carné does everything to evoke sympathy for his characters. Camille and his mother are physically and morally repulsive. Camille resembles a rat and exhibits qualities associated with a deceitful middle-class morality. In contrast, Thérèse and Laurent are beautiful and beaming with love for one another, not an animal love that pushes an unsatisfied woman and a strong and lonely man together, but a true, great love. Thérèse, in the adaptation, is not by any means Laurent's partner in crime. She had no chance to stop him. But she worked with him to escape the consequences, and, despite the odds, to have a life together.

Thérèse, as Spaak and Carné saw her, could only evoke sympathy and compassion. She is shown consequently as a noble person, a victim of her mother-in-law's autocratic behavior and her husband's egotism. From the first shot sequence, a relationship is established among the three and it never changes. During a family walk along a river, Madame Raquin's masterful despotism is revealed, as are Camille's submissiveness to his mother, and his hypochondria and complete indifference towards Thérèse. Thérèse behaves as she is expected to, doing what her mother-in-law and husband demand; however, she is lacking spirit and keeps her thoughts and dreams to herself. Thérèse, Madame Raquin's niece, was adopted after her parents died. The old woman reminds Thérèse constantly of this debt of gratitude and stresses that she will never be able to repay everything that was done for her. Thérèse agrees with humble submission and takes on the role that is imposed upon her, that of a nurse rather than a wife for her weak, sickly husband Camille. She is gentle, submissive, calm, and she behaves like a victim who has no chance of changing her fate.

Unlike Zola and Cain's heroine, Thérèse does not mind leaving her property and sense of security behind in order to be with the vagabond Laurent. Thérèse believes that her debt of gratitude towards her family, her duty to them and her care are what keep Camille alive. Playing the role of a victim, she cannot muster a spirit of rebellion or come to a decision. She tries to buy time and searches for compromises. She would like to find "a peaceful resolution," something that Camille could accept. A typical (fictional) woman in the most traditional sense of the word, she allows herself to be steered and looks to others for guidance. Thérèse makes a decision on her own only once when, after the death of Camille, she leaves Laurent. But she retreats when the blackmailer appears. Once again, she turns to a man and depends on him as she did earlier when her life was compromised by a sense of social and economic pressure.

Laurent loves Thérèse and wants to conquer her as a man gains (fictional) mastery over a woman, but he also wants to free her from her class and gender-based shackles. At one moment in time he tells her that her fate is worse than death, and we are inclined to agree with him. We might even agree with the screenplay's suggestion that the crime inflicted upon Thérèse is worse than pushing Camille off the train.

Winning the love of an enslaved woman and the fear of life under deceitful conditions are what make Carné's film close to Zola's work. However, this similarity is not so obvious since the context is different. While looking for visual solutions, Carné and his cinematographer decided to gamble on a claustrophobic effect of enclosure. We almost never see characters in any other way than behind closed doors. For the Raquins, "the world" is a threat to the safety of their home, which, in contrast, is orderly and cannot be infected by chaos. We see this perception in the aforementioned shot sequence of the river walk. Camille and his mother watch as men bowl, while Thérèse observes the flowing river. It is a chilly winter day and Madame Raquin demands to go back home, complaining that the outing was a bad idea and Camille will get a cold and must be put in bed immediately. In order to meet with Laurent, Thérèse must find a plausible excuse because she never leaves the house on her own. Even Laurent, who is the only free character in the film, is shown behind four walls of his room when he is alone, "imprisoned" by his love that forces him to remain in one place near his chosen one.

The action takes place mainly in the Raquins' residence (as in Zola's novel) and in the store that is located in the same building. In rare instances, it takes place in Laurent's room, a bar where he meets Thérèse, or in the end, on the train. In every one of these places what is evident is the sense of claustrophobic enclosure, an impression unrelated to the actual size of the space. These enclosures are dark and gloomy, filled with objects, and they seem to affect/possess their residents. The Raquins, together with Thérèse, fit ideally with these unappealing spaces; they appear to move according to sketched lines and repeat the same actions. When the tall and muscular Laurent appears, it is as if a wind full of life comes rushing through, ready to blow up the enclosures, threatening their very existence.

The difference between Zola's text and Carné's adaptation is shown most expressively in the final shot sequences. In the novella, novel and theatrical play, the characters turn against each other in a series of attempted murders. Would the murder have been committed if they had not known what the other was thinking? Finally they forgive each other and choose death in the form of a double suicide. In the novel this action takes place before the eyes of Camille's paralyzed mother: "Et, pendant près de douze heures, jusqu'au lendemain vers midi, Madame Raquin, roide et muette, les contempla à ses pieds, ne pouvant se rassasier les yeux, les écrasant de regards lourds."[6]

In the theatrical text, the scene is dramatized sharply. Madame Raquin regains her voice and gets up and Thérèse drops to her feet pleading for forgiveness. The mother says she will not turn the couple over to the authorities; she would rather see their pain. When they drink their poison, she comments: "They died too fast."

In the novel and the play, this final scene is played out as a dramatic triangle: Thérèse, Laurent, and Madame Raquin. The scene suggests to us that the couple, alone, were responsible for their death. The adaptation ends differently. Fate reaches them when they are finally free, when they are not aware of a fatal set of circumstances. The blackmailer dies. Laurent heard him whisper something about "a letter," and can only guess what the threat could mean. As a bell tolls, the shot cuts to a girl throwing a letter into a mailbox. Very often films of poetic realism end in a similar fashion, with no specific resolution of all the dramatic effects.

Carné follows iconographic points related to characters in Zola's novel through the representation of their physical state, their behavior, and their actions. However, the metaphoric character of the novel contains visual details that Carne's film lacks: portraits painted by Laurent, all of which remind us of Camille; a glowing fire in the fireplace, as an allusion to passion; the demonic role of the cat feared by Laurent; and many other situations where the visual is accentuated. As Andre Rothwell points out:

> The backgrounds and settings generally are certainly calculated to appeal primarily to our visual imagination, but at certain key moments in the book Zola goes much further and actually works up his description, including those of the characters, into properly pictorial compositions. Of course, the old idea that a writer must "paint a picture" of the things and people he describes can never be literally true, since the process of representation works in quite different ways in words and in pictures. However, Zola was deeply interested in and committed to the avant-garde painting of his day, particularly the work of Manet, and certain of the descriptions in *Thérèse Raquin* are clearly designed to echo both the wider aesthetic principles defended by the modern painters, and even individual canvases.[7]

Rothwell furthermore expands the idea that Zola's writing technique interrelates with impressionist painting, emphasizing Zola's close ties to Degas, Renoir, Whistler and Pisarro, as well as the inspiration he derived from Monet's work. Incomparable media, different ways of "illustrating" in literature and in art make this comparison an effective metaphor rather than a point of entry for tracing eventual inspirations that can be uncovered by a film artist in Zola's prose. Cinematic poetic realism, although traditionally associated with the French (late) silent cinema and especially the 1930s, has been credibly connected to impressionism. It is characteristic that literary criticism does not describe the visual method of the movement from which Carné gained inspiration and to which he was faithful in *Thérèse Raquin*. The term "poetic realism" is described on the ideological level with emphasis placed on the undertone of content by Robert Sklar, who defines it as:

> A broad term with many meanings, yet with an overall clarity of purpose. It implied first of all fidelity to milieu: to the settings of everyday life, usually of working people and lower classes, rather than the lavish fantasy worlds that Hollywood created and the fascist cinemas of Germany and Italy emulated. Within these authentic atmospheres, characters were driven by destinies larger than themselves, by implacable fate. This could be understood through political ideology, or as a form of social determinism. Yet the "poetic" aspect of this realism was attained not only through the aesthetic evocation of social ambiance, but also by the characters' struggles to transcend fate and achieve important life goals.[8]

Carné remains in the circle of this world vision, which is characterized by a dark atmosphere, tone of nostalgia and bitterness. He continues to poeticize his characters, something that Zola's novel does not attempt to do. He backs up to his cinematic past, consequently leading his characters towards doom and bringing disaster to them at the exact moment when a hint of salvation appears before them. In a way comparable to the earlier films, every meeting becomes an unexpected decree of fate, every decision and move on the chessboard of life are steps towards disaster.

Thérèse Raquin differs from Carné's earlier films in its transparent style. The persistent significance of details, played out, for example, in *Le jour se lève* or in his films from the 1940s, is replaced by simplicity in *Thérèse Raquin*. The camera's attention is concentrated predominantly on the characters and rarely does it record their surroundings. The visual techniques are simple, and the tone of picture is gray with an occasional streak of light. The play of light is generally concentrated on the faces of the characters. However, despite these changes, dictated by the natural evolution of film form and language in the 1950s, Carné remained faithful to his own cinematic style and not to Zola's novel.

Notes

1. Carlo Testa, *Italian Cinema and Modern European Literature 1945–2000* (Westport, CT: Praeger, 2002).
2. Grażyna Stachowna, *Niedole miłowania. Ideologia i perswazja w melodramatach filmowych* [*The Despairs of Love: Ideology and Persuasion in Cinematic Dramas*] (Cracow: Rabid, 2001), 107.
3. Émile Zola, *Thèrese Raquin* (Paris: Éditions Fasquelle, 1970), 8. "I chose to portray individuals existing under the sovereign dominion of their nerves and their blood, devoid of free will and drawn into every act of their lives by the inescapable prompting of their flesh. Thérèse and Laurent are human animals, nothing more. In these animals I set out to trace, step by step, the hidden workings of the passions, the urges of instinct, and the derangements of the brain which follow from a nervous crisis." Émile Zola, "Preface to the Second Edition," *Thérèse Raquin*, trans. Andrew Rothwell, (New York: Oxford University Press, 1998), 1–2.
4. Tadeusz Miczka, *10000 km od Hollywood* [*10,000 miles from Hollywood*] (Cracow: Oficyna Wydawnicza, 1992), 53.
5. Adam Grabicz and Jacek Klinowski, *Kino, wehikuł magiczny. Przewodnik osiągnięć filmu fabularnego. Podróż druga 1950–1959* [*Cinema, Magical Vehicle: A Guide to Accomplishments of Feature Films. Second Voyage, 1950–1959*] (Cracow: Wydawnictwo Literackie, 1987), 45.
6. Zola, *Thèrese Raquin*, 265. "And for more than twelve hours, until around noon the following day, Madame Raquin, stiff and silent, contemplated them there at her feet, feasting her eyes and annihilating them with the hatred in her gaze" (Rothwell trans., 205).
7. Andrew Rothwell, "Introduction," *Thérèse Raquin*, xxix.
8. Robert Sklar, *Film: An International History of the Medium* (New York: Harry N. Abrams, Inc., 1993), 236.

Translation by Anna Chilewska.

9

Ideology and Focalization in *Gervaise*: The Aurenchébost/ René Clément Treatment

RUSSELL COUSINS

Zola's *L'Assommoir* has undergone several transformations for the cinema since Ferdinand Zecca first brought the novel to the screen as *Les Victimes de l'alcoolisme* in 1902. Of the nine subsequent film versions,[1] none has enjoyed the critical acclaim accorded to *Gervaise* directed by René Clément from a script by Jean Aurenche and Pierre Bost.[2] Indeed, this screen adaptation has come to be regarded as a model rendering of the author's socially committed realist text, and a traditional auteurist approach has naturally privileged René Clément's role in this achievement. However, the reworking clearly owes much to those practiced traducers of literary works, Aurenche and Bost, whose prolific partnership was instrumental in the creation of a whole generation of well-crafted, post-war film scenarios.[3] Their contribution to *Gervaise* merits further consideration, not only in terms of the ideological inflection given to Zola's working class narrative but also in terms of the film's dramatic development and more specifically the issue of *focalization*.[4]

At an ideological level, the attractiveness of *L'Assommoir* for the left-wing director and his screenwriters may be self-evident, but neither should the seductiveness of the inherent scenic qualities of the text be discounted. The potential for theatrical or cinematic representation is characteristic of all the Rougon-Macquart novels, as the ever-growing number of stage and screen adaptations testifies.[5] Powerful dramatic structures, sharply observed characters and detailed evocations of milieu,

9. Ideology and Focalization in Gervaise (Cousins) 133

make Zola's fiction immediately accessible to the writer of screenplays. The author's method of exploring key themes through shaded variations of character and situation is, at the same time, conducive to the traditional selective processes of adaptation: a reduction to box-office norms of narrative duration can be readily achieved by concentrating the novel's conceptual elements into fewer, or indeed single illustrations. Similarly, those detailed descriptions of location, so important to the writer of deterministic persuasion, "[c'est] le milieu qui détermine et complète l'homme,"[6] translate readily into a realist conception of mise-en-scène. At the same time, the author's documentalist imperatives can be automatically satisfied in sequences primarily geared to forwarding plot or character elements.

This pre-cinematic quality of Zola's writing is noted by Valerie Minogue in her recent study of *L'Assommoir*, where she concerns herself with "the shifts of focus Zola makes throughout the novel, alternating 'wide-screen' shots of crowds with close-up shots of groups or individuals."[7] Comparisons with the medium of film are again offered in an account of Zola's "sophisticated narrative strategies, his use of a wide range of 'cinematic' techniques (panorama and close-up, fades, flashbacks, etc.), and his studied manipulation of 'point-of-view.'"[8] As several other critics have noted, Zola's writing shares considerable affinity with filmic discourse.[9]

An examination of the unpublished scenario which Aurenche and Bost produced for Clément leaves little doubt either about the political inflection *L'Assommoir* receives in its transition to *Gervaise* or the demands of a medium more comfortable with exploring personal dramas than concerning itself with broader thematic studies.[10] The character-focused film title already indicates much about the re-orientation of the Zola narrative. The more general exposition of the pressures facing the working class, so brilliantly encapsulated in the symbolic title *L'Assommoir*, is diminished in what appears to be a regression to the author's initially more limited conception of his subject, when he penciled in the working title, *La Simple Vie de Gervaise Macquart*. Aurenche and Bost justified their character-centered reworking as follows:

> Nous avons resserré l'intrigue au maximum. Il nous semble qu'une histoire gagne en ne jouant pas trop sur le temps. Cette position nous a donc obligé à sérier dans les manifestations de la déchéance de l'homme. Ceci d'autant plus que nous n'avons pas appuyé sur ce côté *Assommoir*.... Nous avons choisi dans l'oeuvre de Zola ce qui concernait la vie de Gervaise. L'histoire à laquelle nous avons collaboré n'est pas un manifeste anti-alcoolique, c'est l'histoire d'une femme.[11]

This position is restated by Clément:

> ... pour être fidèle à l'esprit de Zola, il n'y avait qu'un moyen, braquer le projecteur sur un personnage en qui se joue, comme dans un miroir sensible, tout le drame. J'ai choisi *Gervaise*.... J'avais envie depuis longtemps de tourner un film sur la condition des femmes.[12]

Not surprisingly, the dense, symbolic narrative contained within Zola's five-hundred page novel is pared down in a number of ways. Selection is a *sine qua non* in the screen adaptation of a literary work, but cuts and transpositions may be particularly indicative of the inflected reading the filmmakers seek to produce. This much is certainly true of the Aurenche and Bost undertaking and, by the same token therefore, even more revealing are the additions they saw fit to work into the scenario. A few examples will suffice to indicate the general direction of the ideological shift. A much-reduced time-scale for the action does not extend to the final phase of Gervaise's life. Widowed and deprived of her shop, she has turned to drink, but she is spared the final degradations recorded in Zola's account of her life. The earlier foreclosing of the drama also leaves Nana a young and relatively innocent child, though the final shots already point to her later sexual escapades. Many minor, if memorable, figures will be lost, and in particular the least attractive working class characters, those most closely associated with scenes of heavy drinking and drunken violence, such as Bénard or Bijard.

The reorientation of the narrative around Gervaise and the men in her life brings a much more substantial part to Goujet who injects a newfound political edge. Republican views, once discredited in the mouth of the disreputable Lantier, are given a fresh status when articulated by the principled, gentle Goujet. Of major significance in the creative extension of this character's role is his participation in a strike which results in a punitive prison sentence. The episode is a typical example of the Aurenchébost concept of "inventer sans trahir" ("to invent without betraying") when transposing an established work for the screen.[13] While not entirely misrepresenting Zola's political stance, they have worked into the narrative their own ideological commitment. Since the author of *Germinal* clearly understood the need to take a stand against exploitative employers, the sequence, they might argue, is legitimate in its generality if not in its particularity. Zola, however, had carefully distinguished between his two working class novels: "Le roman *Gervaise* n'est pas le roman politique, mais le roman des moeurs du peuple."[14] In developing the role of Goujet as the aware, sensitive, moral voice of the community and the text-book father figure to Gervaise's neglected sons, the scriptwriters have further distorted an already unrealistic character portrayal that Zola himself had come to recognize: "Je crois bien d'avoir un peu

Gervaise (Maria Schell) shares a tender moment with Gouget (Jacques Harden) in *Gervaise* (1956).

menti avec Goujet, car je lui ai prêté parfois des sentiments qui ne sont pas de son milieu."[15] The ideological stance implicit in the re-ordering, expansion, and contraction of material becomes evident. The general tendency is to prune away the darker elements and to provide a less brutal account of the lives of Zola's working class characters. Gervaise emerges as the almost faultless victim of a scheming rival, Virginie, and of her male burdens, Lantier and Coupeau, whereas Zola had subjected her actions and attitudes to a tougher scrutiny in her regression to the lifestyle of the milieu she had sought to reject. Progressive views are given more prominence and find a more positive articulation through the patient and understanding Goujet. In many ways then, the scenario represents Zola, but a Zola filtered through the ideological screen of his radical adapters intent on politicizing a compassionate, but hardly revolutionary, text.

The Aurenche and Bost fondness for character-centered plots developed through flashback is the key to the narrative construction of *Gervaise*.[16] Though the original scenario points to a much more complex manipulation of time and perspectives than that witnessed in the film itself, the main intention of binding the viewer into Gervaise's perception of events remains the same. The principal strategy is to mirror events through the consciousness of this hard-working, hard-done-by woman. From the establishing voice-over, which then proceeds to comment on character and to interpret events, it is clear that Gervaise is attempting to make sense of her unhappy situation. But at what point in her downfall does the heroine begin the painful process of reviewing her life?

Following the destruction of the shop by the drink-crazed Coupeau, Gervaise temporarily disappears from the screen. The narrative moves on without her, until she is finally pictured besotted with alcohol in Père Colombe's drinking den. A wide-eyed Nana fails to gain any reaction from her withdrawn, senseless mother, seemingly lost in a world of her own. As Claude Trémois has suggested, it is perhaps in these desperate circumstances that Gervaise starts the whole process of reviewing her unhappy life.[17] From this it would follow that the beginning is found at the end, as though the whole film were one multi-layered flashback.[18]

Though the conventions of voice-over narration designate Gervaise as the narrative's shaping force, her perspective is not an omniscient one. This much is evidenced from the very beginning of the film. Many of the focalizing features of this opening sequence correspond to the modulated viewpoints Valerie Minogue has identified in her discussion of the text. The camera suggests Gervaise's perspective while remaining independent of her. The personal circumstances of the focalizing character are set against the general background of workers flooding into Paris. Gervaise will enjoy all the privileges of the first-person narrator as the audience is immediately drawn into her world though her voice-over and the insights she offers into her situation: "Le matin était revenu. Il n'était toujours pas là. Pas rentré la nuit. C'était la première fois. J'étais tellement fière d'avoir le plus garçon du quartier, moi, la boiteuse."[19]

Her commentary is not attached to any of the images in particular, though the changing perspectives can been seen to reflect her search for her missing partner, the as-yet-unspecified "il" (he). Audience identification is achieved with her emotional perspective, though the camera angle cannot literally be from her spatial location perched high above street level. This is confirmed by the angled perspectives in her subsequent conversation with Mme Boche in the street below. Her voiced recollections spell out her disadvantaged situation as an abandoned female, and it is apparent that she has interiorized the cruel jibe of others when she refers to herself as "la boiteuse" (the lame one). The voice-over in the past tense establishes the process of reconstruction in Gervaise's mind, but what the camera reveals is that she is not aware, at least at the time, of the events as they take place. Parallel montage discloses Lantier's presence in the flat opposite, but even if Gervaise strongly suspects Lantier's infidelity, she is hardly likely to have been aware of the scene played out for the audience.

The privileging of the viewer with information denied Gervaise can only increase sympathy for the deceived protagonist. She is making do in her dingy room with her two children while, in a deliberately contrastive mise-en-scène depicting much more congenial surroundings, Lantier amuses himself with Adèle and Virginie. The camera turns the audience into Pudovkin's posited observer of events "ideally mobile in space and time."[20] The viewer knows for certain what Gervaise can only surmise.

The visual account of Lantier's return is instructive in terms of how camera position and framing bind the audience to Gervaise's point of view.[21] As focalizer, she is framed with her back to the camera capturing Lantier's entrance. This is how she sees him, but if the audience shares that perspective it does so with the knowledge of Lantier's infidelity, as yet only suspected by the exploited Gervaise. A supportive bonding is further developed as her emotions of hurt, then relief at seeming reconciliation, are captured in close-up. Gervaise's ensuing voice-over not only serves as a narrative bridge for the journey to the *lavoir* (washhouse), but also confirms her emotional dependence on the worthless Lantier.

The scope of this article does not permit a detailed discussion of the function and effect of all fifteen voice-overs, which structure the narration.[22] Suffice it to note, at this stage, that some mark a simple ellipsis, some record Gervaise's reactions to events, while others her assessment of individuals. These are effectively key moments in her developing insight into her tragic destiny. Each represents her foregrounding of the episodes she deems to have been important in her life and the viewer, by and large, is guided by her interested point of view. However, it clearly remains the case that the camera frequently relates events outside her knowledge, or conveys a different slant to the story she is recounting.[23]

The present analysis will focus on selected examples of voice-over, which are major structuring devices in the narration. The first concerns two interlinked voice-over presentations, which illustrate the Aurenche-bost formula for narrative development through flashback. Taken together, these scenes form part of the intricate pattern of associative recall in Gervaise's reconstruction of events.

Marriage to Coupeau

The fight with Virginie in the *lavoir* is over and, as Gervaise leaves with Claude and Etienne to face a future without Lantier, her voice-over carries the narrative forward to her marriage with Coupeau. Her commentary runs as follows:

> Eh bien, puisque c'est somme ça je me défendrai, et toute seule avec mes deux petits. Et puis, d'abord, je n'ai pas de mari, vous dites. Mais si, je me suis mariée. Je me suis mariée, oui! Il m'a épousée, Monsieur Coupeau. Mais naturellement pas en blanc comme celle-là, je ne pouvais pas. Ma robe, je l'avais empruntée à la soeur de Coupeau. Ah, celles-là, quelles avares! Ce sont des gens qui travaillent dans l'or. Ils fabriquent de petites chaînes. Il faut que travailler dans l'or vous rend méchant.[24]

This voice-over (V.O) can be broken down into a series of segments together with the screen images (S.I.) they cover:

(1)   S.I: Gervaise leaving the *lavoir* with her children.
            V.O: Her reflection on her situation (present tense) and her resolution to meet any challenge (future tense).
(2)   S.I: Gervaise and Coupeau dressed for their wedding. Gervaise observes a bride in a white dress. A shoe is passed between Coupeau and Mes Bottes.
            V.O: She addresses the viewer directly concerning her marriage to Coupeau. This is an event about to be witnessed but formulated in the past tense. She compares the bride's dress with her own borrowed from the Lorilleux.
(3)   S.I: The mean-spirited Lorilleux work at their gold, with an embarrassed Coupeau and an amused Gervaise foreground in close-up.
            V.O: Gervaise's negative commentary on the couple complements the screen images.

The narrative chronology is teasing, for here there is an episode within an episode, brought to Gervaise's consciousness by the associative trigger of the observed wedding dress and her own borrowed from Coupeau's sister. There is, then, a flashback within an existing flashback, as memory takes her further back in time. This means that the next scene, the morning of the wedding in which she recalls her feelings for Coupeau, takes place after the Lorilleux flashback, but before the initial flashback introducing the wedding-day sequence. Gervaise's commentary runs: "Evidemment, il n'était pas aussi distingué que ... mais, il était si gentille, et couvreur, c'est un bon métier."[25]

The screen images confirm Coupeau's nature, and his charge that *Mes Bottes* (My Boots) has stolen one of his shoes ties in with the images of the shoe passed from man to man as the bridal couple await the ceremony. At the end of this scene a simple cut returns the narrative to the signing of the wedding register. A strictly linear chronology would mean that this scene follows on from that depicting Gervaise and Coupeau waiting to become man and wife. However, contained within this chronological period of waiting is the endlessly elastic duration of psychological time, which sanctions the introduction to the Lorilleux and Gervaise's reflection on her feelings for Coupeau.

The Return of Virginie

Within Zola's text there is a strong sense of circularity and entrapment as characters, moving within the narrow confines of the *quartier* (neighborhood), regularly encounter one another. In Clément's re-telling of the story, this closed world persists in repeated meetings between key players placed in parallel circumstances. Such is the case with Gervaise and Virginie, whose shared past is inextricably linked with Lantier and the fight in the *lavoir*. Years after successfully establishing her *blanchisserie* (laundry), Gervaise meets up again with Virginie, now Madame Poisson. Their chance encounter, as Gervaise delivers laundry to her clients, inevitably re-opens the past. The focalizing voice-over passes quickly over the acquisition of the shop to focus on the meeting with Virginie: "Et je l'ai eue, ma boutique. Et puis voilà qu'un jour qu'est-ce que je vois? Virginie. Ah, elle m'était bien sortie de la tête, celle-là!"[26]

The discovery that Virginie now lives in the rooms she had previously occupied with Coupeau triggers a spate of memories covering her marriage and the birth of Nana. According to the original scenario, such recollections were to be recaptured visually through a series of associative flashbacks; however, in the film itself the recall is simply verbal. It becomes apparent that material from this sequence has been displaced to Gervaise's earlier account of her marriage. Nevertheless, the audience is still treated to a second rehearsal of established information. The significance of this further recounting lies not so much in the details themselves but in the briefing of Virginie. The camera records not only Gervaise's disarming openness with her former antagonist, but also reveals Virginie to be calculating and untrustworthy.

Children as Surrogate Focalizers

In the work of Zola and Clément children provide key perspectives in the demonstration of a given value-system. They represent the future, the next generation, and as such it is in their destinies that society's formative influences will be seen. For the determinist author they are the final expression of cause and effect now stretching beyond one generation into the next and, sadly, perpetuating the malevolent influence of

Young Nana (Chantal Gozzi) stares at the filthy feet of her father in *Gervaise* (1956).

society's evils.[27] For Clément, children serve a similar function as briefly innocent observers of adult wrongdoings or damaging attitudes. Their presence is established at every key moment: Gervaise's tearful argument with the unfaithful Lantier; the degrading fight with Virginie in the *lavoir*; the wedding visit to the Louvre marked by ribald comments and sexual innuendos.

More significantly, as they grow up, the children regularly witness the drunken behavior of adults, while after Gervaise's feast, Etienne, in particular, suffers the confusion of his natural father moving back into the family home. His realization that Gervaise has once more shared Lantier's bed is clearly distressing.[28] If his role is essentially as a recipient of painful truths, his half-sister Nana comes to play an increasingly active role in the unfolding of events. It is she who initially registers for the audience the disgusting sight of Coupeau lying in his own vomit, and in her wide eyes is reflected the knowledge of her mother's capitulation to Lantier. Thereafter, she becomes implicated in Coupeau's drinking, smuggles in bottles for him and reveals to Gervaise that he has pawned clients' sheets to finance his craving for alcohol. Shortly afterwards, she

9. *Ideology and Focalization in* Gervaise *(Cousins)*   141

The infamous fight between the washerwomen: Gervaise (Maria Schell, left foreground) and Virginie (Suzy Delair, right foreground) in *Gervaise* (1956).

watches in bewilderment the antics of Coupeau in the grip of *delirium tremens*, and is subsequently caught up in the trauma of his violent destruction of the shop.

Gervaise, as the original focalizer, has fallen silent. Her story has run its course; she has lost control, and her voice is no longer heard making sense of the screen images. It now falls to the abandoned Nana to provide the narrative thread through the closing elliptical sequence in which a wine glass ominously serves as the visual link. It is the wandering child—and the lower camera angles confirm this—who in turn has become the character/communicator. It is she who, in the closing scenes, discovers for the audience the solitary, stupefied Gervaise slumped in the corner of the drinking den. If the tragedy of Gervaise has been played out, for Nana, the product of deficient parenting and a disastrous environment, a woefully short life of sexual adventure is about to begin. The endless cycle of social misery continues unbroken, as the focus now shifts from mother to daughter.

Throughout the film, by means of the voice-over presentation, framing that foregrounds Gervaise as the participant/observer, camera angles that associate action with her viewpoint, and close-ups that identify with her pain or pleasure, the audience is locked into her version of events. It is her interested, and sometimes limited, viewpoint as the character/narrator, which is shared with the viewer. This focalization is essential to Clément's purpose of moving the cinema audience to question the intolerable pressures placed upon women such as Gervaise in an uncaring, happy-go-lucky, male-structured society. Where the director's camera privileges the audience to knowledge the heroine does not possess, invariably to expose the machinations of malevolent characters intent on undermining Gervaise, the effect is to strengthen identification with the somewhat disingenuous, good-hearted victim. The calamitous life-style of the *quartier* (neighborhood) finds its ultimate expression in those final chilling shots of a virtually parentless Nana roaming the streets. The sequential images of a drunken mother and an unsupervised child translate, in a memorable visual form, the moral conclusion that Zola hoped would be drawn from *L'Assommoir*: "Fermez les cabarets, ouvrez les écoles!"[29]

Appendix to Chapter 9: Voice-overs in Gervaise

1. Gervaise on the balcony of the Hôtel Boncoeur: "Le matin était revenu. Il n'était toujours pas là. Pas rentré la nuit. C'était la première fois. J'étais tellement fière d'avoir le plus beau garçon du quartier. Moi, la boiteuse." ("It was already morning. He still wasn't here. Didn't return during the night. It was the first time. I was so proud to be with the most beautiful boy in the neighborhood, me, the lame one").
2. Inside the Hôtel Reconciliation with Lantier: "Ca s'est arrangé encore une fois. Il n'avait qu'à me regarder, faire un sourire, et je finissais par dire 'bon.'" ("Once again, it all worked out. He just had to look at me, smile, and I'd end up saying 'fine.'")
3. Gervaise leaves the *lavoir* after her fight with Virginie and recalls her marriage to Coupeau together with the attitude of the Lorilleux: "Eh bien, puisque c'est comme ça, je me défendrai, et toute seule avec mes deux petits. Et puis, d'abord, j'ai pas de mari, vous dites. Mais si, je me suis mariée. Je me suis mariée, oui! Il m'a épousée, Monsieur Coupeau. Mais naturellement, pas en blanc comme celle-là, je ne pouvais pas. Ma robe, je l'avais empruntée à la soeur de Coupeau. Ah, celles-là, quelles avares! Ce sont des gens qui travaillent dans l'or. Ils fabriquent de petites chaînes. Il faut que travailler dans l'or vous rend méchant." ("Well, if that's how it is, I will defend myself, all alone with my two little ones. And then, first of all, I have no husband, you say. But yes, I got married. I got married, all right! He married me, Mister Coupeau. But naturally I was not in white, like her, I could not.

9. *Ideology and Focalization in* Gervaise *(Cousins)* 143

My dress, I borrowed it from Coupeau's sister. Ah, those ones, so miserly! These people work in goldmines. They make small chains. Working in goldmines has to make you mean").

4. The morning of the wedding, and Gervaise recalls her feelings for Coupeau: "Evidemment, il n'était pas aussi distingué que ... mais, il était si gentille et couvreur, c'est un bon métier." ("Obviously, he wasn't as distinguished as.... But, he was kind, and a roofer, that's a good profession").
5. At the visit to the Louvre, Gervaise recalls her feelings for Goujet: "Ah non! Il n'était pas comme tout le monde. Il me disait, et pourquoi est-ce qu'ils tiennent à l'avoir pour une noce. Il n'est pas gai, il ne fait pas rire tout le monde. Il a l'air de penser à autre chose. Et puis tout d'un coup je me suis dit, ça doit être parce qu'ils l'estiment bien." ("Oh No! He was not like everyone else. He would tell me, and why do they want him for a wedding. He isn't cheerful; he doesn't make everyone laugh. He seems to be thinking about some other things. And then all of a sudden, I said to myself that it must be because they respect him").
6. At the Coupeau household, Gervaise returns from a hard day's work, tired but content: "Le temps a passé. Les enfants ont grandi, et puis j'ai eu Nana. Ah pour ça on travaillait dur, lui sur les toits, moi à la blanchisserie, parce que je m'étais mis dans la tête à louer une boutique et devenir patronne à mon compte." ("Time went by. The kids grew up, and then I had Nana. Oh, for that we worked hard, him on the roofs, me at the laundry, because I took it into my head to rent a store and become my own boss").
7. In the Coupeau household, after her husband's fall from the roof, Gervaise is exhausted and dispirited: "Six mois après il était guéri, seulement avec le docteur à cent sous la visite, tout avait passé." ("Six months later he was cured, only with a hundred cents a visit, all had passed").
8. On the street, Gervaise recognizes Virginie: "Et je l'ai eue, ma boutique. Et puis voilà un jour, qu'est-ce que je vois? Virginie. Ah, elle m'était bien sortie de la tête, celle-là." ("And I finally opened my store. And then, one day, what do I see? Virginie. Ah, that one, I had completely forgotten!").
9. In the shop, Gervaise tells Virginie how she set up in business: "Est-ce que j'avais besoin de lui faire toutes ces confidences? Et je lui ai même raconté que c'était M. Goujet qui nous avait prêté l'argent pour la boutique. Et je lui ai dit, je ne voulais pas trop; c'était Coupeau qui avait voulu." ("Did I need to tell him all these secrets? And I even told him it was M. Goujet who had loaned us the money for the store. And I told him, I didn't really want to; it was Coupeau who wanted to").

10. In the street, Gervaise and Goujet are walking together. She explains her problems with Coupeau and her financial embarrassment: "Ce jour-lé il se passait deux bonnes choses. D'abord, il a voulu m'embrasser, et il m'avait laissé à quoi faire mon dîner." ("That day two good things happened. First he wanted to kiss me, and he had left me something to have for dinner").
11. In the shop, on Gervaise's feast day, Virginie tells her that Lantier is back in the area: "Et, moi, qui croyait de ne penser plus à Lantier, un homme qui vous a eue à quinze ans et qui vous a rendu si malheureuse, ça s'oublie pas." ("And I had hoped not to think about Lantier anymore, a man who had you at fifteen and who made you so unhappy is impossible to forget").
12. In the shop, followed by a dissolve to the Music Hall, Gervaise recalls the evening, which led to her renewed relationship with Lantier and the consequential loss of Goujet's friendship: "Il y a bien une âme qui lui dira ce que j'ai fait pendant qu'il était en prison, Virginie, elle en est capable. C'est bien elle qui a voulu tout ce qui est arrivé." ("There must be someone who will tell him what I did when he was in prison; Virginie is capable of that. She is the one who wanted all that happened").
13. In the shop, Gervaise cleans up Coupeau's vomit, as Etienne realizes his mother's infidelity. Then, dissolve to Gervaise and Goujet at the *bal populaire* (local dance): "Et mon pauvre petit, qu'est-ce que je pouvais lui dire? Rien. Il n'aime plus sa mère, c'est tout. Et le seul qui m'aimait, le seul qui aurait pu empêcher ça, il fallait qu'il soit en prison. Et maintenant qu'il est revenu, comment lui expliquer. Il comprendra jamais." ("And my poor little one, what was I to tell him? Nothing. He doesn't like his mother anymore, that's all. And the only one who loved me, the only one who could have prevented this, he had to be in prison of course. And now that he has returned, how am I to explain it to him. He will never understand").
14. In the shop, Gervaise, off-screen, comments on Lantier's advice to Coupeau to drink less: "Il avait raison, Lantier, Coupeau crèverait à force de boire et, ma foi, il y avait des jours où je pensais au bon débarras." ("Lantier was right, Coupeau would drink himself to death, and well, there were days when I thought to myself that it would be a good riddance").
15. At the railway station, Goujet leaves with Etienne: "Il n'y a que ces deux de propre dans ma vie. C'est peut-être pour ça qu'ils partent." ("These two are the only decent ones in my life. That may be why they are leaving.")

Notes

1. In his study of *L'Assommoir*, Roger Clark lists the following films that owe their inspiration to Zola's text: *Les Victimes de l'alcoolisme*. Ferdinand Zecca, France, 1902; *A Drunkard's Reformation*. D.W. Griffith, U.S.A., 1909; *L'Assommoir*. Albert Capellani, France, 1909; *Les Victimes de l'alcool*. Gérard Bourgeois, France, 1911; *Le Poison de l'humanité*. Émile Chautard, France, 1912; *Drink*. Harry T. Roberts, England, 1917; *L'Assommoir*. Charles Madru and Maurice de Marsan, France, 1922; *The Struggle*. D. W. Griffith, U.S.A., 1931; *L'Assommoir*. Gaston Roudès, France, 1933; *Gervaise*. René Clément, France 1956. For further details of these films, see Roger Clark, *Zola, L'Assommoir*, Glasgow Introductory Guides to French Literature, no. 13 (1990): 81–82.
2. *Gervaise* opened in Paris on 5th September, 1956 to enthusiastic reviews. Credits: Gervaise (Maria Schell); Coupeau (François Périer); Virginie (Suzy Delair); Lantier (Armand Mistral); Goujet (Jacques Harden); Mme Lorilleux (Jany Holt); Mme Boche (Mathilde Casadessus). Director, René Clément; producer, Agnès Delahaie; scriptwriters, Jean Aurenche and Pierre Bost; music Georges Auric; costumes: Mayo. Major film awards: Best Film and Best Actress (Venice Film Festival, 1956) and Best Foreign Film of 1957, New York Film Critics. Selected reviews: *Cahiers du Cinéma*, no. 63 (Oct. 1956): 42–44; *Film Culture*, no. 5 (Dec. 1957): 14–15; *Films and Filming* 3 (Feb. 1957): 22; *Films in Review* 8 (Dec. 1957): 525; *Image et Son*, no. 98 (Jan. 1957): 8–10; *The New Yorker* 33 (Nov. 23, 1957): 149; *The New York Times*, Nov. 12, 1957: 46; *Les Nouvelles Littéraires*, Sept, 20, 1956; *Sight and Sound* 26 (Winter 1956-7): 148–50; *The Times*, Dec. 10, 1956: 5; *Variety*, Sept. 19, 1957.
3. For an account of the partnership between Jean Aurenche and Pierre Bost, see my essay on Jean Aurenche in James Vinson, ed., *The International Dictionary of Films and Filmmakers*, Vol. 4, Writers and Production Artists (Chicago and London: St. James Press, 1987), 24–26. The writers' successful partnership brought about the elision of the two names to form Aurenchébost (Aurenche et Bost).
4. For this article, I worked with Genette's definition of *Focalization*—"The perspective in terms of which the narrated situations and events are presented; the perceptual or conceptual position in terms of which they are rendered" and of *Focalizer*—"The subject of focali[z]ation; the holder of point of view; the focal point governing the focali[z]ation." In Gerald Prince, *A Dictionary of Narratology* (UK: Scolar Press, 1991), 31–32.
5. The most frequently adapted texts by Zola are *L'Assommoir* and *Nana*. The most recent major screen adaptation is Claude Berri's *Germinal* (1993), starring Gérard Départdieu.
6. "Man is shaped and made whole by his environment." Émile Zola, 'De la description', in Aimé Guedj, ed., *Le Roman experimental* (Paris: Garnier-Flammarion, 1971), 232.
7. Valerie Minogue. *Zola, L'Assommoir*, Critical Guides to French Texts, no. 87 (London: Grant and Cutler, 1991), 48.
8. Ibid., 94.
9. See, for example, Leo Braudy, *Yale French Studies*, no. 42 (1969): 68–88; *Sergei Eisenstein, Film Form*, trans. Jay Leyda (London, 1963); René Jeanne in *Présence de Zola* (Paris, 1953), 204–213; Maurice Leblond, *Visages du Monde*, no. 17 (1934): 154–55; Joy Newton, *The French Review*, vol. 44, no. 2 (1971): 106–116; Georges Sadoul, *Europe*, no. 30 (1952): 158–69.
10. The original scenario for *Gervaise* may be consulted at the Institut des Hautes Études Cinématographiques, Paris. Découpage no. 2205 S.
11. "We tightened the plot to the maximum. It seems to us that the story gains by not playing too much with time. This standpoint therefore required us to set aside certain displays of man's decline. This is also because *L'Assommoir* was not centered

on this aspect.... From Zola's work we chose what was related to Gervaise's life. The story we collaborated on is not an anti-alcoholic manifesto, it is the story of a woman." *Le Film Français* 636–37 (24 August 1956): 23.

12. "... There was only one way to stay faithful to Zola's tone and that was to aim the spotlight on a character within whom, just like in a sensitive mirror, all the drama is played out. I chose Gervaise.... For a long time, I wanted to make a film about the condition of women." André Farwagi, *René Clément* (Paris: Seghers, 1967), 33.

13. François Truffaut, "Une certaine tendance du cinéma français,"*Les Cahiers du Cinéma* (January 31, 1954): 15–28.

14. "*Gervaise* is not the political novel, but the novel about a people's morals." The ébauche for *L'Assommoir*, Bibliothèque Nationale, Nouvelles acquisitions françaises, MS. 10.271, fol. 171.

15. "I believe I may have lied a little regarding Goujet, for I sometimes ascribed feelings to him that are not in his environment." Zola's letter to Yves Guyot, editor of *Le Bien public*, published 13 Feb. 1877, *Correspondance*, éditée sous la direction de B.H. Bakker, vol II (Les Presses de l'Université de Montréal, 1980), 538.

16. In many respects *Gervaise* is typical for the Aurenchébost approach to adaptation, a style of sympathetic reworking and invention supposedly geared towards fidelity to the original but which invariably resulted in character-centered, formulaic constructions imbued with their own political persuasions. The packaged sameness which they engineered for a whole range of disparate works, from *Le Rouge et le Noir* to *Le Diable au corps*, earned the scorn of the young critic François Truffaut, who contemptuously dismissed their approach as textual abuse and a denial of cinema's potential for originality in expression.

17. Claude-Marie Trémois, *Gervaise*, Fiche no. 282, *Téléciné* (Oct. 1956): 28–40.

18. In the novel Gervaise frequently recalls happier times as her fortunes decline.

19. "It was already morning. He still wasn't here. Didn't return during the night. It was the first time. I was so proud to be with the most beautiful boy in the neighborhood, me the lame one."

20. V.I Pudovkin. *Film Technique and Film Acting*, trans. Ivor Montagu (New York, 1970), 254.

21. The same camera position is adopted more than once to seal identification with Gervaise's point of view. See, for example, Goujet's trial sequence or the scenes at the railway station when he leaves with Etienne. In contrast, the final shot of Gervaise in the drinking den is of her face. She is no longer the link observer, but the observed

22. A transcription of the voice-overs in *Gervaise* is given in the appendix.

23. For example, the bogus nature of the blind/deaf beggar on the steps of the church is humorously revealed to the viewer while, as the wedding party tours the Louvre, the incongruity of the working class presence is suggested by the focus on the muddy shoes.

24. "Well, if that's how it is, I will defend myself all alone with my two little ones. And then, first of all, I have no husband you say. But yes, I got married. I got married, all right! He married me, Mister Coupeau. But naturally I was not in white, like her, I could not. My dress, I borrowed it from Coupeau's sister. Ah, those ones, so miserly! These people work in goldmines. They make small chains. Working in goldmines has to make you mean."

25. "Obviously, he wasn't as distinguished as ... but he was so kind, and a roofer, that's a fine profession."

26. "And I finally opened my shop. And then, one day, what do I see? Virginie. Ah, that one, I had completely forgotten her!"

27. In *L'Assommoir*, the themes of promiscuity and violence are demonstrated in the destinies of Nana Coupeau and Lalie Bijard.

28. After discovering that Lantier has slept with Gervaise, Etienne reacts petulantly

to Goujet's well-intended paternal advice with, "'J'ai trop de pères!'" ("'I have too many fathers!'"). The child's displaced hurt is self-evident.

29. "Close the cabarets, open the schools!" Zola's letter to Yves Guyot, editor of *Le Bien public*, published 13 Feb. 1877, *Correspondance*, 537.

10

The Female Reader in *Pot-Bouille* and Duvivier's Cinematic Representation

ELISABETH-CHRISTINE MUELSCH

In his 1989 essay "Recasting Zola: Gérard Philipe's Influence on Duvivier's Adaptation of *Pot-Bouille*," Russell Cousins argues that the portrayal of the Marie Pichon—Octave Mouret relationship in the film is indeed a betrayal of the message Émile Zola wanted to convey, namely, that female education is inadequate, leaving women defenseless against unscrupulous males.[1] Cousins and earlier reviewers of the film have pointed out that Duvivier's (1957) adaptation of the novel shows less harshness in tone and imagery than the original text; it focuses more on representing a "light-hearted satire of bourgeois transgression,"[2] than on depicting social injustices and the morbid world of bourgeois hypocrisy in naturalist effrontery.[3] However, my contention is that Duvivier addresses Zola's concern for female education through his attention to a particular element of it: reading. The pros and cons of female literacy were the subject of educational and literary debates throughout the nineteenth century and this issue also becomes a structuring element of the film. The intent of this article is to investigate Duvivier's shaping of reading scenes, by focusing on the reading woman in the film and contrasting her with the female reader in the novel. However, it is not only the female reader in the text/film, but also the female reader of the text/film who will be important for this interpretation. Nevertheless, Zola and Duvivier employ similar strategies to reach a large audience with their novels/films,[4] clearly taking female reader/viewer expectations into consideration[5] and targeting women as potential consumers of their works: yet the ideal reader of Zola's novel and the ideal spectator of Duvivier's film, because of their respective socio-historical circumstances, are not the same.

The representation of female reading in the novel *Pot-Bouille* serves as a metonym for the dismal education women received in nineteenth-century France. Well before the publication of *Pot-Bouille*, Zola had written articles on female education and the bad reading habits of bourgeois daughters. In 1880 he had published "La Moralité en littérature," an essay criticizing the romantic readings devoured by young women, whose heroines provided, in Zola's eyes, unsuitable role models for a nineteenth-century woman:

> Il n'en est pas une de vivante parmi elles, j'entends qui se conduise raisonnablement, en bonne et simple créature. Ce ne sont qu'abnégations sublimes, qu'ignorances ridicules, que bêtises emphatiques et volontaires. Notre jeune fille française, dont l'instruction et l'éducation sont déplorables, et qui flotte de l'ange à la bête, est un produit direct de cette littérature imbécile, où une jeune vierge est d'autant plus noble qu'elle se rapproche davantage d'une poupée mécanique bien montée.... Walter Scott a fait toute une génération de rêveuses et de raisonneuses insupportables.[6]

The female character in *Pot-Bouille* who most closely fits the above description is, of course, Marie Pichon, a naive and sentimental reader, defined by her inability to read and interpret either text or reality critically. However, other female characters are represented as being affected differently by romantic literature. Mme Josserand, aware of the fact that reading functions also as an indicator of social status, reads Lamartine's epic poem *Jocelyn*, originally spelled "Josselin," a name alluding to one of the most best-known noble families in France, thus revealing her own aspirations for social ascent.[7] In order to gain recognition, Mme Josserand makes every effort to let others know about her readings. Her romantic readings, unsubstantial in the first place, are soiled by the pragmatics of everyday life: Adèle, her servant, drags the book into the kitchen to do her accounting on the cover. The parallel to the marketing/prostitution of the Josserand daughters is striking. The romantic desires of the Josserand girls, conceivably also molded through idealistic literature, are subjected to the materialistic preoccupations of the mother, who keeps her accounts at the expense of her daughters' well-being. Just as Adèle keeps her accounts on the backs of romantic novels, the mother keeps her accounts on the overleaf of her daughters' romantic desire. This sarcastic presentation of self-important behavior among bourgeois female readers, intimately linked to the world of bourgeois hypocrisy unveiled in Zola's novel, is taken up in Duvivier's film adaptation.

Like many of his contemporaries,[8] Zola viewed inappropriate readings and insufficient education as the leading causes for adulterous behavior: "Chez une femme qui prend un amant, il y a toujours au fond la lecture d'un roman idéaliste, que ce soit *Indiana* ou le *Roman d'un jeune homme pauvre*,"[9] blaming foremost romantic literature for women's adultery. It is therefore no surprise that reading plays an important role in the process of seduction of married female characters in both the novel and the film. While Zola exemplified three different types of adulterous women in *Pot-Bouille*,[10] Duvivier focuses mainly on the hysteric and the woman who is seduced through reading,[11] an activity, which Gérard Philipe, in the role of Octave Mouret, either participates in or initiates. The high frequency of reading scenes in the film is striking, particularly in light of the fact that many other important passages of the novel are not duplicated in the movie. Not only does Duvivier reproduce many of the reading scenes of the novel, to a certain extent even problematizing the merit of different literary genres, but he also adds further reading scenes to the film. Clearly the film thrives on the image of reading as a dangerous cultural practice, able to compromise the virtue of women.

This emphasis is in keeping with Gérard Philipe's role as the charming seducer Octave Mouret.

The issue of appropriate readings for young women is first addressed in the film when Mme Josserand (played by Jane Marken) and her daughters return from a ball, where the girls had once again been unsuccessful in finding suitable husbands. Frustrated by the failure, Mme Josserand turns on her daughters, scolding them for not being more aggressive in their pursuit of eligible bachelors and telling them to make more concessions toward suitors. This is clearly an invitation to immoral behavior, which Mme Josserand seems to justify by her goal: marriage. She then proceeds to

Gérard Philipe and Dany Carrel prepare for love in *Pot-Bouille* (1957) (courtesy *bfi*, film stills).

attack her husband with the remarks, "Ne laissez pas traîner le journal, il y a dedans des articles qui ne sont pas pour les jeunes filles" and "Vous n'avez vraiment aucune moralité."[12] For the viewer of the film, Mme Josserand's hypocritical educational endeavors are apparent since she teaches her daughters seduction but does not allow them to read the newspaper, a genre often coded as belonging to the male domain, not only because newspaper readers connect through their reading with the public sphere—the world of politics and finance—but also because they gain access to the world of crime and passion described in the *faits divers* (short news items).[13] The film mirrors closely tone and content of a scene described in the second chapter of the book, in which the shy M. Josserand tries to escape the outbursts of his wife by hiding behind the newspaper *Le Temps*. Zola depicts M. Josserand as one of the few integral characters of *Pot-Bouille*, a man working a second job to support his abusive wife who keeps up a world of appearances. The shallowness of Mme Josserand's true interests is displayed in her attempt to establish her superiority in educational matters vis-à-vis her husband. She criticizes M. Josserand for his lack of ambition, his unprestigious job, and for the little concern he shows for what she considers their daughters' proper education. Through the sarcastic presentation of Mme Josserand emphasizing her family's long-standing interest in female education epitomized by a father who was responsible for a *pensionnat* (boarding school), Zola expresses his contempt for the educational values of the bourgeoisie.[14] He particularly disliked the education young women received in convents.

Zola's criticism of bourgeois female education in nineteenth-century France is mirrored in Duvivier's portrayal of the dysfunctional Josserand family. Through the presentation of a scheming Mme Josserand, who views her daughters as commodities and education as a necessity to place them on the marriage market and who shields them from "inappropriate" newspaper readings while simultaneously training them to be refined seductresses, the inadequacies of nineteenth-century female education become apparent to a twentieth-century audience.

An important reading scene in the movie, which is not represented as such in the novel, forms the basis of the first erotic encounter between Octave and Berthe (played by Dany Carrel). At one of her *soirées* Mme Josserand tries to set up Octave with her daughter Berthe, inviting him to look at Berthe's photo album. Again, Mme Josserand reveals hypocritical moral standards, since she shields her daughters from reading newspapers but encourages Berthe's perusal of a photo album with an eligible bachelor, clearly illustrating to the viewer that, for bourgeois women like Mme Josserand, reading is entirely functionalized. In this latter event, reading only serves the purpose of seducing eligible bachelors.

Berthe's physical development, displayed in the photographs, becomes the two readers' topic of conversation. Here, as in other parts of the film, visual and verbal clues imply a connection between the body of the text and the body of the woman reading the text/images. The textual body is subjected to Octave's interpretation: "J'aurais l'impression de vous avoir connue toute petite.... Et l'album fermé nous sommes devenus de vieux amis,"[14] to achieve his main goal: the seduction and manipulation of the female body. Octave points to the milestones displayed in the album, the first step, the first dance, to justify his physical seduction: giving Berthe the first kiss. Evidently, reading together is understood by both readers as an erotic activity, and the book/photo album is seen as an agent of seduction.

Another notable reading scene in the film, which is not a reading scene in the novel, focuses on the refusal to read. The scene occurs during Octave's first encounter with his new employer Mme Hédouin, owner of the store *Au Bonheur des Dames*. Mme Hédouin, played by the very successful actress Danielle Darrieux, who had starred as a partner of Gérard Philipe previously,[15] is a woman who comes across to Octave as "froide" ("cold"), and who "ne vit que pour le magasin"("lives only for the store"). When Octave hands her two reference letters, she refuses to look at them, saying that she only relies on her own judgment: "Je ne me fis qu'au propre jugement"("I only trust my own judgment"). This scene serves to illustrate Mme Hédouin's character. She is a woman anchored in reality who forms her opinion based on observation rather than on hearsay. Her judgment of reality is not impaired through (mis)readings of literature. As Wai-Chee Dimock argues, reading understood beyond the boundaries of the literary text is a phenomenon peculiar to modernity.[16] Since the mid-nineteenth century people have had to become readers of sorts, interpreting the increasingly complex world surrounding them. At the same time, late nineteenth-century France saw a rise in professional groups, whose members successfully instituted new reading conventions.[17] This culture of professionalism affected not only men, but also women. Legal and social reforms influenced women's ability to pursue professional careers, which allowed them, at least in theory, to become expert readers and interpreters of signs. Mme Hédouin represents this new type of professional woman, whose ability to read and interpret her surroundings is formed through her education and professional experience. She reads the facts rather than the impressions of other people.

In this aspect, the film mirrors the character of Mme Hédouin as developed in the novel. Zola, too, represents Mme Hédouin as the "new woman," whose sense of pragmatism is not altered through romantic readings and social pretense. Her work is an important part of her self-understanding. Zola designed her as an antidote to the many bourgeois

10. The Female Reader in Pot-Bouille (Muelsch)

Left to right: Gérard Philipe, Dany Carrel and Danielle Darrieux discuss merchandise and exchange familiarities in *Pot-Bouille* (1957).

and petit-bourgeois adulterous women in *Pot-Bouille*,[18] who are easily seduced by Octave, while Mme Hédouin hardly seems to notice him: "Octave était blessé qu'elle ne le regardât pas davantage."[19] Even though she remains levelheaded throughout the novel, the film shows her as soon seduced by Octave's charm; like all the other women, she is unable to resist him. Because of her awakening desire for Octave, she forgoes her business-like approach to life and begins to manipulate the people around her. In the interval between the publication of the novel and the first screening of the film, professional women had certainly become more established in French society than they had been in 1882, when the novel was first published. Many post-naturalist novels represent a new female reader, who reads to increase her knowledge and to further her professional career instead of escaping reality and seeking romantic fulfillment through literature.[20] Why does the film first underscore so emphatically the professional woman refusing to be influenced by recommendation letters, only to set Mme Hédouin up as a vulnerable, jealous and manipulative female? The answer lies with Gérard Philipe in the role of Octave Mouret and with assumptions about gender-specific reading behavior.

In the film, to be a professional, Mme Hédouin only has one option: not to read text/books. The moment she takes the liberty of reading or allows Octave to read and interpret text for her, she succumbs to his charm. Thus, Duvivier's film links reading and interpreting text with male power. It is the quality of Henri Jeanson's "dazzling dialogues" as Jacques Siclier calls them, which furthers this interpretation.[21] The film emphasizes that Octave's strategies of seduction are always linked to language and text. It is also his ability to wrap women into his fabric of words that eventually allows him to seduce Mme Hédouin. In due time, he sits with her over the books, interpreting the rather factual material by creating a seductive scenario. Mme Hédouin actually identifies this phenomenon in an off-hand comment, calling him "le poète lyrique de la bonneterie" ("the lyrical poet of the hosiery"), after he has presented to her his plans for expansion and his marketing strategies. This development activity is also accentuated cinematographically. They both take their eyes off the books and move toward the window to imagine the extent of the possible enlargement.

The communal reading of the accounting books is an equally focal scene of attempted seduction in the novel: "Il en était arrivé à étudier l'affaire au point de vue des chiffres, à établir déjà un devis approximatif, de l'air passionné dont un page romantique aurait déclaré un amour longtemps contenu."[22] However, Zola's Mme Hédouin is mainly intrigued by Octave's commercial abilities; in another place their relationship is described as "une sorte d'intimité commerciale"[23] ("a sort of commercial intimacy"), while Duvivier's Mme Hédouin has a distinctly sexual interest in her employee, whose many girlfriends she perceives as rivals. The film underscores the seductive nature of Octave's language, his manipulative use of not only romantic but any kind of text, and his intentional confusion of the boundaries between fiction and reality. He appears as the creator and agent for the dissemination of romantic literature. While Zola mainly addresses young women's inability to make a distinction between fiction and reality and their uncritical transposition of romantic fiction onto the realities of French bourgeois nineteenth-century life, the film underscores Octave's role as the creator of seductive scenarios and his ability to use books and other kinds of written materials to seduce women.

The most prominent female reader in the novel and film remains Marie Pichon. The film, unlike the novel, does not develop the breadth of the psychological reasons that led to Marie's strong desire for romantic literature. Zola designed Marie to illustrate the effects of an inadequate education, in which the intellectual horizon of young women was purposefully limited. When Marie's parents, M. and Mme Vuillaume, visit their daughter, Octave is invited for coffee and made aware of the education Marie has received: "La fierté ne vaut rien, déclara Mme Vuillaume. Nous lui avons toujours recommandé la modestie."[24] Mme Vuillaume underscores that it is much more difficult to raise a girl than a boy, because she believes that a daughter has to be kept under constant surveillance. Marie is hermetically shut off from the outside world:

> L'honnêteté d'abord.... Les portes fermées, les fenêtres closes, jamais de courants d'air, qui apportent les vilaines choses de la rue.... Puis, quand elle a grandi, prendre des maîtresses, ne pas la mettre dans les pensionnats, où les innocentes se corrompent; et encore assister aux leçons, veiller à ce qu'elle doit ignorer, cacher les journaux bien entendu, et fermer la bibliothèque."[25]

Knowledge was intentionally withheld from her, which explains how she could remain so ignorant as a married woman. As a child, her access to reading materials was severely restricted. While the mother, who herself never read for pleasure, censured Marie's readings: "des lignes que sa mère raturait à l'encre sur leur journal de mode, et dont les barres noires la faisaient rougir,"[26] it was the father who ultimately controlled her access to books and to the library, where Marie herself never set foot. Indeed, men monitor Marie's reading throughout her life.[27] First her father supervised her reading, allowing her to read romantic novels only shortly before the marriage. The father, who views himself as a liberal educator,[28] explains that: "...malgré les craintes de sa mère, je me suis décidé à lui permettre, quelques mois avant son mariage, la lecture d'*André*, une oeuvre sans danger, toute imagination, et qui élève l'âme.... Moi je suis pour une éducation libérale."[29]

His "liberalism" is displayed in his educational slogan: "pas de romans avant le mariage, tous les romans après le mariage."[30] While the father considers reading novels dangerous for an unmarried woman, certainly because of the passionate passages contained in them, and Marie's very emotional reaction to the reading seems to prove him right, he considers it an acceptable pastime for a married woman who by social and legal norms is allowed to know about sex and passion. But Marie, precisely because of her cloistered existence and her uncritical readings of romantic novels, which contribute to her highly romanticized notion of gender relations, is little prepared for real life and real marriage. Legally and emotionally she remains a minor.

Zola's bored and boring Marie, "toute une solitude monotone de femme tournant du matin au soir dans les mêmes soins d'un ménage d'employé,"[31] a *grande rêveuse* in the tradition of Madame Bovary,[32] becomes the willing victim of her seducer, Octave Mouret, by reading romantic literature. Octave calls her a *pimbêche*"[33] ("stuck-up"), alluding to the fact that she aspires to a different life, thereby forging for the reader a link between Mme Bovary and Marie Pichon, and sustaining a rather condescending description of the archetypal female nineteenth-century reader.

At this point in Marie's development, the film begins. Spectators do not see Marie's parents, and the shortcomings of their educational maxims are only alluded to in a displaced form in the representation of Mme Josserand. For the viewer, then, there is no causal relationship between Marie's education and her personality. The spectator only sees her gracious loneliness, which Duvivier's Octave Mouret addresses by saying, "J'ai appris votre solitude par les Campardon"("I learned about your loneliness from the Campardons"), when she hands him the book she had borrowed. Throughout the film, Octave's attitude toward Marie is that of charming politeness and inconsequential seduction, with no trace of contempt in either his words or actions. He appears as the kind seducer, clearly set up as a rival to a harsh and unreasonable M. Pichon, whose insignificance is documented in his complete absence from the film. The viewer only hears about him through Marie Pichon: "Mon mari me défend de lire des livres" ("My husband forbids me to read books"), because her husband believes that "la lecture développe trop les sentiments"("reading develops feelings far too much"). Marie tells Octave that when she started crying while reading a book: "Il [her husband] m'a fait une scène de jalousie." ("He [her husband] exploded at me in a fit of jealousy").

Zola's M. Pichon never has attacks of jealousy. Indeed, he finds books for Marie in the "Cabinet de lecture au passage Choiseul"[34] ("the reading room in the Choiseul passage") to fill the void in her life. Duvivier's Octave listens to Marie's confessions, expanding on the bridge she has already built for him. He closes the gap between fiction and reality by telling her that "On ne trompe pas son mari avec un héros de roman" ("You can't cheat on your husband with a hero from a novel"), and kissing her, thereby usurping the position of the hero of the novel. Again, Duvivier's Octave demonstrates the interpretive skills that allow him to use the content of the novel to achieve his main goal—the seduction of women. When Octave leaves Marie's apartment, after having kissed her passionately, she hastily asks him "[v]ous m'en prêtez d'autres?" ("Would you lend me some others?"). Octave flirtatiously plays with the ambiguity of the question—kisses or books—by asking her, "d'autres?" ("others?"). Evidently, she answers "des livres" ("books"). In the eyes of the spectator, Octave's behavior seems justified as an absurdly possessive M. Pichon deserves little sympathy. Unlike Zola's Octave, who believes that he should bring husband and wife together again, this one has no feelings of guilt.

Duvivier's Marie resembles very little the pale wallflower designed by Zola. Anouk Aimée, not yet risen to the heights of her stardom, plays the role of Marie and her traits certainly remain engraved in the memory of the viewer. Instead of a pale, hardly noticeable blonde, spectators see an attractive brunette with trademark eyes. Her appearance not only suggests repressed sensuality but also a physical link to her readings. When Marie attempts to return a book to Octave, the viewer notices that Marie's dress has the same pattern as the cover of the book, implying that book and dress might cover a similar content, linking the novel to Marie's character. This reading is furthered in another scene in which Octave Mouret comments on Marie's questions and interprets the texts he has lent to her. When she asks him what the book is about, he replies that this is the story of a man, "qui aime une femme vertueuse" ("who loves a virtuous woman"), and Marie interrupts, saying "[n]e me racontez pas la fin" ("don't tell me the ending"), to which Octave in turn comments "C'est une histoire sans fin" ("It is a never-ending story"), implying that their story too is never ending. The entire dialogue remains a constant play on the content of the book and their own relationship, which Octave presents to Marie and the viewer as intertwined. In this case, it is not Marie who transposes her reading experiences onto her surroundings, but it is Octave who creates a seductive scenario, craftily interpreting fiction to influence Marie's behavior.

The two Maries not only differ in physical appearance, but also in the social roles they occupy. Zola's Marie is a mother, and the narrator, and consequently the reader of *Pot-Bouille*, judges her reading in light of this fact. In the novel, Marie is a passionate and fast reader, devouring the book like an appetizing dish. It is certainly no accident that the book is frequently mentioned in connection with a meal, alluding to the assumed consumer behavior of the female nineteenth-century reader. When Octave visits Marie's apartment during his lunch break he sees, indeed, the effect the book has on her. Entirely absorbed in her reading, she neglects everything around her:

> Marie lisait, les coudes sur la table, les deux mains au fond de ses cheveux dépeignés. Elle venait de manger, sans nappe, un oeuf dans un plat de fer-blanc, qui traînait, au milieu de la débande d'un couvert mis à la hâte. Par terre, Lilitte [Marie's daughter] oubliée, dormait, le nez sur les débris d'une assiette, qu'elle avait cassée sans doute.[35]

Marie reads to escape her dull existence and abandons all responsible behavior. She is unable to reconcile her unfulfilled romantic desire with the banality of everyday life. In her constant search to experience passion and romance, she tells Octave that the passages she really likes in a novel are those where people declare their love to each other. Octave, though disgusted by her sentimentality, seizes the opportunity to seduce her. At night, Marie waits for him to pick up his book: "Elle semblait ivre, le visage gonflé comme au sortir d'un sommeil trop lourd,"[36] and she proceeds to explain her reading experience to him: "Quand ça vous prend, on ne sait plus où l'on est."[37] She is so ecstatic that she kisses Octave and from there it is only a small step to Octave's possessing her on the kitchen table, "entre l'assiette oubliée et le roman, qu'une secousse fit tomber par terre."[38] The damaged book symbolizes Marie's moral fall, but also, as Nicholas White has pointed out, the fall of the romantic culture to which Marie subscribed.[39] After the consummation of their sexual desire, the content of the book is no longer the agent of seduction; the physical book represents Marie and Octave's destroyed relationship and the so important loss of value in bourgeois society.

The cinematic Marie is a surprisingly responsible person. In the film Marie is childless; her apartment is neatly kept, and she never appears frowzy or distraught. Octave never belittles her readings; therefore, the viewer does not look down on her for reading novels, but rather perceives her as a woman who appreciates literature. Literature—the spectator never quite knows whether she reads romantic or realist novels—is represented as an enrichment of her daily life rather than as a means to escape it. This is clearly the message conveyed in the final scene between Octave and Marie. After she is discovered in Octave's room, Berthe has to escape the rage of her jealous husband and she hides in Marie's apartment. Marie does not treat Berthe as a rival; she is free of jealousy. Indeed, she respects the love that existed between Berthe and Octave. When Octave seems to notice a hint of sadness in Marie, afraid that she might be upset because of his relationship with Berthe, she dispels his fears by saying, "Grace à vous ... je ne serais plus jamais seule" ("Because of you ... I will never be alone again"). Again, this sentence is ambiguous. On the one hand, she refers to the world that has opened up for her thanks to reading; on the other hand, she thanks Octave for having brought sensuality and happiness to her life, if only temporarily, well aware of the fact that a man like Octave Mouret cannot be possessed but only be shared.

Marie clearly strikes a relationship with the woman in the audience who, like her, has to share Gérard Philipe/Octave Mouret. Like Marie, the female viewer is happy that, for a while, Gérard Philipe comes to life as her hero, not necessarily as the hero of a novel read, but as the hero of the new medium of entertainment, film.[40] For a couple of hours the female spectator can leave her monotonous life and imagine herself as taking on the role of Marie, whose needs resemble those of a French housewife in the 1950s. Zola's Marie, who is treated by Octave with contempt, could not have provided a suitable identification model for a female spectator of the 1950s. The average French wife in the 1950s, even though mostly confined to home and family life and in financial matters often still dependent on her husband, was significantly more educated than Marie Pichon in the novel *Pot-Bouille*. Evidently, the cinematic Octave Mouret can no longer belittle Marie's readings, because the cinematic Marie is cleared of naïveté and uncontrolled sentimentality, character traits that would affect the female viewer's identification process adversely. Russell Cousins has demonstrated that Duvivier had good financial reasons for presenting *Pot-Bouille* in a comic slant during a time period he identifies as the "less socially conscious, late fifties."[41] Forging an identification process between female spectator and female lead roles in the film became a necessity to guarantee full movie theaters.

Duvivier's cinematic adaptation of *Pot-Bouille* did not entirely betray Zola's message of inadequate nineteenth-century female education, but displaced it. For marketing reasons, the inadequacies of female nineteenth-century education are taken up in the representation of the Josserand family. However, Zola's understanding that female adultery is intimately linked to (uncritical) reading becomes an important element throughout the film. The film solidifies the notion that women, whether professional women (Mme Hédouin) or housewives (Marie Pichon), cannot be critical readers of text, as both types of women are vulnerable to and seduced by male interpretation (Octave Mouret). Mme Hédouin and Marie Pichon, because of their implied continuous relationship to Octave—Mme Hédouin marries him and Marie remains eternally grateful to him—provide the most attractive identification models for the female spectator. The anti-emancipatory quality of this movie may lie exactly in the fact that Mme Hédouin and Marie Pichon could provide strong identification models for a Frenchwoman of the 1950s. Unlike Berthe, who appears to be the product of a female nineteenth-century education, or Valérie Vabre, the standard nineteenth-century hysteric with whom Octave engages briefly in an erotic relationship, Mme Hédouin and Marie Pichon appear to be taken out of their nineteenth-century context. They bear the traits of the professional woman and housewife of the 1950s, without mirroring their actual reading behavior. Unanchored in a clearly defined historical context, these two women represent female readers as uncritical and vulnerable decipherers of text, susceptible in their turn to male interpretation.

Notes

1. Russell F. Cousins, "Recasting Zola: Gérard Philipe's Influence on Duvivier's Adaptation of Pot-Bouille," *Literature/Film Quarterly* 17.3 (1939): 146.
2. Ibid., 144.
3. Duvivier himself acknowledges this in his article "Pourquoi j'ai trahi Zola," *Les Lettres Françaises* (31 Oct. 1957) when he underscores the comical and satirical aspect of his film.

4. See Cousins, who points out that *Pot-Bouille* was the most popular and profitable film of the 1957 season ("Recasting Zola": 148).

5. Anne-Simone Dufief argues that Zola intentionally created melodramatic scenes and cultivated pathos to target the female reader. To support her argument Dufief quotes from a draft of *Travail*, in which Zola states: "Mais je fais un roman, il faut surtout que je passionne les femmes" ("But I am writing a novel, I have to fascinate the women especially"). Quoted in Anne-Simone Dufief, "La Lectrice, personnage et destinataire dans les romans de la deuxième moitié du XIXe siècle," in Angelica Rieger and Jean-François Tonard, eds., *La Lecture au féminin/Lesende Frauen. La lectrice dans la littérature du Moyen Âge au XXe siècle/Zur Kultur-geschichte der lesenden Frau in der französischen Literatur von den Anfängen bis zum 20. Jahrhundert*, Beiträge zur Romantik 3 (Darmstadt: Wissenschaftliche Buchgesellschaft, 1999), 211. Duvivier clearly targets the emotions of the female viewer by attributing the lead role to Gérard Philipe. Cousins phrases it aptly, "As the romantic lead he is assured of the attention of every female: neither other men's wives nor their mistresses can refuse him" ("Recasting Zola":147), unlike Roy Armes who believes that the directors of the 1950s were not concerned with "the relevance of their stories to the contemporary world, in which they, and their audiences, lived" [*French Cinema* (London: Secker & Warburg, 1985), 147]. Duvivier addresses contemporary values and concerns through his interpretation of Zola's novel.

6. Quoted in Henri Mitterand, "Etudes, notes et variantes: *Pot-Bouille*," in Émile Zola, *Les Rougon-Macquart: Histoire naturelle et sociale d'une famille sous le Second Empire*, ed. Henri Mitterand, vol. 3 (Paris: Gallimard, "Bibliotheque de la Pléiade," 1960–1966), 1604–05. "Not one is alive among them, I mean who would act reasonably, like a good and simple creature. They are no more than sublime self-denials, no more than ridiculous acts of ignorance, no more than pompous and voluntary stupidity. Our young French girl, whose instruction and education are deplorable, and who wanders from an angel to a beast, is a direct product of this thoughtless literature where a young virgin gets nobler the closer she gets to a well made up mechanical doll.... Walter Scott made a whole generation of unbearable female dreamers and quibblers."

7. The argument could also be supported by drawing attention to the similarities between the two names. I thank Philippe Moisan for providing information on the Josselin dynasty.

8. See Theresa McBride's example of the appeals court judge Louis Proal who connected female adultery to "new women's fashions, novels and popular theater, which featured fictional stories of romance and illicit sexual relationships." "Divorce and the Republican Family," in Elinor A. Accampo, Rachel G. Fuchs and Mary L. Stewart, eds., *Gender and the Politics of Social Reform in France, 1870–1914* (Baltimore: The Johns Hopkins University Press, 1995), 70.

9. Quoted in Mitterand, "Etudes, notes et variants," 1604–05. "In a woman who takes a lover, there basically always is a reading of an idealist novel, whether it is *Indiana* or the *Roman d'un jeune homme pauvre*."

10. Preceding the publication of *Pot-Bouille*, Zola had published "L'Adultère dans la bourgeoisie" in *Le Figaro*. Reprinted in Émile Zola, *Œuvres complètes*, ed., Henri Mitterand, vol. 15 (Paris: Cercle du Livre Précieux, 1968), 531–37.

11. In this context it is worth mentioning Zola's three types of *adultère*: the hysterical woman, who is for Zola the result of spatial enclosure (Valérie Vabre in *Pot-Bouille*); the woman who is enticed by her mother to prostitute herself to find a suitable husband (Berthe Josserand); and the woman who is adultère by stupidity (Marie Pichon). They are also all linked to female reading. For a good analysis of nineteenth-century medical discourses on female reading and hysteria, see Janet Beizer's "Reading Women: The Novel in the Text of Hysteria," *Compar(a)ison: An International Journal of Comparative Literature* 1 (1993).

12. "Don't leave the paper lying about, there are articles inside that are not for young girls" and "You really have no morality."

13. See also Martyn Lyons who points to the notion that "newspapers, which connected the reader with the public world of politics and finance, were often seen as a male preserve, read and discussed in the bar or the cabaret, those favorite sites of masculine sociability." Martyn Lyons, *Readers and Society in Nineteenth-Century France: Workers, Women, Peasants* (New York: Palgrave Publishers, 2001), 85.

14. "I would have the impression of having known you very young ... and the album closed we became old friends."

15. Danielle Darrieux played Mme Rénal and Gérard Philipe played Julien Sorel in Autant-Lara's 1954 adaptation of *Le Rouge et le noir*. Incidentally, Roy Armes considers "the beginning of the film depicting Gérard Philipe and Danielle Darrieux as lovers separated ... by both age and social position" (*French Cinema*, 152), one of the most successful scenes of the film.

16. Wai-Chee Dimock, "Feminism, New Historicism, and the Reader," in Robyn R. Warhol and Diane Price Herndl, eds. *Feminisms: An Anthology of Literary Theory and Criticism*, revised ed. (New Brunswick, NJ: Rutgers University Press, 1997), 635–50. Dimock bases her argument on Steven Marcus's essay "Reading the Illegible," in H. J. Dyos and Michael Wolff, eds. *The Victorian City: Images and Realities*, vol. 1 (London: Routledge & Kegan Paul, 1973), 257–76.

17. Dimock interprets this phenomenon for nineteenth-century America, but a similar phenomenon can be observed in France.

18. In a letter to the critic Henry Fouquier, dated April 26, 1882, Zola wrote in response to some questions the critic had raised concerning the character development in the story: "Mme Hédouin n'est pas très distinguée. C'est une marchande que j'ai fait parler avec une simplicité voulue. Votre continuelle erreur est d'incarner tous mes bourgeois dans le type unique que vous vous faites d'une bourgeoisie raffinée (la vôtre), tandis que ma bourgeoisie, à moi, à part du peuple, passe par le commerce et l'administration, pour arriver aux professions libérales" ("Mrs. Hédouin is not very refined. She is a shopkeeper; I willingly wanted her to speak with simplicity. Your continuous mistake is to embody all my bourgeois as the only type of refined bourgeoisie you know (your own), while my bourgeoisie, mine, aside from the people, goes through trade business and administration to attain liberal professions"). Quoted in Mitterand, "Etudes, notes et variants," 1632. Zola had a very differentiated view of the bourgeoisie, in which the individual would gradually progress through different social strata.

19. Émile Zola, *Pot-Bouille. Les Rougon-Macquart. Histoire naturelle et sociale d'une famille sous le Second Empire*, ed. Henri Mitterand, vol. 3 (Paris: Gallimard, "Bibliothèque de la Pléiade," 1964), 16. "Octave was injured and even then she wouldn't look at him."

20. Paul Bourget's novel *Un Divorce* (1904) illustrates this phenomenon in an exemplary way. The novel deals with the socio-cultural changes that took place in *fin-de-siècle* France, and, even though Bourget interprets the new female reader negatively, his representation clearly documents the fact that a different female reader had emerged in French society.

21. Jacques Siclier, *Télérama* (15 March 1977).

22. Zola, *Pot-Bouille*, 172. "He became able to study the matter from the point of view of figures, to already approximate the passionate air with which a romantic page would have declared a love suppressed for long."

23. Ibid., 165.

24. Ibid., 64. "Pride is worth nothing, declared Mrs. Vuillaume. We have always recommended modesty to her."

25. Ibid., 66. "Honesty first.... The doors shut, the windows closed, never any light breezes that bring those villainous things from the street.... Then, when she grew up,

find teachers, not place her in boarding schools where innocents are corrupted; and also attend the lessons, see to what she needs to ignore, hide the papers of course, and close the bookcase."

26. Ibid. "lines that her mother crossed out with ink in the fashion journal, and whose black bars would make her blush."

27. As Martyn Lyons has pointed out, this was indeed quite common for the first half of the nineteenth century, when even publishers assumed male buyers would select the books for their wives or daughters (*Readers and Society in Nineteenth-Century France*, 82).

28. We have to keep in mind that conservative educators at the beginning of the nineteenth century advocated that women be denied access to reading materials because—they argued—reading would detract housewives from necessary and useful domestic labor. The same argument would be used against the female reader of novels during the second half of the nineteenth century.

29. Zola, *Pot-Bouille*, 67. "...Despite her mother's worries, I decided to allow her, a few months before her marriage, the reading of *André*, a work devoid of danger, all imagination, and that elevates the soul.... Me, I am for a liberal education."

30. Ibid. "No novels before marriage, all the novels after marriage."

31. Ibid., 62. "A woman's whole monotonous solitude circling from morning till night in the same cares of a household worker."

32. "A big dreamer"—See, in this context, Jean-François Tonard's article on the daydreaming, solitary female reader in nineteenth-century French literature: "Les rêveries d'une lectrice solitaire: Emma Bovary," in Rieger and Tonard, eds. *La Lecture au féminin/Lesende Frauen.*

33. Zola, *Pot-Bouille*, 60.

34. Ibid., 67.

35. Ibid., 71. "Marie was reading, her elbows on the table, both hands deep down in her tousled hair. She had just eaten, without a tablecloth, an egg in a tin plate lying around in the middle of spread out silverware hastily placed. On the floor, Lilitte [Marie's daughter] forgotten, was sleeping, her nose on what was left of a plate, which she most likely had smashed into pieces."

36. Ibid., 75. "She seemed drunk, her face swollen like upon waking up from a very deep sleep."

37. Ibid. "When it comes over you, you lose yourself completely."

38. Ibid., 76. "Between the forgotten plate and the novel that a jolt made fall on the floor."

39. See Nicholas White, *The Family in Crisis in Late Nineteenth-Century French Fiction* (Cambridge: Cambridge University Press, 1999), 33. When Octave lends Marie novels by Balzac, she returns them with the comment: "Tenez, je vous rapporte votre Balzac, je n'ai pas pu le finir.... C'est trop triste, il n'a que des choses désagréables à vous dire, ce monsieur-là!" (211). "Here, I brought back your Balzac, I wasn't able to finish it.... It is too sad, he only has unpleasant things to say to you, that man!" As Brian Nelson has pointed out, Marie is indeed a discriminating reader ["Explanatory Notes," Émile Zola, *Pot Luck*, trans. Brian Nelson (Oxford: Oxford University Press, 1999), 380] who rejects realist literature and who asks for "des histoires où il y a eût beaucoup d'amour avec des aventures et des voyages dans des pays étrangers," *Pot-Bouille*, 211 ("stories where there was lots of love with adventures and journeys to unknown countries"). She rejects Balzac as too close to life: "[ç]a ressemble trop à la vie" ("it resembles life too much"), 211.

40. Michelle Perrot indicates, in her book *Les Femmes ou les silences de l'Histoire* (Paris: Flammarion, 1998), that movie-going was a pastime for both sexes in twentieth-century France. However, women seem to have embraced this activity more so than men (289).

41. Cousins, "Recasting Zola": 144.

11

The Fabrication of Claude Berri's *Germinal*

ANNA GURAL-MIGDAL

A great number of articles devoted to Claude Berri's 1993 adaptation of Zola's *Germinal* have criticized the director for having betrayed the novel, particularly in regards to the mythical dimension of Zola's writing which inscribes him in the horizon of great cosmogonies and gives it "une atmosphère dantesque [faisant] de la mine un véritable enfer, une 'fosse' hantée par les 'ombres' des morts."[1] Moreover, studies pertaining to the reception of the film have put emphasis on the marketing strategies that were deployed to guarantee its popular success, accusing Berri of having made his *Germinal* into a vast myth-glorifying enterprise aiming to commercialize the nostalgic figure of the mine and the miner. Also denounced was the "deadly" character of this adaptation of *Germinal,* which was said to have relegated the working class to "the drawers of history."[2]

All these commentaries indicate to us that the manner in which *Germinal* has been dealt with here is restrictive because it has been evaluated merely as an adaptation of Zola's novel, or purely as a marketing product. One does not go without the other, however, because adapting a novel for cinema, especially when it comes to a classic or a bestseller, allows one not only to recuperate its literary prestige but also to be guaranteed a large audience of already persuaded consumers. And Zola's *Germinal* has the peculiarity of being an already consecrated, in fact canonical work, which still at this time appears on the bestseller list in paperback.[3] Wanting to make *Germinal* when one is, like Claude Berri, a director and producer renowned for his expertise in film adaptations

Gérard Depardieu challenges the troops during the strike in *Germinal* (1993).

of literary works and their commercialization, seems to indicate at first glance a desire to take the easier road.[4] This, not to mention the risk incurred by the director of being criticized for exploiting a literary heritage that carries the colors of the broad mass of French people, of standing in the long line of directors who have transferred Émile Zola's work to the screen and of being unable to escape the comparison, of seeing his film judged not for what it is but for what it should have been according to its fidelity to the spirit or to the letter of the novel.[5]

The objective of our study is to look at *Germinal* not as film adaptation or as a "film-événement" (blockbuster), but according to a genetic perspective aiming to re-evaluate the importance and significance of this feature film through a number of materials that will constitute here a sort of filmic pre-text. More precisely the intent is to invalidate or to qualify the comments made by critics about Claude Berri's *Germinal* by analyzing the origin of this film with the help of three works: *Germinal, L'Aventure d'un film* by Pierre Assouline, *Germinal Blues: Souvenirs de tournage* by Benoît Barbier, and *Autoportrait* by Claude Berri. Berri's *Autoportrait* shows that in his conception of the making and shooting of the film, the famous French director, far from betraying Zola, remained faithful to the manner in which the writer had conceived and made his novel.

From Zola to Berri: Interaction between the Literary and the Cinematic

This study would not reach its objective without first emphasizing the interaction between the literary and the cinematic in Zola and Berri's work method. An examination of the novelist's preliminary project files done by Colette Becker in "*La Fabrique de Germinal*" allows us to observe, for example, that Zola, while composing his character sketches, did not envision them otherwise than in terms of casting.[6] Casting involves establishing a set of selection criteria, which will allow the director to choose the actors or extras that best correspond with the profile of the character to be played. Pierre Assouline reveals to us on this subject, that when the shooting of Berri's film was being prepared, Evy Figlioni, responsible for casting the extras, chose them according to a desire for authenticity related to their native environment and to their personal experiences as miners. Their faces had to be marked, worked, as if to show the hardships of a miner's labor transmitted from father to son and the permanence of the suffering forming one body with the North of France. Zola proceeds in a similar manner, composing sketches that allow him to establish a civil status, a portrait and a history for his characters, displaying their genealogical filiations and their association with a particular milieu. Like a filmmaker, he puts emphasis on facial expressions through which the true soul is revealed but, in the manner of a naturalist writer, he inscribes the trace of a predestination on the features: "Avec cela, quelque chose de détraqué dans le regard, un vacillement par moment, qui pâlit l'oeil noir: et alors une légère crispation nerveuse passant sur le visage. C'est la marque de la lésion nerveuse qui augmentera plus tard, qui tournera son hérédité d'ivrognerie en folie homicide. Laisser deviner ainsi d'un bout à l'autre, l'inconnu qui s'exaspère en lui."[7] Therefore, Berri's own process of selecting actors could have been strongly influenced by the reserves of memory made up by Zola's character files. While reading the "fiche-personnage" (character file) of Étienne Lantier, written by Zola in his novel's preliminary project files, the director is convinced that Renaud will be that man: "taille moyenne, joli garçon, un galant sourire sur des dents blanches, quelque chose de détraqué dans le regard, un vacillement par moment, une légère crispation nerveuse, un rien le grise, intelligence vive mais obstruée par des idées toutes faites."[8] It seems that the director wants to show us here to what degree the naturalist writer has influenced him. However, already in this description of Lantier, Berri offers us a personal vision since he does not confer any kind of deterministic meaning to the unsettlement of this character. In this respect, one can wonder if the director of *Germinal* does not use Zola's files also as a literary source, a necessary reference, to justify in this case a possibly questionable casting choice, since the role of Étienne was played by Renaud Séchan who is not an actor but a singer by profession.

Even if there is an interaction between the literary and the cinematic in Zola and in Berri's work method, it is important to mention that the writer and the filmmaker have both, nonetheless, been able to take advantage of the two forms of artistic expression that are literature and cinema. Zola's pre-text for *Germinal,* according to Becker, allows readers, "d'assister au spectacle d'une gestation *romanesque*"[9] ("to witness the spectacle of a gestation of the novel") through which the writing already attains the mythical by the repetition and the importance of the symbol.[10] It is, however, with its open-set conception of filming that the fabrication of Berri's *Germinal* invokes the mythical dimension of cinema, because allowing visitors to watch this super-production being made, has undeniably contributed to its transformation into a spectacle of a spectacle and to have the film preceded by its legend. But what is of interest in the scope of our study is not so much to determine the specificity of the literary and the cinematic but to divulge certain points of convergence in the conceptual approaches to the preparation and the fabrication of a novel and a film. An analysis of the conception and the shooting of the film *Germinal* leads us to make reference to a theory proposed by Pierre Sorlin about cinema as a "miroir et fabrique" (mirror and factory), which simultaneously involves the insertion of a catalogue of images known or recognizable as pieces of life, and the production of an imaginary world which incorporates fragments of the real and the unreal into the confined logic of film directing.[11] Altogether, the visible appears as the place where the mirror and the factory meet. And it seems to us that it is this very notion of the visible that constitutes a basis for the *romanesque* (technique of the novel) in Zola because his massive documentation of things seen, read or heard is filtered and mixed by a screen-like gaze directed upon the world. The fabrication of a film also demystifies the destiny of cinema which is to be decided between the artistic will and a series of economic-industrial constraints: above and beyond the outlined fact of a confrontation between unbound expression and profit obligations, it brings up the antagonism between a director and the funds, thus echoing the underlying dialectic in the novel *Germinal*. And, is it not evident that Zola and Berri share an ability to accept their own ideological contradictions, along with the constraints of popular success? Nonetheless, apart from these kind of similarities concerning the way to conceive artistic creation, three major elements deserve a deepened comparison when it comes to the preparation of the novel *Germinal,* and of its film adaptation: firstly, the research work as an integral part of the literary and cinematic fabrication of *Germinal,* which at the same time becomes an autonomous creation; secondly, the function of the location and of the setting of the film, both at the same time vehicles of authenticity and carriers of a special and geographical imagery conveyed in the act of writing or filming; finally, the issues associated with Zola and Berri's conception of the character of Étienne in relation to the father figure. These elements, it seems, all contribute to establish, in the writer as much as in the filmmaker, an effect of authenticity in the very gestation of their work, which indicates a will to abolish frontiers between reality and fiction.

The Research Work and the Work's Gestation

Colette Becker clearly demonstrated in *La Fabrique de Germinal* that Zola prepared all his novels according to a systematic research and composition process.[12] When it comes to the documentation, the author of *The Rougon-Macquart* seems to be doing the work of a researcher as it is presently done in television or cinema. In the case of *Germinal* it then becomes a matter of acquiring informative material from books, newspaper clippings, visual documents, on-site observations and testimonies on a chosen subject, in this instance on the mine.[13] Afterward, the informative material is assembled and well arranged in order to allow the creation of preliminary project files. The latter appear in Zola as the equivalent of a report because the information is treated, that is integrated in the form of knowledge and at the same time interpreted as well as made into a spectacle in the outline of a fiction in the making. In this regard, the writer does not only claim the function of researcher but also that of a studio director, as a result of his involvement in the administration and management of the material preparation of his novel as well as in its conception as a staged representation. One notes, for example, after reading the preliminary project files that Zola meticulously plans all the phases implicated in his research work, including the phases of reading, of searching for informants, as well as of the planning of his visit to the coal field in Anzin. Moreover, the novelist simultaneously undertakes the research work along with the work of fictional construction, which institutes interferences between these two types of exploration. Therefore, the elaboration of *Germinal* echoes the naturalist program and the experimental method where note taking, observation is directly related to knowledge, and where experimentation originates in the staging of a possible world by the author. As it is rightly pointed out by Claude Duchet in his preface to *La Fabrique de Germinal,*

> Partout cependant la maîtrise ne cesse de s'affirmer (le mot-clé est ici "poser"), une maîtrise de créateur, qui parle à la première per-

> sonne, qui dispose souverainement de ses ouvriers, commande aux catastrophes comme aux foules ... *Germinal* ... apparaît ainsi, dans l'intimité relative d'un texte en devenir, comme projet et procès d'écriture.... Affleurent ici ou là les manifestations d'une zone plus secrète, quand sont abordés les abîmes de la sexualité ou les territoires enfouis de l'imaginaire.[14]

The sketch as well as the various successive plans that complement the writing of *Germinal* show that Zola, akin to a film director, constructs every chapter of his novel like a continuation of successive projects of scenarios and of cutting that go along with the writing. In this system of composition by stratifications, directing instructions are an integral part of the rhythm and of the dramatic result proper to a script. The cutting for each chapter remains open, seeing that Zola incessantly adds notes collected along the way. In this regard a device comparable to a scaffold assures the construction of the novel as an ensemble made of diversely formed materials, to allow it to be read through its exterior relations. The novelist elevates the foundations of his *Germinal* up to the crossroads of the past and the future because he uses a massive documentation to compose it simultaneously as archives and as an evolving text. A play on echoes and on expansions also inscribes the fabrication of *Germinal* in those larger ones reminiscent of *The Rougon-Macquart*, while a reading of the sketches indicates to us that they can escape from the writer and become autonomous. As a result the work of imagination rescues Zola from all rigors associated with the construction of his novel.

The shooting of the film *Germinal* is also based on impressive research and preparation work assigned to numerous members of the film crew. Firstly, in a singular effect of "mise-en-abyme," Éric Bartonio, first assistant director, investigates Zola's own research, which leads him not only to read the books the novelist used to extract his information from, but also to try and find the unknown sources that could have inspired him. The gathering of the archives and of the internal documentation for the film thus puts emphasis on the passing down of a legacy of knowledge. The importance given to the idea of cultural heritage also becomes obvious due to the desire to rediscover, before the filming, the popular traditions and local songs. Following the many advertisements printed in *La Voix du Nord*, Bartonio collected photos of homes and of locations sent in to the production department by the readers of that regional paper. But beyond this museum-like preparation work and desire for exactitude, a need to take liberties with the story and with Zola's novel also manifests itself, in order to make room for imagination. The two costume designers, Sylvie Gautrelet and Caroline de Vivaise, describe their vision to the director when it comes to the color of the film. According to them, "ce sera celle de la brique, de la terre et de l'ab-

11. The Fabrication of Claude Berri's Germinal (Gural-Migdal) 169

sence de végétation."[15] Therefore, the miners' clothing won't be black and will play a part in the construction of an atmosphere specific to the film rather than highlight the dramatic character of the narrative. In this way Berri moves away from the tradition of novels about the mine specific to the nineteenth century, to give preference to a mining film.[16] One will not be astounded to learn that the director organized a screening of Pabst's *La Tragédie de la mine* (1932) for his crew, a film which corresponds with his vision as filmmaker due to its universal message, one that stimulates the solidarity between men, and its aesthetic strongly tinged with poetic realism. Berri therefore finds his cinematic inspiration in the work of a German filmmaker while he aspires to inscribe his *Germinal* in the tradition of French cinema as a tribute to it, in addition to marking it with his own imprint.

The director has therefore made all the necessary arrangements to have the entirety of the making of his film documented. He gave the journalist and writer Pierre Assouline carte blanche to facilitate an uncontrolled access to the set so he could write on a daily basis a diary-like document of the filming. In this regard the interest of a work such as *Germinal, L'Aventure d'un film*, seems to lie in its journalistic and at the same time novelistic dimension. The major part of the book amounts to a live report from a filming location during which Assouline writes down rather than composes his impressions, thus showing the hastiness and pace of the annotations. At the same time, we see that this on-the-spot investigation simultaneously gives life to a novel in which the writing is nourished by the actual adventure of the film. Assouline's book, besides the fact that it seeks to dismantle the wheels that created *Germinal*, hands the film back to its legend because it recounts a collection of risky, new and coincidental experiences to which the author gives a human value: "Ce livre est le récit d'une aventure, celle d'un homme, avant d'être celle d'une équipe, puis de leur film."[17] Like Zola, Assouline has a sense for dramatization and his work is about succeeding to transform the story of a man into that of a film and also illustrating a daily fight for survival.

Another privileged witness of the film's fabrication, stills photographer Benoît Barbier also followed the filming of *Germinal* from beginning to end to later make a photo album, *Germinal Blues: Souvenirs de tournage*:

> Anticipant la nostalgie qui nous envahirait sans doute au terme de notre vie commune, j'ai souhaité constituer l'album de cette famille disparate née de la nécessité. Pour le photographe de permanence, il s'agissait de retrouver le charme de ces images jetées en vrac dans de vieux cartons à chaussures, aussi imparfaites qu'émouvantes. Ils feraient donc leur cinéma et je tenterais tant bien que mal d'en con-

A worker attacks the machines and the system in *Germinal* (1993).

server quelques traces. Histoire de nous faire des souvenirs pour quand on sera vieux.[18]

These remarks emphasize the documentary and nostalgic aspects of photography. The photographic report has ethnographical aims here since it was a question of observing for several months the communal life of a "tribu d'artistes" (tribe of artists) on the set of a film. As in Zola, this tribe makes up a separate world, in this case that of the vast family of cinema whose moments at work, of rest or of leisure were to be recorded. And is it not the primary principle of an ethnographical investigation to be limited to an observation of groups confined to a specific location in order to draw up a documentation of descriptive nature about Man? As Barthes has said, "... contrairement au texte qui, par l'action soudaine d'un seul mot, peut faire passer une phrase de la description à la réflexion, la photographie livre tout de suite ces 'détails' qui font le matériau même du savoir ethnologique."[19] According to the author, photography is also linked with reality and the past because it makes of the instant an "avoir-été-là" (to have-been-there) experience, and behind every negative shows the accomplishment of death.

In his investigation of the filming of *Germinal*, Benoît Barbier reveals cinema in the making by capturing snapshots that correspond to the notes taken from real life by the author of *The Rougon-Macquart*. Those photos taken with a little Minolta also seek to capture a meaningful image of what will become the film, thus echoing the manner in which Zola thought ahead about the scene to be done while he was writing in his notebook. Made in a panoramic format dear to the photographer that was Émile Zola, Barbier's black and white snapshots come across as an autonomous creation in comparison with the film's shots that he refuses to copy. The photographer rather tries to create an image within an image and to take advantage of the static and fixed aspect of photography. He completes his album by using only off-the-set views through which he also tries to transmit the truth and the poetry of the photograph.

The investigative and research work done to prepare the film *Germinal* along with the open-set filming establish the "mise-en-abyme" of a multiplicity of texts and images that aim to perpetuate Zola's work and at the same time to archive the work of Berri:

> ... il y a quatre équipes de filmeurs qui se font face: celle de la caméra fixe, celle de la "steadycam," celle du "making-off" chargée par la production de réaliser un film sur les coulisses du film et celle d' "Envoyé spécial,"l'émission de *France 2*, qui en fait autant. A force de se marcher dessus dans l'espoir de s'éviter, ils vont finir par se filmer les uns et les autres.Une étrange sensation naît de ce cinéma qui se mord la queue. Comme un fascinant jeu de miroirs. Seul un caricaturiste pourrait rendre la vérité de cet instant. Cabu vient d'arriver. *Charlie-Hebdo* lui a demandé un reportage, textes et dessins, sur le film. Il ne pouvait pas tomber mieux.[20]

Such a procedure also generates comings and goings between reality and fiction because the simple fact of awareness about being photographed or filmed on the set and off the set transforms the whole crew into extras and the filming into a spectacle. For that reason the acting of real actors who are aware of being observed from the outside sometimes appears less authentic than that of the false extras, all this while a kind of truth imposes itself in this falseness, that of cinema in the making.

Searching for Locations and Geographical Setting

The desire for authenticity, when it comes to the choice of filming *Germinal* in the North of France, does not only seem to us a promotional strategy aiming to make this region into of place of worship and pilgrimage.[21] The fact that Claude Berri wanted to film all the scenes with Jean Bart on the old mining site of Arenberg seems more emblematic of his own vision since the closed down mine is in itself a figure of memories and death. The construction of the mine of Voreux set, the most important one in the film, right in the middle of a beetroot field in Paillencourt, contributes to plant life in the heart of death, as well as allows an interpretation of the filming site as a suspended world and concentration camp-like universe since it is compelled to be razed to the ground right after the filming. The elimination of boundaries between reality and fiction, besides supporting the very nature of cinema, shows all the truth that can be extracted from the artificial, the big machine, the scaffold of the false Voreux making visible the truthfulness of work and of sweat. "L'enfer du décor" (The hellishness of the setting), to borrow a term from Assouline, is therefore also a necessity to satisfy both the requirements for authenticity and those of creation. The set designers of *Germinal* have certainly found inspiration for their Voreux in an engraving from that epoch found in a mine museum in Lewarde; however, the fabrication of their Voreux, "ce chevalement surpomblant le puits de mine, cet espèce de beffroi dont les charpentes supportent les molettes où s'enroulent les cables des cages d'ascenseur,"[22] was much more than that of an imposing setting, because it was necessary to work on creating the filmic image of a machine of exhaustion. In contrast to Zola, who endows his Voreux with a performing material force and grants it the mythical figure of a Minotaur devouring every morning his ration of human flesh, Claude Berri and his team prefer to give it sort of visual and mechanical coldness that invades a screen inscribed with the imminence of death.

In this respect, when the producer-director chose to shoot in France rather than in Poland where after all it would have cost him much less, it is not uniquely to preserve the authenticity of the geographical setting but also because, in a foreign country, he wouldn't have as deeply experienced or been affected by the setting and by the landscapes. Therefore, he may not have had the same ability to create, to portray with such truthfulness the silent suffering on the faces emerging from the natal ground, from this immense and flat earth contrasting the massive construction of the mine. Like Zola, Berri has a sense for the geographical setting, and he knows how to exploit its geometric possibilities. Is it not true that the author of *The Rougon-Macquart* represented the city of Paris when it was undergoing massive drainage and reconstruction work undertaken by Lord Hausmann, like a vast building site offering the spectacle of a world in transition? One needs only to reread *Nana*, for example, to see that Zola's universe is a threatening one, one that tends towards empty spaces. Hence, the evocation of "ces hôtels en construction dressant leurs échafaudages sous le ciel noir au travers de cette plaine glaciale et vide du nouveau Paris."[23] This kind of spatial representation positions the subject on the periphery and not in the center as if to convey him in his fleetingness, in his upcoming disappearance. A similar positioning of the character can be found in Berri since, just like the actress in *Nana*,

11. The Fabrication of Claude Berri's Germinal (Gural-Migdal)

this provisional actor-miner that is the Lantier of his film progresses amid the burial of beings and of things, to eventually disappear in the void of the screen.

The preliminary project files for *Germinal* allow us to note that Zola was searching for location before a single word was written not only to investigate, notebook in hand, the places where the action was taking place but also to find a framework for his novel that would allow him to create a setting that would relate to his aspiration. After having considered the coalfield of Saint-Étienne, he decided to travel to Valenciennes four days after the triggering of a strike by the miners of Anzin, on the 19th of February 1884. Despite the briefness of his visits to the location, the region conquered the novelist because of the symbolic power of the landscape and of its mining topography. On the subject, Assouline points out that,

> en parfait architecte du roman, [Zola] était conscient du parti qu'il allait tirer de ce paysage à trois dimensions, de cette perspective à trois étages: chevalements, plaines, galeries. Sous l'acuïté de son regard, tout avait immédiatement valeur de symbole: le Voreux tel une bête malfaisante, le puits tel un gouffre, les mineurs noirs comme la nuit, les bourgeois blancs comme le jour. [...] Aux riches la lumière, aux pauvres les ténèbres.[24]

This quote brings us back to the image in Zola's work; after all, is it not, as suggested by Mitterand, undoubtedly linked with the symbol, since the latter "naît avec la sensation et parce qu'il est dans les choses"?[25] Likewise, Pasolini emphasizes that in reality "raw" objects do not exist because they are all significative in their natural state in order to become symbolic signs.[26] The leader of naturalism works on the figural dynamic of the landscape to organize its codification. Thus, when Zola writes in *Carnets d'enquête* that "le caractère du pays à Anzin est plat et morne, tandis qu'il est pittoresque et tragique à Valenciennes,"[27] he manipulates a shift through which the sensation of the horizontal gives birth to a symbol of flatness, to which he confers a contrasting effect by opposing it to "pittoresque et au tragique" (the picturesque and to the tragic). Such an observation allows us to infer that the description of the landscape in Zola's novels is also to be considered in terms of effects. After a careful reading of his outlines and preliminary sketches, we note that Zola gives great importance to the tragic effect that emerges from inscribing the symbol into the geographical setting: "J'aimerai bien à ne pas oublier à la fin le décor tragique de la fosse écroulée. Le représenter à la fin sous un éclairage nouveau."[28] Here the tragic acquires the powerfulness of its effect due to the inscription of the symbol into the settings, which underlines the idea of environmental determinism.

Berri, unlike Zola, seems to want to elude the deterministic conception of a milieu. Evidence of that can be found in his character of Étienne who comes out unchanged and even less initiated from the ruins of the mine. No gray hair to mark him with the hardships of the passage. Lantier exits the mine, the way he entered it, like a figure making an appearance. Similarly, Berri refuses heightened effects that give an immediate depth to the tiniest event, just like he rejects the spectacle of a disaster.

It is therefore rather in the poetic effect that one should look for Zola's influence on Berri, because for both artists the framework, the landscape, the setting, and the costumes all contribute to a certain poetic quality. At the time of his search for locations, the director:

> sait qu'il veut un canal près du chevalement de son puits de mine. Il pourrait tricher en filmant un canal à part et des champs à perte de vue également à part. Il n'en serait jamais satisfait. Dans le roman, le cours de la Scarpe avait son importance.... Zola jugeait même que le canal contenait toute l'âme de la plaine, dans "cette eau géométrique qui la traversait comme une grande route, charriant la houille et le fer."[29]

It is because he remembered this that Berri and his crew ended up in Paillencourt. For a film director guided by his visual instinct, it is a revelation. Everything is there in one single shot: the waterway, the fields, and the landscape. This effect of alignment through juxtaposition foresees possibilities of a "trompe-l'oeil" perspective. The director of *Germinal* succeeds in extracting from this setting a vision that is harmonious with the harsh and dry tone of the *Carnets d'enquête,* which in turn endorses the paratactic style of the film script.[30]

The setting of the Voreux, despite all the efforts deployed by local authorities and the associations of miners to preserve it or to relocate it on the mining site of Wallers-Arenberg, will have to be destroyed and burned so that the fields on which it had been planted be returned to nature. No material trace will be preserved. It is therefore in the earth's nudity that the memory of *Germinal* will be inscribed, in unison with its death. Even the abandoned film site took on the appearance of a ghost city; this time the setting created a landscape of death. The photos taken on the set by Benoît Barbier, in addition to collecting the memories of this concentration camp-like, insalubrious universe, open to the four winds and where one flounders in mud, captured faces resembling fugitives emanating from the Northern plains and out of the violent history of the dark country. And, as it is written in *Germinal Blues: Souvenirs de tournage*:

> Le clan *Germinal* né le 25 août, premier jour du tournage, [sera] dispersé au début 93, avec le départ des derniers camions de matériels transportant les projecteurs et autres rails de travelling loués pour l'occasion. Le groupe [sera] désormais dissolu puisque les membres partiront chacun de leur côté pour contribuer à la fabrication d'autres histoires.[31]

The Character of Étienne and the Father Figure

However, if the notions of searching for locations and for settings are in a way the source of veracity, they nevertheless differ in the significance they attain. While Zola practices a form of writing that carries the novel towards the future, at the end of his outline and in the character sketch of Étienne, Berri offers us a more pessimistic vision centered on an inexorable disappearance of everything, because nothing will germinate under the footsteps of his Lantier. There is no renaissance on the horizon for the broken earth he chooses to film. In this respect, the director conveys his freedom of expression in his manner of conceiving the last sequence of his film: on one hand, a voice off reads an excerpt from the ending of *Germinal*, on the other, the image contradicts the meaning of the passage being read by showing an April field where nothing is growing. The vision of the world that becomes apparent from this sequence allows us to retrospectively re-evaluate the entirety of the film and to view the very meaning of its filming as a figure of memory and death. The evidence is provided at the beginning of *Germinal*, which Berri dedicates to his deceased father, Hirsh Langmann, a Polish Jew, craftsman and furrier as well as survivor of the big raids of the Occupation and member of the French Communist Party henceforth on its way to extinction.

The father as a figure of memory and of death seems indeed very important for the writer and for the director. As Henri Marel has said:

> Si le récit se déroule entièrement au travers d'Étienne et que l'expérience terminée, Zola et Lantier sortent ensemble du livre, le héros principal n'est-il pas en définitive Maheu? Même après sa mort, il reste le moteur de l'œuvre.... Pourquoi la Maheude revient-elle à son tour à la fosse? Le chef de famille n'est plus là. La famille est détruite.[32]

Correspondingly Berri dedicates his film to his father, pays homage to his memory and to his Jewish roots, as if to repair the mistake of having denied part of his heritage by having changed his name. In his *Autoportrait*, Claude Berri says: "Je n'ai pas su être une mère. À peine un père. Je suis resté fils."[33] It is not surprising then that he identifies with the character of Lantier whose fugacity and effervescence he emphasizes. On that subject, doesn't he mention: "Une phrase de mon père me revient en mémoire: on est juste sûr de mourir"?[34]

Perhaps it is in such statements that can be found the differences between Zola and Berri's vision. The latter indeed refuses the inevitable character of determinism engendered by the environment, just like the utopian idea of germination. The director rather seems to emphasize an immanent conception of death, which manifests itself not only in the film's subject, but also in its pre-text and intertexuality. In this respect, Berri's autobiography is saturated with an obsessional presence of death in the heart of life. The director begins his book with: "Je vais essayer de me souvenir dans le désordre. La vie continue. Je dois me dépêcher. Je dois mourir mais comment? Il faut mourir et vivre encore. Il faudrait écrire ses mémoires une fois mort."[35] While compiling his memoirs, he is also writing those of his dead father, his dead wife and his dead son. Berri writes for all those no longer living because it is necessary to continue this burial of beings and things, despite the scream of la Maheude, which, in the film *Germinal*, appears as the most intense expression of pain.

In a summary of his project on *Germinal* prepared for subsidies commissions, Berri underlines not only his will to make a film containing the powerful cry of Zola's novel, but also to honor the memory of his working-class father through that of the miner:

> J'ai eu une vie différente de celle de mon père. Matériellement, j'ai basculé de "l'autre côté," mais je crois que mon coeur bat encore à l'unisson avec le sien. Quand je lis *Germinal*, quand je pense à *Germinal*, je suis à côté de mon père, aux côtés des mineurs qui crient parce qu'ils ont faim.[36]

Berri wanted to become a filmmaker because of a father who also loved cinema and dreamt about becoming an actor, so it is told in *Le Cinema de Papa* (1970). This film negatively consecrates Claude Berri as an author incapable of having his own style or of escaping his autobiography. But if *Le Cinema de Papa* had been a success, maybe the director would not have felt the need to adapt one of the cult novels of French literature and to take considerable risks to carry out the filming of *Germinal*. By accomplishing this project, Berri desired to undertake a challenge through which he could show his father that he had been right to believe in him. To console himself in moments of despondency, Berri repeated this sentence: "Avec un père comme son père, c'est pas possible, il doit réussir."[37]

Germinal was certainly a big popular success; the accusation of being a film without a style set aside, it nevertheless reveals the brilliance with

11. The Fabrication of Claude Berri's Germinal (Gural-Migdal) 177

which Berri creates his own vision of the world through a story that does not belong to him. As it is shown in the film director's autobiography, it is his father who passed on this vision to him. Claude Berri has the merit of having taken over Zola's heritage and the tradition of French cinema with great virtuosity, in spite of the fact that he admitted to having been largely inspired by the German film *La Tragédie de la mine*. By its fragmentation in short sequences, by the expressionism of its close-ups and by its changes in points of view allowing the emotion on the faces to be captured, Berri's *Germinal* certainly echoes French cinema of the twenties, particularly the film adaptation of *La Terre* by Antoine. The reflection of French cinema from the thirties can be found in a trace of poetic realism in the style of Renoir accentuating the aesthetic of sobriety and rigor, and the exploration of the content. Finally, the film is indebted to cinema for the French quality, such as practiced in the fifties by René Clément, where technical perfection, the beauty of the setting, of the costumes and photography prevail. Born from a reaction to those important moments of history that were the fall of the Berlin Wall and the closing of coal mines in France, *Germinal* is in the end a film about a condemned world rooted both in history and posterity.[38]

Notes

1. "A Dantesque atmosphere turning the mine into a true hell, a 'pit' haunted by the 'shadows' of the dead." Quoted in Patricia Carles and Béatrice Desgranges, "Le Germinal de Claude Berri, entre hommage et trahison," *Excavatio* 6-7 (1995): 5.
2. *Humanité* (29 Sept. 1993): 5.
3. *Germinal* remains a bestseller because 180,000 copies of the book continue to be sold each year in paperback. See on this subject an article devoted to Zola on the centenary of his death in *Le Nouvel Observateur* (Nov. 14–20, 2002).
4. We know of the great success that Claude Berri has had with his two adaptations based on Pagnol's work, *Jean de Florette* and *Manon des Sources*. *Jean de Florette* ranks at number thirteen on the list of the biggest successes of French cinema with FF7,182,000 in box office sales and *Manon des Sources* at number eighteen with FF6,604, 000.
5. Most works devoted to the film consider it only as a film adaptation or as a "blockbuster." The problem exposed by the commentaries on Berri's fidelity to the novel *Germinal*, is that instead of analyzing his film for what it is, attempts have been made to reconstruct it following Zola's approach; as a result, the personal vision of the filmmaker has been ignored.
6. Becker mentions in *La Fabrique de Germinal*, "[a]près avoir mis 'l'Ébauche' dans une chemise, il passe à ce qu'il appelle 'les Personnages.' C'est, à proprement parler, l'état civil des divers personnages. Il reprend chacun de ceux qu'il a trouvés, en écrivant l'Ébauche, et lui dresse des actes: histoire, âge, santé, aspect physique, tempérament, caractère, habitudes, alliances, etc. En un mot, tous les faits de la vie." *La Fabrique de Germinal, Dossier préparatoire de l'oeuvre*, 2 vols. (Paris: SEDES, 1986), 23. ("After having put the 'sketch' in a folder, he moves on to what he calls the Characters.' It is, strictly speaking, the civil status of the diverse characters. He goes back

to all the ones he has found by writing the sketch, and draws up his deeds: history, age, health, physical aspects, temperament, character, habits, alliances, etc. In a word, all the facts of life").

7. Ibid., 297. "Along with something unsettling in the gaze, a swaying now and then which makes the dark eye grow pale: and then a gentle nervous twitch overtaking the face. It is the mark of a nervous lesion that will increase with time, turning his hereditary drunkenness into a homicidal madness. Making noticeable in this way, from one end to the other, the exasperating stranger inside of him."

8. Quoted in Pierre Assouline, *Germinal, L'Aventure d'un film* (Paris: Fayard, 1993), 78–79. "Average height, good looking boy, a gallant smile with white teeth, something unsettling in the gaze, a swaying now, a gentle nervous twitch, the slightest little thing goes to his head, lively intelligence but obstructed by preconceived ideas."

9. The French term *romanesque* refers to the technique of the novel ("roman") and should not be confused with the architectural style designated by the English word "Romanesque."

10. Becker, *La Fabrique de Germinal*, 6.

11. According to Marel, "*Germinal* s'établit donc au confluent des intentions de Zola et de sa documentation sur place, du roman et de sa 'fabrique'. Zola n'oublie jamais que le romancier est un savant. Il en garde l'objectivité, montrant une froideur scientifique, faisant abstraction de ses passions. Et surtout il a l'oeil et l'esprit du journaliste. Comme tout grand écrivain, il se trouve libéré de sa documentation par la magie de son imagination." *Germinal: Une Documentation intégrale* (Glasgow: University of Glasgow French and German Publications, 1989), 111. ("*Germinal,* therefore, establishes itself somewhere in between Zola's intentions, his on site documenting, the book and its 'fabrication.' Zola never forgets that the writer is a scholar. He remains objective, showing a scientific coldness, leaving his passions aside. But most importantly, he has the eye and the mind of a journalist. Like all great writers, he finds himself liberated from his documentation by the magic of imagination").

12. On this subject, Colette Becker tells us that Zola, in the preliminary project files for his work, "a voulu donner l'image d'une création logique et rationnelle, ce que viennent corroborer les titres qu'il a donnés aux parties composant invariablement ses dossiers: 'Ébauche,' 'Liste des personnages,' 'Fiches-personnages,' 'Plan général,' 'Plans'." Becker, *La Fabrique de Germinal*, 7. ("wanted to present the image of a logical and rational creation, something that confirms the titles he chose for the parts that invariably make up his files: 'Sketch', 'List of characters', 'Character-sketches', 'General plan,' 'Shots'").

13. After reading Zola's *Les Carnets d'enquête*, we note that *Mes Notes sur Anzin* is divided into five parts: "Regard sur les terris" ("Glancing at the coal tip"); "Descente aux enfers" ("Descent into hell"); "Le travail à la mine" ("Work in the mine"); "Habitudes et rituels" ("Habits and rituals"); "Glanes" ("Gleaning"). We also notice that the last part of *Mes Notes sur Anzin,* partially stemming from explanations given by an engineer named Lévy, contains information about the history, the topography and the administration of mines by the Anzin Company. The notes are complemented by visual documents like drawings, sketches, topographies, documentary outlines, etc. Émile Zola, *Carnets d'enquête, Une ethnographie inédite de la France* (Paris: Plon "Coll. Terre humaine," 1986).

14. "The control, however, continually asserts itself everywhere (the key words here are 'to set'), the control of a creator, who speaks in the first person, who sovereignly orders his workers, who issues commands to catastrophes as to crowds ... *Germinal* ... appears thus, in the relative intimacy of a constantly evolving text, as a project and a writing process.... Here and there emerge manifestations of a much more secret place, when contact is made with the abysses of sexuality or the hidden territories of the imaginary." In Collette Becker and Véronique Lavielle, *La Fabrique des Rougon-Macquart, Edition des dossiers préparatoires* (Paris: Champion, 2003), 8.

15. "It will be that of the brick, of the earth and of the lack of vegetation." Quoted in Assouline, *Germinal, L'Aventure d'un film*, 128.

16. Henri Marel is right to suggest that *La Ville noire* (1860) by George Sand may have been the initiator of the mine novel in the 19th century (*Germinal: Une Documentation intégrale*, 264). *La Vie souterraine ou la mine et les mineurs* (1866), by an engineer named Louis-Laurent Simonin, was also an important scientific and technical source for the mine novel. Among the other 19th century novels concerned with the subject that need to be mentioned are: *Les Indes noires* (1877) by Jules Verne, *Sans famille* (1878) by Hector Malot, *Le Grisou* (1880) by Maurice Talmeyr, or *Scènes de l'enfer social. La Famille Pichot* (1882) by Yves Guyot. Among the mining films, apart from *La Tragédie de la mine* (1931) by Georg Wilhelm Pabst, the masterpiece that has attracted Berri's attention, we can cite *Germinal* (1913) directed by Albert Capellani with the collaboration of André Antoine, *Borinage* (1933) by Joris Ivens and Henri Storck, *Le Point du Jour* (1948) by Louis Daquin, *Germinal* (1963) by Yves Allégret, et *Le Brasier* (1991) by Éric Barbier. Moreover, Berri makes the following comment about Spielberg's *Schindler's List*: "C'est la conscience des origines qui remonte. Il a le droit de se faire plaisir. C'est son *Germinal* à lui." ("It is a consciousness about one's origins that arises. He has the right to please himself. It is his own *Germinal*"). Quoted in Assouline, *Germinal, L'Aventure d'un film*, 327.

17. "This book is the story of an adventure, that of a man, before being that of a team, and then the story of their film." Assouline, *Germinal, L'Aventure d'un film*, 11–12.

18. "Anticipating the nostalgia that would doubtlessly invade us towards the end of our communal life, I wanted to compose an album of this disparate family born out of necessity. For a photographer of permanency, it was about rediscovering the charm of these pictures loosely thrown together in old shoeboxes, as imperfect as they are touching. They would put on their act and I would attempt to the best of my ability to preserve some of its traces. Just to have a few memories for when we will grow old." Quoted in Benoît Barbier, *Germinal Blues, Souvenirs de tournage* (Paris: Hoebeke, 1993), 1.

19. "... In contrast with the text which, by the sudden action of a single word, is able to have a description become a reflection, photography immediately conveys those 'details' that make up the very material of ethnographical knowledge." Roland Barthes, *La Chambre Claire, Note sur la photographie* (Paris: Éditions de l'Étoile, Gallimard, le Seuil, 1980), 52.

20. "... There are four teams of cameramen that face each other: the one with fixed cameras, the one with the 'steadycam,' the 'making-of' team put in charge by the producers to make a behind the scenes film about the film, and the 'special correspondent' team from the program *France 2* that is doing the same. By treading on each other's toes in the hope of avoiding each other, they will end up filming one another. A strange sensation is born out of a cinema chasing its own tail. Like a fascinating play of reflections, only a caricaturist could represent the truth of that instant. Cabu has arrived. *Charlie-Hebdo* has asked him for a report with a text and drawings about the film. He couldn't have been luckier." Assouline, *Germinal, L'Aventure d'un film*, 324–25.

21. It is important to mention, nevertheless, that at the beginning there was an intention to preserve the set of the film *Germinal* after the shooting to make it an accessible historic site for visitors.

22. "The shoring overhanging the mine shaft, a kind of belfry of which the structures support the toothed wheels with winding cables of elevator cages." Assouline, *Germinal, L'Aventure d'un film*, 134.

23. "These hotels under construction raising their scaffolds towards the dark sky through the frozen plains and emptiness of the new Paris." Émile Zola, *Nana* (Paris: Fasquelle, "Le Livre de Poche," 1972), 316.

24. "Being a wonderful architect of the novel, [Zola] was conscious of what he could gain from this three dimensional landscape, from this three-stage perspective: shoring, plains, galleries. Under his watchful eye, everything immediately had a symbolic value: the Voreux became a harmful beast, the shaft became the abyss, the miners black like the night, the bourgeois white like the day.... Light for the rich, darkness for the poor." Assouline, *Germinal, L'Aventure d'un film*, 118.

25. "Is born out of sensation and because it is in things." Henri Mitterand, "Le regard d'Émile Zola." *Europe* 468-69 (Avril-Mai 1968): 187.

26. Why, from the start, do naturalism and film seem to have the same realistic basis? Because a naturalist writer's observation nourishes itself with "raw" nature, while the gaze of the film director, as is shown by Pasolini in *L'Expérience hérétique* (Paris: Payot "Coll. Langues," 1976), in the absence of a dictionary, of a language, is forced to extract images from the chaos of the universe.

27. "The character of the land in Anzin is flat and gloomy while the one in Valenciennes is picturesque and tragic." Émile Zola, *Carnets d'enquêtes, Une ethnographie inédite de la France* (Paris: Plon "Coll. Terre humaine," 1986), 489.

28. "I would very much like not to forget at the end the tragic setting of the collapsed pit. To represent it at the end under a new light." Quoted in Becker, *La Fabrique de Germinal*, 238.

29. "Knows that he wants a waterway close to the shoring of his mineshaft. He could cheat by filming a waterway separate from the infinite plains. He would have never been satisfied by it. In the novel, the watercourse of the Scarpe had its importance.... Zola even believed that the soul of the plains was contained in the stream, 'this geometrical water that crossed it like a main road, hauling the coal and iron.'" Assouline, *Germinal, L'Aventure d'un film*, 124.

30. The *paratactic style* is based on parataxis. Parataxis is the juxtaposition of syntactic units without the use of a conjunction or the juxtaposition of clauses or phrases without the use of subordinating or coordinating conjunctions. Film scripts are usually written in a paratactic style similar to the sketches of Zola's novels.

31. "The *Germinal* clan born on the 25th of August, first day of shooting, will be dispersed at the beginning of 93, with the departure of the last equipment trucks transporting projectors and dollies rented for the occasion. The group will henceforth dissipate, each of the members going his or her own way to contribute to the fabrication of other stories." Barbier, 4.

32. "Even if the narrative unfolds completely through Étienne and once the experience comes to an end, Zola and Lantier come out of the book together, isn't it Maheu who is in fact the primary hero? Even after his death, he remains the driving force of the work ... why does the Maheude in turn come back to the pit? The head of the family is no more there. The family is destroyed." Marel, *Germinal: Un Documentation intégrale*, 218.

33. "I was not able to be a mother. Hardly a father. I remained a son." Claude Berri, *Autoportrait* (Paris: Éditions Léo Scheer, 2003), 25.

34. Ibid., 21. "One of my father's sayings comes to memory: we are only sure to die."

35. Ibid., 11. "I will try to remember in the disorder. Life goes on. I must hurry. I must die but how? It is necessary to die and to live again. One's memoirs should be written once dead."

36. "I had a different life from my father's. Materially, I fell over to the 'other side,' but I believe that my heart still beats in unison with his. When I read *Germinal*, when I think about *Germinal*, I am next to my father, alongside the miners that scream because they are hungry." Quoted in Assouline, *Germinal, L'Aventure d'un film*, 36.

37. "With a father like his father, it's not possible, he has to succeed." Berri, *Autoportrait*, 21.

38. The following texts were influential to this study: René Ballet, "Présence

ouvrière dans les arts et la littérature de l'après-guerre," in *La France ouvrière: De 1968 à nos jours*, ed. Claude Willard (Paris: Les Éditions de l'Atelier/les Éditions ouvrières, 1995); Jacques Noiray, *Le Romancier et la machine*, vol. 1 (Paris: José Corti, 1981); Tangui Perron, "Nitrate et gueules noires ou le filon minier" *Positif* (Novembre 1993): 24–31; Pierre Sorlin, *Sociologie du cinéma: ouverture pour l'histoire de demain* (Paris: Aubier Montaigne, 1977); Émile Zola, *Germinal* (Paris: Garnier-Flammarion, 1968).

Translation by Alexandra Miekus.

12

Nostalgia Is Hard to Let Go: The French Communist Party's Reception of Claude Berri's Filmic Adaptation of *Germinal*

LAURENT MARIE

The hype that surrounded the release of *Germinal*,[1] on 29 September 1993, was by no means a coincidence. Such an exceptional film—the adaptation of a popular classic of French literature, with a prestigious cast and the highest film budget in the history of French cinema (FF160 million)—deserved an exceptional reception. Along with television, the French press, both daily and weekly, dedicated impressive coverage to the film: 7 pages in the *Nouvel Observateur*, 6 pages in *Télérama*, 5 pages in *Le Figaro magazine* and *Le Monde*, 4 pages in *Le Point*, *L'Express* and *La Croix*.[2] This came after a first wave of reports in the autumn 1992, when the adventures of the film shooting were given abundant coverage.

The French Communist Party (PCF), through its daily newspaper *L'Humanité*, added its voice to this media and publicity hype, after having welcomed the film crew on the central stage of the "Fête de *L'Humanité*" two weeks previously. I will analyze the specificity of the Communist reception, in those aspects that might be considered problematic but also symptomatic of the unease of the party in the face of a rapidly changing French society. In order to do this, I will firstly place this reception within a historical dimension, comparing it to previous opinions held by the PCF on Zola and on previous film adaptations of *Germinal* or on films dealing with the mining community.

12. Nostalgia Is Hard to Let Go (Marie) 183

The strike leader (Jean-Roger Milo, left foreground) and fellow mine workers plan for action in *Germinal* (1993).

Following the example of a great section of the French press, the Communist reception was twofold, dealing, on the one hand, with the occasion that was *Germinal*, and on the other, with the film itself. Whether in *L'Humanité*, *l'Humanité-dimanche* or *Revolution*, the three main Communist newspapers, the occasion took precedence over the film itself. The "surprising echo of *Germinal* one century later" was highlighted, and evidenced, according to the paper, by an opinion poll published when the film was released which confirmed that "61 percent of workers and 54 percent of French people consider that things have not changed dramatically" in a century.[3] Journalists lauded the film director and lead actors for their sincerity and good faith. On the basis of Pierre Assouline's book,[4] film critic Jean-Pierre Léonardini hastened to point to the impeccable record of Berri, Depardieu, Renaud and Miou Miou, all from a working class, mining and Communist background where "one didn't eat meat every day."[5] He then paid tribute to the extras, those former miners who were reduced to unemployment by "the sharp phase of the modern social crisis" and who totally identified, as the readers were told, with the Zola characters.[6] These extras were the very same people that Françoise Colpin, journalist with *Revolution*, had met during her visits to the mining provinces: "These men are made of the same stern stuff as those who led the Anzin strike for 56 days, from which Zola borrowed the documentary elements of this fresco of the concrete." Moreover, she had found in this film the "permanence of suffering" and the "dignity" that characterize this region.[7] The reservations, quite ridiculous when all is said, expressed by a big industrial boss from the north of France, who feared that *Germinal* might give the region a bad image, became evidence of the "strange dialectic backlash" provoked by the film.[8] I could multiply *ad infinitum* these examples of laudatory arguments that, as will have been noted, did not take *Germinal* for what it actually was, that is, a feature-length film, and a very long one at that.

Indeed, taking a closer look at the numerous pages dedicated to the event that *Germinal* represented, it is striking that the actual reviews of the film were allocated a most limited space, as they were drowned in a tidal wave of publicity. In the five pages that *L'Humanité* dedicated to the release of the film,[9] only one column was taken up by the review itself. The rest of the coverage described the people from the North who "had tears in their eyes"[10] during the film premiere in Lille. It promoted Cavanna's book *Les Enfants de Germinal* and reproduced an interview with Marcel Barrois, president of the CGT mining union in the Nord-Pas de Calais region who, "like Zola's Lantier, is immediately likeable."[11] The same scenario was to be found in HD where, alongside a three-page investigation called "Impressions on the country of *Germinal* today" and a two-page interview with Claude Berri, the article by Gilles Le Morvan only spread over one column.[12]

The content of these reviews might explain the small space allocated to them. Apart from Françoise Colpin,[13] the judgments cast on the film were ambivalent, to say the least. Leonardini considered that "*Germinal* is slightly laborious," that it didn't reach the "indispensable pathos, the sublime emphasis all the way through," that the crowd scenes "always exhale an odor of artificial mise-en-scène," that "every detail is relevant," but that "it never really reaches a symphonic unison."[14] The reviews clearly lacked enthusiasm. In their insistence on the accuracy of the settings, on the conformity of the places and movements, it is obvious that neither Gilles le Morvan, nor Luce Vigo in *Revolution* had been truly won over by the film. The former was quite harsh in his judgment of the choice and the directing of the actors and actresses, and openly severe when it came to the dialogues that were merely "quaint exchanges verging on the stereotypical."[15] The Communist film critic thus denounced the stultifying character of the new adaptation of *Germinal*, which contributed to "tucking the working class world away in the drawers of history."[16] In an apparently contradictory manner, Luce Vigo expressed the same reservations when she regretted that "Claude Berri owes the modernity of his topic purely to the reproduction, word for word, of Zola's sentences."[17]

Thus the reception within the Communist press was dual. The filmic reservations were overshadowed by the glorifying and mystifying enterprise surrounding the miners and the mine, in which the Communist Party played an active role. The film was not a masterpiece, far from it, but one was almost duty-bound to go and see it. The comparison with the 1963 film adaptation of the same novel by Yves Allégret will help to emphasize what was at stake in the Communist reception of *Germinal* by Claude Berri.

It became clear very quickly that in cinematographic terms, the reception given to Allegret's film was not so different. Some of the criticisms of that adaptation of the novel echoed those voiced against Berri's *Germinal*. However, instead of being lost in a promotional tidal-wave, these criticisms were the very body of the reception, which was left solely to the film and literary critics. In *Les Lettres françaises*, Armand Lanoux said that the director and scriptwriter, Charles Spaak, had betrayed the novel if not the ideology.[18] There was a touch of anger in the manner in which Lanoux attacked this mining tale, this empty carcass where two of the main characters, Le Voreux and the crowds, disappeared in the case of the former and were only featured in a "skinny, anecdotal and puny"[19] manner in the case of the latter. Lamenting that this was no new *Potemkin*, the critic deemed the film unworthy of "the entry of the social war into world literature."[20] In the same issue of the paper, Marcel Martin was also quite lukewarm: the film lacked "magnitude and fire ... and also the miracle of an original artistic creation."[21] And if one felt some emotions, "it was thanks to Zola more than to the director."[22] The writer and the novel were far more present in the assessment of Allégret's film. What also differs most from the manner in which the new adaptation was received is the established link between the film and the contemporary reality of its release. While Marcel Martin made this link to the present,[23] he did try to be objective: "One hundred years after the events that it describes, the novel keeps a painful contemporary dimension: not so much in France (indeed) but in many places in the world, places not so far from our own borders."[24]

In *L'Humanité*,[25] Samuel Lachize was happy to see that a filmmaker should focus on the working class, which was indeed a rare theme in the French cinema of that time and whereas, just like Marcel Martin, he displayed some degree of discomfort faced with the coldness and the lack of epic of the film, he praised the director for having "almost overcome all [the hurdles] and kept intact the spirit of Zola without indulging in arbitrary parallels with present-day reality."[26] How are we to understand such a divergence of attitudes on the parallels with contemporary reality? Some answers can be found in a survey of the positions of the PCF regarding both the novel and its author as well as the politics of the PCF regarding the miners since the Liberation of France.

The start of a real Communist mythology surrounding the mining world can be traced back to the years 1945–47. Being the first political party in France in 1946 in terms of votes, the influence of the PCF was felt throughout the country. On 21 July 1945, Maurice Thorez, Secretary General of the party and member of the government, talked to the miners of Waziers in the following terms: "To produce, to make coal, is the highest form of your duty as a class, of your duty as Frenchmen."[27] The "Production Battle" was thus launched.[28] The miner, savior of the homeland, and therefore national hero, had to be ready to make all kinds of sacrifices. The speeches of the Communist or trade union leaders of that time—which were necessarily numerous in order to galvanize workers for whom the fruits of labor were slow in coming—rarely mentioned *Germinal*. Moreover, Zola's work was not quoted in the Communist reviews of the film directed by militant filmmaker Louis Daquin, *Le Point du Jour*, made in 1948 and released in 1949.[29] This absence, which may seem surprising at first, can quite logically be explained if the context of the time is taken into account. With the nationalization of the *Houillères de France* and the vote on the statute of miners, measures the PCF was proud of, it would have been quite inappropriate to refer to the miserable conditions once experienced by the miners as described by Zola.[30] In 1947, the miners were not these uncouth and politically illiterate individuals who were caught up in violent passions, but proud, industrious workers, the saviors of the nation. To recall their past living conditions would have meant above all forgetting the social advances won after a hard-fought struggle by the miners and their organization, namely the PCF which got, let it not be forgotten, almost 25 percent of the votes of the nation.[31]

Indeed any initiative that did not confirm the pious and positive image of the hard-working, honest worker was systematically denounced by the PCF as anticommunist propaganda. The wrangles of Marcel Pagliero with the CGT and the Communist Party in 1949 about his film, *Un Homme marche dans la ville*, testify to this.[32] This relationship to work was to be found in Jean Fréville's *Zola, semeur d'orages*, in which the writer praised Zola as the "glorifier of labor."[33] At the time, the party was absorbed by the Cold War and was promoting the aesthetics of Socialist Realism, which dominated the manner in which Fréville read Zola.[34] If we were to caricature what was already presented in a caricatured form, history had a meaning, that of progress. Thanks to Socialism, miners would thrive in happiness and mining accidents would no longer be fatal.

The political strength of the PCF and its influence within a powerful working class also explain the reception of Yves Allegret's *Germinal*.[35] Once again, it would be counterproductive to insist on a possible parallel between the conditions of 1963, the year of the last mass movement of this corporation, and these described by Zola.[36] Those were not yet nostalgic times. The number of workers in France would reach its peak in 1975 (8.5 million), the year when André Marc Vial's *Germinal et le «socialisme» de Zola* was published, and in which the analysis attempted to be more complete, more measured, and more objective than the one that prevailed in the 1950s.[37] However, three years later, André Wurmser's preface to the *Germinal* edition edited by Henri Mitterand was published, and pointed to a tendency to revert to the spirit of previous rhetoric.[38] In this text, André Wurmser focused on Zola the journalist whom he deemed worthier of praise than the novelist: "What Zola reports pleads in favor of the miners. They are only condemned by what he invents."[39] And while it was, as far as the class struggle was concerned, "the only novel fundamentally true, an unprecedented novel never equaled since,"[40] he nevertheless named heirs to Zola's book: André Still's admirable short stories, or Louis Aragon's *Les Communistes,* for the simple reason that the lower classes that *Germinal* had introduced to the novel genre disappeared from French literature along with Zola and only resurfaced in those works.[41] This argument was again developed in his article "Marxists, Zola and Balzac" published in the *Cahiers naturalistes* in 1964.[42] This exaggerated lineage, to say the very least, between the writer of *Germinal* and those who had reached the peak of their Stalinist period demonstrates an enduring and flatly dogmatic take on Zola. Being in the eyes of the PCF the first novel to deal with the class struggle, the denunciation of capitalism, *Germinal* belonged, to a certain extent, to the French Communists, as they are the real defenders of the working class.

It is in this restricted and limited vision of the novel as well as its indefensible appropriation that the origins of the reception of Berri's adaptation can be traced. But this new *Germinal* was on all cinema screens at a time when the French Communist Party was going through one of the most difficult stages of its eighty years of existence.[43] The PCF was facing a major existentialist crisis. On the one hand, it had lost, in the space of a generation, a substantial section of its electorate, dropping from 21.6 percent of votes in 1963 to 6.4 percent thirty years later.[44] On the other hand, the party was competing directly with the extreme-right for the working-class vote in a number of its traditional strongholds. Lastly, and more significantly, with the implosion of Communist Europe, a whole system of references had collapsed, leading to the end of those models that were deemed "globally positive" not so long before. Full of bitterness, on the edge of the abyss, the French Communists (re)discovered nostalgia. What could better convey this feeling than cinema, especially in the case of the adaptation of a so-called "founding text"? At a conference on Scorsese's *New York, New York,* Jacqueline

Wealthy Madame Hennebeau (Anny Duperey) prepares for love in the midst of the labor conflict in *Germinal* (1993).

Nacache stressed that "the nostalgic feeling, both as an awareness of loss and as an aspiration to find again a lost ideal, is intrinsically linked to utopia, to a longing for a harmonious world because it is whole, free from any fracture."[45]

"Lost ideal, utopia, longing for a harmonious world": all these terms echo former illusions or define quite accurately the Communists' state of mind in 1993. The extent to which the film adaptation of *Germinal* was symbolic for the French Communists is thus quite obvious, irrespective of its qualities or faults. Of course, *Germinal* and its revolutionary message justified past struggles and, more to the point, justified the survival, the very existence of the PCF in 1993. The welcome given to the original socialist fiction, written thirty years before the Bolshevik revolution, must be seen as a purifying act, as an unconscious desire for renewal. This focus on a writer from before bolshevism enabled the PCF, by forcing the contemporaneous echoes, to obliterate fallen models from abroad, while stressing the national dimension of its past.

Therefore, the explanation for the Communists' reception of Claude Berri's film is to be found in internal reasons—more precisely, in the party's internal justifications. If this were not the case, how could one possibly make sense of this reception that differed so little from that of the press once described as "bourgeois"? How could one explain the defense of a film in which, as was common knowledge, the extras had been paid below union rates? How could one explain the fact that a brief article published in *L'Humanité* announced that *Germinal* would be shown, in the presence of the film director and the Minister of Culture, Jacques Toubon, in the cinema multiplex of Thais in the Val de Marne department, when it was well known that this new breed of cinemas would inevitably lead to the disappearance of those in the town centers which were the only guarantee of pluralist distribution?[46]

The industrial and economic dimension of the Communist reception of *Germinal* must not be underestimated. The PCF, which was deeply involved in the GATT debate that was taking place in artistic circles, was very active in the campaign for the European cultural exception. By the magnitude of its production and the expected extent of its success, *Germinal* represented for the French Communists a response to the American hegemony in the field of blockbusters. As *Le Figaro* pointed out, what was being witnessed was indeed a duel between the French and American blockbusters, *Jurassic Park* and *Germinal*.[47] The fact that the adaptation of a classic of French literature was holding its own against the latest Spielberg production was in itself enough to satisfy the advocates of the "exception culturelle."[48]

The contradictions of the Communists' reception of *Germinal* contain its very limitations. *Germinal* could not compete with American cinema, and great historical reconstructions, derived from the national heritage, were not going to inspire future talents.[49] Indeed, the film was hugely successful at the box office. But was this a sign of political awareness, as the film critics would have had us believe? In the context of such advertising hype, this is doubtful. As Marc Vernet put it, "the film institution cannot be solely conceived as a dream factory; it is also a machine that switches off dreams";[50] *Germinal* can therefore be viewed as the elevation of a working class that no longer exists as such,[51] a sort of "national funeral of the mythical worker,"[52] to use René Ballet's phrase. But any misunderstanding must be avoided. The point here is not to go along with Louis Pauwels who saw "no structural link whatsoever" between the society in *Germinal* and his own, and contended that the standard of living of a couple on the minimum wage is vastly superior to that of an average "rentier" under Napoleon III, a comparison which was both stupid and revolting.[53]

In 1993, France was going through a serious economic crisis, the effects of which were particularly felt among the most deprived sections of the community. It was, as *L'Humanité* frequently reminded its readers, a France of exclusion, of social fracture, of unemployment and of precariousness. But to put it simply, Claude Berri's commemorative choice and grandiloquent style did not appear to represent the best vehicle for an awakening, for a new awareness, and more importantly, could not reach a young audience. Berri's *Germinal* was like a school trip to the mining museum. This latest adaptation, which must have disappointed Henri Mitterand's expectations as he hoped that the film would capture and transpose the excesses of an epic, fantastic, lyrical, crazy work, did not constitute, in 1993, the cinematographic translation of a live Marxism.[54] Was it not André Wurmser himself who wrote thirty years previously that "realism is a link between a moving reality and its observer, who is also mobile, who changes along with the world that he transforms," concluding that this perpetual variation implied the perpetual invention of new modes of expression?[55]

These new modes of expression existed. French cinema in the 1990s experienced a "return of the real," showing a new interest in the portrayal of France's social situation and its effects on its people. This was to be found in first films, or in films made by young directors who speak about a contemporary reality without corny sensitivity or painful nostalgia, but with a lot of subtlety, doggedness and hope for the future. This is the case of Laetitia Masson's *En avoir ou pas* (1996), the Belgian Dardenne brothers' *La Promesse* (1996), Manuel Poirier's *Marion* (1997), to quote but a few. Above all, anyone looking for the trace of *Germinal* in French cinema would have to see Bruno Dumont's first film *La Vie de Jésus* (1997). Although it does not portray a mining community, this film contains the violence and the force of Zola's work, set as it is in a working class community, ravaged by the unemployment which destroyed Northern France's textile industry. From the pinch-mark competition to the blinding sun, from the animal-like love to the pointless crime, the whole working class community is unraveled as it is seven years after the closure of the last shaft that took place not far away from it.[56] The expected germinations have been replaced by an industrial wasteland, and more seriously, a human wasteland. This is no longer the hopeful month of *germinal*, in the revolutionary calendar; instead it is the winter month of *nivose* under a blazing sun.[57] Since the second half of the 1990s the French Communist critics have embraced wholeheartedly this new wave of filmmakers—those mentioned above have been warmly welcomed in the Party's press—while it has viewed the big-budget productions with a much more critical and circumspect eye. The evolution of the Communist critical discourse took place alongside a larger transformation in the PCF, which began at the very moment Berri's *Germinal* was released. A turning point in the history of the PCF, Georges Marchais announced that he would not stand for re-election as secretary-general after twenty-two years as leader of the Party, and was replaced by Robert Hue. The following week, *V.O.—La Vie Ouvrière*, the CGT weekly, changed its title to *L'Hebdo de l'actualité sociale-la vie ouvrière CGT*. The "mutation," launched by the new leader, has not led to the PCF's recovery, in spite of having been part of Jospin's left-wing government between 1997 and 2002. Indeed, at the turn of the new century, the PCF itself may run the risk of becoming another French '*lieu de mémoire*' alongside Zola's mine shaft.

Notes

1. *Germinal*, dir. Claude Berri, Le Studio Canal+, 1993.
2. *Le Nouvel Observateur* (16 Sept.1993); *Télérama* (29 Sept. 1993); *Le Figaro Magazine* (18 Sept. 1993); *Le Point* (25 Sept. 1993); *L'Express* (23 Sept. 1993); *Le Monde* (30 Sept. 1993); *La Croix* (30 Sept. 1993).
3. *L'Humanité* (29 Sept. 1993): 2–6.
4. It is rather surprising that the Communist journalist should approve of Assouline's book, as the author seems to have more advertising skills than journalistic talent. This is evidenced by the two following examples: Assouline compares Berry to the director of *La Bête humaine*: "His *Germinal* is under the sign of Jean Renoir," and he almost rejoices at the failure of Eric Barbier's mining film, *Le Brasier*, a failure which Berry appeared to have hoped for himself. This is a (counter-)example of cinematographic solidarity lacking in « germinalesque » spirit. Pierre Assouline, *Germinal ou l'aventure d'un film* (Paris: Fayard, 1993), 394.
5. Jean-Pierre Leonardini, "Etonnant écho de *Germinal* un siècle après," *L'Humanité* (29 Sept. 1993): 2–3.
6. Ibid.
7. Françoise Colpin, "Ma vision de *Germinal*," *Révolution* (7 Oct. 1993): 11.
8. Leonardini, "Etonnant écho de *Germinal*": 2–3.
9. *L'Humanité* (29 Sept. 1993): 2–6.
10. Ibid.
11. "On ne peut séparer le passé de l'avenir," *L'Humanite* (29 Sept. 1993): 4.
12. *L'Humanité-Dimanche* (23 Sept. 1993).
13. Colpin, "Ma vision de *Germinal*": 11.
14. Leonardini, "Etonnant écho de *Germinal*": 2–3.
15. *L'Humanité* (29 Sept. 1993): 5.
16. Ibid.
17. *Révolution* (7 Oct. 1993): 4. Luce Vigo was surprised to see her report, in which her disappointment is tangible, introduced by a very large black headline stating: "Vive *Germinal*," and published alongside a large photograph of the film.
18. Armand Lanoux, "*Germinal* ou le nouveau Maître des Forges," *Les Lettres françaises* (26 Sept. 1963).
19. Ibid.
20. Ibid.
21. Marcel Marin, "*Germinal*," *Les Lettres françaises* (26 Sept. 1963).
22. Ibid.
23. Claude Berri was at odds with Yves Allégret and refuted this interpretation. On the contrary, he stated that this film constituted a testimony on the past. Patrick Apel-Muller, "Berri et les enfants de *Germinal*," *L'Humanité* (30 Sept 1993).
24. Marin, "*Germinal*."
25. A private screening of the film was held for the managers of the CGT, the trade union close to the PCF. They subsequently praised the director. Thus, Henri Krasucki, future secretary general of the CGT, thanked the film director on behalf of the union for having made, with this film, "something good for the workers," in *L'Humanité*, (11 Oct. 1963).

26. *L'Humanité* (21 Oct. 1963).
27. Maurice Thorez, "Discours de Waziers, 21 juillet 1945," in *Œuvres choisies, vol. 2, 1938–1950* (Paris: Éditions Sociales, 1966), 393.
28. On this period, see more particularly : Évelyne Desbois, Yves Jeanneau, Bruno Mattéi, *La Foi des charbonniers: les mineurs dans la bataille du charbon 1945–1947* (Paris : Éditions de la Maison des sciences de l'homme, 1986). The authors question the role of the CGT and the PCF, accused of having appropriated the memory of the miners. According to them, the statute of the miners and the nationalization, for instance, did not emancipate the miners but rather consolidated their continued dependency on the workplace (181). Moreover, the authors quote one of the rare writers, a miner, who strongly protested against this "one way" imagery. This was Constant Malva, who was at the time very critical of Louis Daquin's film (77–79).
29. This film, which is often cited as the only French realist-socialist film, is a tribute to the solidarity of the miners and to their work (The young man of the family who did not want to "go down" ends up by proudly going inside the mine).
30. The nationalization was voted on 17 May 1946, and the statute of miners, which introduced the right to accommodation and free heating, on 14 June of the same year.
31. On the occasion of the 27th Congress of the PCF, *L'Humanité* published a special report in which various French regions were presented, such Le Martinet, a small village of the Alesian mining region, where "the miners immediately identified with this young party and, in September 1921, for their first election, they entrusted it with the leadership of the municipality," in *L'Humanité* (18 Dec. 1990).
32. Filmed in Le Havre, *Un Homme marche dans la ville*, located in working class circles, dealt with alcoholism and domestic violence. A campaign of protest against the film was organized by the CGT and the PCF and played an important part in the commercial failure of the film.
33. Jean Fréville, *Zola semeur d'orages* (Paris: Éditions sociales, 1952), 71–72.
34. Ibid.
35. 21.8 percent of the votes cast in the 1962 legislative elections.
36. The workers represented two-thirds of the French workforce in 1966 (excluding the self-employed).
37. André Marc Vial, *Germinal et le « socialisme » de Zola* (Paris : Éditions sociales, 1975).
38. André Wurmser, "Preface," *Germinal*, ed. Henri Mitterand (Paris: Gallimard, 1957), 9–46. André Wurmser was literary critic for *Lettres françaises* from 1947 to 1972 and from 1954, editorialist for *L'Humanité*.
39. Ibid., 26
40. Ibid., 16.
41. Ibid., 15–16.
42. André Wurmser, "Les Marxistes, Balzac et Zola," *Cahiers naturalistes*, no. 28 (1964):137–148.
43. "The PCF is in the lowest ebb of its electoral influence, making the percentage obtained in March 1993 (6.4 percent of the voters) one of the worst results of all its legislative electoral history." Roger Martelli, "1993: un résultat Communiste en demi-teinte," *Société française*, no. 46 (Spring 1993): 2–9.
44. Ibid.
45. Jacqueline Nacache, "L'hommage et la nostalgie," in Jacques Aumont, ed., *Pour un cinéma comparé* (Paris: Cinémathèque française, 1996), 299–317.
46. *L'Humanité* (29 Sept. 1993): 4. See also AFP 280800 (Sept. 2003).
47. "The heaviest French production (FF160 million).... *Germinal* wins its bet and has been seen today by a total of 5,500,000 spectators. *Jurassic Park*, 6,300, 000 (released on 20 October)," *Le Figaro* (29 Dec. 1993).
48. "Cultural exceptions." Others expressed their reservations: "What films are on offer to fight against Uncle Sam's famous imperialism? At random, *Germinal* by

Claude Berri who combines the roles of director and producer.... Let us just remark that this is one more episode in the restoration of a cinema somewhat contrived and purely illustrative at the heart of which the director-producer tends to replace the actual directing problems by administrative issues." Thierry Jousse, "Vices publics et vertus privées," *Cahiers du cinéma*, no. 472 (Oct. 1993):4–5.

49. It is Luc Besson's *Fifth Element*.

50. Marc Vernet, *Figures de l'absence* (Paris : Cahiers du cinéma, 1990): 7.

51. See Michel Verret's article, "Classe ouvrière, mouvement ouvrier. Où va le mouvement ouvrier français?" *Communisme*, no. 28 (1990), 40–48: Massive decline of the working class: from 8.5 million workers in 1975 to 7 million today, of which only 6 million work. The deconcentration is as massive: regarding production (after the mining and textile industries, the steel and metal industries, and the shipyards have all been blown to pieces); regarding location (active depopulation in traditional working class regions such as Nord-Pas-de-Calais, Lorraine, shipyard areas, to which one must add, in the whole of the territory, the continuous transfer of working class population from concentrated collective settlements to individual, scattered housing); regarding culture (productive and residential dispersal corresponding to the disappearance of a whole association-based working class organization).

52. René Ballet, "Présence ouvrière dans les arts et la littérature de l'après-guerre," in Claude Willard, ed., *La France ouvrière. Tome 3: De 1968 à nos jours* (Paris: Les Éditions de l'Atelier/Les Éditions ouvrières, 1995), 25.

53. Louis Pauwels, "L'Assommoir," *Le Figaro* (16 Oct. 1993): 29.

54. *Le Quotidien de Paris* (28 Sept. 1993). Indeed, he is disappointed; see Henri Mitterand, *Zola, la vérité en marche* (Paris: Découvertes Gallimard, 1995), 72.

55. Wurmser, "Les Marxistes, Balzac et Zola": 139.

56. 21 December 1990, closing down of the last shaft, no. 9 in Oignies, "La Terre se referme à Oignies," in the headline of *L'Humanité* on that day.

57. See Laurent Marie, "La Vie de Jésus: Nîvose au pays de *Germinal*," *Excavatio*, Vol. XII (Spring 1999): 162–168.

13

"At the Still Point": Framing the Naturalist *Moment*

ROBERT SINGER

In 1991, Dutch filmmaker Peter Delpeut released his postmodern tribute to silent film, *Lyrisch Nitraat (Lyrical Nitrate)*, which re-narratized a series of shots of found footage, previously undetected in an Amsterdam cinema storage site, to the newly added accompaniment of operatic arias and classical music excerpts. Delpeut's film recycles the retrieved images of narratives lost, including insects, portraits, travelogues, and excerpts from narrative cinema.

One of the most compelling and extensive shot sequences involves the final moments of two unidentified, gasping miners, apparently preparing for and later united in death, as each clings to the other in a moment of worker and personal solidarity. The extra-diegetic "hymn to friendship" duet, "Au fond du temple saint" from Bizet's *Les Pêcheurs de Perles*, complements the entrapped frenzy. Contrasting shots of workers attempting a rescue of the two struggling miners inspire emotions of hopefulness, anxiety, resignation, and suggest the poetic beauty of a romanticized death. Delpeut's recovered shot sequence was, in reality, found footage from Victor Jasset's *Au Pays des ténèbres* (France, Éclair 1912) a loose adaptation of Émile Zola's novel *Germinal*,[1] which was partially available for research in the Library of Congress, Washington, D.C.[2]

The second reel of Jasset's film begins with a dramatic mining disaster, a cave-in, flooding water, and panicking miners attempting to escape inevitable death. The majority of shots in the second half of *Au Pays des ténèbres* were set in the flooding coal mine and an airless pocket of that mine into which two miners retreat, a most suggestive naturalist

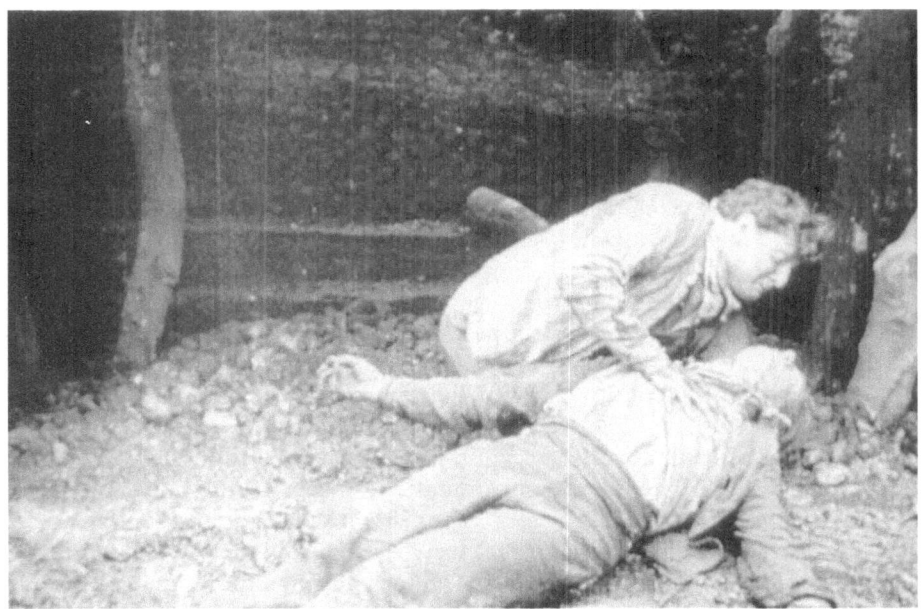

Au Pays des ténèbres (1912): *Top:* Death in the airless mine is imminent. *Bottom:* The rescue is too late to save the former rivals. (Both courtesy Nederlands Filmmuseum, film stills.)

environment. Other contrasting shots introduce two significant social groups, the owners/engineers and the local women—there are no female miners as in Zola's novel—to produce a triangulated series of spatially ordered reaction shots in chronological time. As the owners and engineers debate in a bourgeois, opulent indoor setting, in contrast with the rising waters and tumultuous frenzy of the cave-in, the film cuts to the women initially excluded from the process of decision making, trying to get inside this meeting and, suggestively, the mine itself. The focus is on the rescue and the workers digging away, to get into that airless mine pocket, while listening for life.

What led to this catastrophe? The Library of Congress provides notes about the missing first reel, informing the viewer of a rivalry between two miners, Louis and Charles, over a woman. This causes a split between them. The second reel seems to favor the human drama of survival. In Zola's novel, the cave-in is deliberate. The apolitical emphasis of Jasset's adaptation is on romantic jealousy, brotherhood, worker solidarity, and not the ignored responsibilities of management or the mine owners; Zola's *animalistic* conception of heightened sexual tension and rivalry is evident but significant political machination is underplayed and even sentimentalized in the film narrative, which emphasizes romantic love along established genre parameters. In the Jasset adaptation, these two fighting miners accidentally set off an explosion leading to the mine cave-in. Jasset's shots of all of the trapped miners and their attempted rescue impose a mood of impending, claustrophobic doom. At the end of the second reel, the two miners have died together, reconciled, and are carried off by other miners. These shot sequences from a found narrative, part of a greater whole, suggest multiple and complex intertextual operations to the contemporary viewer, especially as they regard Émile Zola: his theories, fiction, and their subsequent film adaptations.

The two film stills illustrating this naturalist chain of events—the workers' struggle to survive in a flooding, airless coal mine, a failed rescue, and death—are a significant part of the Zola/Jasset/Delpeut *Germinal* narrative. Each shot/film still is a functional "*moment*," an intertext linking narrative to narratives, which, unlike a photograph, "...is part of a unifying whole"[3]: the film from which it emanates. In this case, the "whole" incorporates not only the film texts but also a range of naturalist narratives and precepts. According to Barthes, "In the [p]hotograph, the event is never transcended for the sake of something else.... [I]t is the absolute Particular."[4] This is distinct from the film still, which is an interrelated particular, more than a thing in itself, a prioritized, representative moment. These two film stills from the Jasset/Delpeut texts, shots composed of naturalist moments of working class experience and images of entrapment from Zola's novel, are therefore parts of a greater whole: "The still, then, is the fragment of a second text *whose existence never exceeds the fragment*; films and still find themselves in a palimpsest relationship without it being possible to say that one is *on top of* the other or that one is *extracted* from the other.[5] If perceived only as photographs, these two shots/stills are unlikely to evoke the interpretive level of reaction that *apriori* knowledge of the source narrative generates. As Barthes discovers, the photograph, and as I am suggesting now, the film still, "...animates me [us],"[6] but in different ways; reading the film still suggests an active spectator, engaged in an interpretive process linking text to text, meaning to meaning.

Unlike the traditional photograph, which, "...as it stands alone, presents merely the *possibility* of meaning ... [and] is conceivably open to appropriation by a range of 'texts',[7] the film still *is* a coherent part of a system of representation, with a narrative context that functions beyond the "level of connotation"[8] a photograph implies. Of course, there are significant "naturalist" photographs, such as those accompanying the texts *L'uomo Delinquente* (1889) and *La Donna Delinquente* (1895), by Cesare Lombroso, and *How the Other Half Lives* (1890), by Jacob Riis, and *El Carrer* (1961), by Joan Colom, that are viably read as potential intertexts linked to core naturalist precepts and themes: the facial physiognomies of atavistic criminals, anonymous alcoholics, urban, working class centers of poverty, and other examples. These photographs extend the application of naturalist concepts into the range of the sociological narrative, rather than the literary. This illustrates the broad intersection between theory, the literary and the social sciences, captured in the connotative representation of the naturalist image.

When viewed as an active intertext, the film still, "institut[es] a reading that is at once instantaneous and vertical,"[9] producing a field of narrative linkage to other narratives. The film still is, literally, a visual intertext, a layer upon other layers, leading to the film text and its narrative/cultural antecedents, which invoke varieties of interpretation.[10] Therefore, the original/recycled images of the two film stills from Zola's source text, *Germinal*, with the melodramatic pose and placement of the botched rescue and death of the miners, are fluid entries into a greater narrative, naturalist experience. They are privileged, informing moments.

Specifically, what is the naturalist "*moment*"? What is its relationship to the theoretical function and visual dynamic of the film still selected from the naturalist film text? This process of definition and application incorporates literary theory and practice, beginning with Zola's aesthetic pronouncements. In his essay on "Le Roman expérimental," Zola makes a prescient comparison between the biological circulus, an organic solidarity, with "une sorte de mouvement perpetual, jusqu' à ce que le dérangement ... ait rompu l'équilibre ou amené un trouble ou un arrêt,"[11] and a social circulus. It is the social circulus, the dynamic movement and interaction among people, society, and the respective era, which affects the individual under the scrutiny of the clinical naturalist lens, as viewed by the observer, in the presumed position of knowing.

In the collective life of a society, and the experience of the individual, things go awry, which suggest a naturalist-based reading beyond the metaphysical. Zola's analysis looks toward genetic and environmental causalities, a fusion of scientific and ideological principles. According to Zola, "dans la société comme dans le corps humain , il existe une solidarité qui lie les différents members ... de telle sorte que, si un organe se pourrit, beaucoup d'autres sont atteints."[12] Naturalist literature and film provide insight into the lives and plight of the "tainted," by identifying genetic and/or environmental causal agencies. How does the troubled or entrapped individual—the criminal, the violent, the jealous, the foolish, the drunkard, the deceived, and others—respond to historical and biological "circumstances," which are impersonal, ceaseless, and metaphorically grinding?

In a reading of Claude Bernard's scientific and experimental methodology, Zola derives the concept of the social circulus, and applies theory to naturalist narratives. Issues associated with human heredity (atavism, degenerative alcoholism, idiocy), environmental impediments (saloons, sexual rivalries, unemployment), and modification of milieu (war, strikes), are potential and complicated catalysts in the material world. The *"derangement"* affects human "fate," but these are sociological and scientific causalities. Zola's conceptual *derangement* might lead to a hidden, repressed side of human nature "acting out" as an observable state of the unsettled, troubled personality. The consequences are often deleterious to self and society, and the effects on others within a given environment (home, workplace, neighborhood), can be significant, from seduction, conspiracy, disease, to even murder.

The conceptual *derangement* is critical to an informed reading of literary and film naturalist narratives, and specifically to the relationship between naturalist film and still. The *derangement* facilitates the reaction of the human animal; it is the product of naturalist tensions coalescing, and the naturalist still captures the *moment*. In a photographic sense, the *derangement* can be either the negative (unseen forces of genetic origin) or the positive (visible forces imposed by the social order) affective moment of a naturalist experience for the human animal. The *derangement* produces this immediate effect but also implies broader ideological mechanisms, such as the sociological and scientific facts of the human animal in relationship to history and culture. Zola's *derangement* recalls Barthes' *punctum*, the "sting," or "partial object" in a photograph that literally catches and controls the eye/imagination of the observer. In the naturalist film still, which frames the *moment*, the act or product of the *derangement*, details from the picture are simultaneously informational, symbolic, and now intertextual, suggesting movement among narratives.[13] Unlike the intertextual linkage between film and its still: "When a photograph is cropped, the rest of the world is cut *out*."[14] Of course, with the photograph, there remains an implied field of interpretive context, and the contemporary, experimental film stills of Cindy Sherman suggest that the relationship between still and photograph is blurred, in a postmodern context, and defined by its artificial realism, its "pose." She is her own *punctum*. The naturalist film still suggests a more literal context, from shot to film to narratives beyond.

The aesthetic principles informing Zola's "Le Roman expérimental," the social circulus and the *derangement*, have led to the following analysis of the naturalist *moment*, as it involves reading the film still as an intertext. To illustrate the significance of these critical concepts, I will examine a series of film stills, *moments*, from naturalist film texts, Ferdinand Zecca's *Les Victimes de l'alcoolisme* (1902), based on Zola's *L'Assommoir*; Fritz Lang's *Human Desire* (1954), based on Zola's *La Bête humaine*; and Roger Vadim's *The Game Is Over* (1966), based on Zola's novel, *La Curée*, to establish how these film stills correspond to the visual representation of the *derangement*.

Ferdinand Zecca's *Les Victimes de l'alcoolisme* (1902), based on Zola's *L'Assommoir*, enjoys the status of historical originality; it is the first known film "adaptation" of a Zola novel. Zecca's film, a series of five tableaux, was described by Georges Sadoul as "a pantomime,"[15] that ran for five minutes. The Zola/Zecca narrative of the decline of a working class family due to the effects of chronic alcoholism and encroaching poverty has remained one of the most popular of all the naturalist texts to be adapted into film. Gervaise and Coupeau, the married couple, experience a familiar decline and demise afforded the entrapped naturalist individual, as a result of personal and economic failures, such as his work-related accident and her family and business collapse. However, the single most corrosive *derangement*, as Zecca's title suggests, is chronic alcoholism.

A film still from *Les Victimes de l'alcoolisme* captures the naturalist *moment* of Coupeau's descent into the violence and madness of the *delirium tremens*. Isolated and bound, Coupeau is an object in a padded room. This shot is compellingly recreated in the subsequent adaptation of *L'Assommoir*, *Les Victimes de l'alcool* (1911), by Bourgeois.[16] No longer a man/father/husband, he is the final victim of his own disease. As a photograph, the image is hard to identify and bereft of its naturalist context; it's just a strange picture. The film still, an intertext recalling Zola's naturalist narrative, is a shot compelling for its absence of movement, as if Coupeau were an entrapped body, something like a man, in sheets. As a

Unknown actor offers a case study of delirium tremens in *Les Victimes de l'alcoolisme* (1902) (courtesy *bfi*, film stills).

naturalist *moment*, this still from *Les Victimes de l'alcoolisme* is a study of the decline of the human animal, the product of chronic alcoholism.

If one accepts the premise that "Fritz Lang's cinema is the cinema of the nightmare,"[17] then those naturalist agencies operating in *Human Desire* (1954), the *noirish* adaptation of Zola's *La Bête humaine*, involving the remote environment of the railroad-town, the closed workers' society, corrupt lovers, violence, alcoholism, and the post–World War II historical milieu, actively link the noir aesthetic with naturalism.[18] *La Bête humaine*, Zola's narrative of the declining years of the Second Empire, and the portrayal of Jacques Lantier as tormented bearer of atavistic fury and murderous impulses linked to sexual arousal, is transformed in Lang's *Human Desire* into the noir specifics of anxiety, betrayal, violence, and illicit passion—the substance of bad dreams—of Jeff Warren, portrayed by Glenn Ford. This is also a cursory description of the film noir aesthetic, with its characteristic "central male protagonist ... who is divided, but often lacks self-knowledge ... between femme fatales and domesticating women, both types presented as threats ... [which creates] a mood of pervasive anxiety."[19] Jeff Warren is the prototypical noir male: divided and threatened.

In *Human Desire*, Lang essentially reconstructs select naturalist narrative exteriors of Zola's novel, as well as recalls Renoir's adaptation of 1938, to conform to the noir visual and thematic structures of despair and decline. In this adaptation, (now, Anglicized) railroad worker and Korean War veteran Jeff Warren experiences mounting tension and crises that are rendered visual by Lang's stylized lighting, camera angles and placement, and by the use of objects such as mirrors. The traditional *derangements* suggested by the genetic/environment dialectic take a new direction: In *Human Desire*, Jeff Warren is not the *a priori* vision of atavistic fury of Zola or Renoir's Jacques Lantier. Lang had previously explored the workings of atavistic impulses in the criminal mind in *M* (1931), in which the child murderer confesses that he cannot control the environmentally induced call to kill, the *derangement*, emerging from within, making him the product and the victim of biological and psychological impulses associated with sexual arousal.

Jeff is not a murderer, although he is a veteran and has experienced legalized murder, as the conditions were politically acceptable. He has been affected by the dehumanizing conditions of war; and, now at home, he is "off-center" and seems unprepared to accept the routines imposed by the domesticating social order of the post-war working class. Although "the concept of destiny haunts Lang's work,"[20] it is not a biological imperative in *Human Desire*. The prevailing sense of noir determinism is essentially linked to environmental causalities, and the agency of Jeff's crisis is the sexually frustrated, abused, and entrapped femme fatale.

Although in *Human Desire*, Lang will incorporate a series of traditional naturalist catalysts—alcohol, sexual/work-related frustrations and rivalries, and a troubled male—to facilitate the corrosion of social conditions that lead to murder and further intrigues, the *derangement* is the "dangerous" female. The discontent, atypical 1950s "housewife," Vicki, portrayed by Gloria Grahame, is the totalizing agency. Vickie's working class status, her "past," her unfulfilling marriage, and lack of prospects, make her consistently look for a way out socially, and as it befits the noir visual style, inwardly, at her own suggestive reflection.

In *Human Desire*, there are multiple mirror and glass (transparent and reflection) shots. According to Hirsch, "reflections in mirrors and windows are a recurrent aspect of noir iconography ... suggesting ... masquerade,"[21] which involves psychological and sexual masking and unmasking. In one early shot sequence, as Vicki stares into her bathroom mirror, "fixing herself up," her intensely jealous and alcoholic husband asks, "what went on this afternoon?" The mirror suggests another "side" to her, hidden like a genetic code.

Gloria Grahame reveals multiple sides of self in *Human Desire* (1954).

This *moment* is distinct from Renoir's use of the mirror as prop to reveal "the demon self."[22] In one late shot in *La Bête humaine*, Jacques glares at his reflection after committing murder and sees the beast within revealed.[23] Vicki's particular duplicity, her other "image," involves former sexual intrigues and lying for survival. Her sexual, predatory self, which expresses itself in a less physically violent, more traditional "noir seductress" role, is a different manifestation of the atavistic personality. She gets others to kill for her.

Later, after Vicki and her husband commit murder on a train, she encounters Jeff Warren. In another mirror shot-sequence, she takes out a compact from her purse, and "fixes up" while they speak, thus signaling the emergence of the other *fatale* side. She has targeted the object of her desire; Jeff is a way out and sex is a lure, her controlling weapon.

The film still from *Human Desire* shown in this chapter is a significantly stylized shot, a *moment*, in the life of a working class female murderer/adulterer. Although Vicki looks away, in an indifferent pose, the shot suggests an inwardly pensive gaze. Placed in the foreground of the shot, Vicki casts two images in two separate mirrors: pure noir. As the observer looks at her, nearly undressed, legs up, in subtle, *chiaroscuro* lighting, in the privacy of her bedroom, both the larger and smaller mirror reveal a side-angle shot of her not looking at herself, but casting dual images of self. Therefore, the mirror functions as a revelatory noir agency for the observer, since its traditional function, to reflect its viewer, has not been utilized. There is more to Vicki, as the mise-en-scène denotes. The observer possesses *a priori* information that she plots to ensnare Jeff, as she is ensnared in a dreadful marriage and life with little hope. In the large mirror, the image contains a reflection of a door left open, suggesting a way in for him as well as a way out for her. In both the naturalist and noir narrative, there is little such possibility; doors also close.

In contrast to Lang's working class naturalist narrative, *The Game Is Over* (1966), Roger Vadim's adaptation of Zola's novel *La Curée*, is a study in bourgeois frustration and betrayal, both sexual and economic, and the entrapment of the human, female animal. Like Zola's Saccard family from the era of the Second Empire in France, in Vadim's modern adaptation, the Saccard family is now a wealthy, privileged symbol of post–World War II French class and consciousness. The adaptation also suggests the relationship between Zola's naturalism and its observation of the working class, and realist literature's preoccupation with the foibles of the middle/upper class

Vadim represents the Saccard family as non-communicative and deceptive; more importantly, husband and wife are sexually alienated. The bored wife/stepmother, Renée, played by Jane Fonda, has married an older, indifferent industrialist, Alexandre, and he has a son from the first marriage, the aimless yet very sexual Maxime, who is closer in age to Renée. Their inevitable affair serves as a catalytic *derangement*. With its sitar music, pop art paintings, Maxime's 16mm movie camera and hand-held shots, anti-wrinkle cream, and drugs, *The Game Is Over* situates the naturalist narrative in a 1960s context without eliminating the interrelated themes of adulterous sex, duplicity, and the corrosive effects of money/capital.[24]

In this chapter's film still from *The Game Is Over*, the observer sees the husband, Alexandre, covertly watching his unfaithful wife, Renée. She is a nearly nude figure, lazily sitting under her home salon-style hair dryer, reading a magazine. Renée's pose has interesting structural parallels with the shot of Vicki in *Human Desire*, but Renée lives in a different social environment than Vicki, who is locked in a more primal struggle to survive her enraged husband. Both Alexandre and the observer gaze at this object of desire. This medium, over-the-shoulder shot, facing glass partition doors with hazy, flowing curtains, makes her an inaccessible vision to be looked at. Her husband is an outsider, both to her space in this shot and her life. Renée practices the art of being beautiful for her stepson/lover; as an active intertext, the film still directs the observer to

Jane Fonda as the object of Michel Piccoli's gaze in *The Game Is Over* (1966).

the previous awareness of her adulterous liaison and her husband's discovery of the facts. This is not a magazine photograph of a bored housewife. The shot is set after the affair has been consummated. There are competing tensions in this still, suggesting dual readings of the naturalist *moment*: the (sexual) animal in repose, and a hunter's future prey. In *The Game Is Over*, guns, hunting, and the act of "shooting" (both guns and camera), are significant recurring motifs linked to the strategy, confrontation, and survival of the more corrupt. Renée's deception and betrayal are juxtaposed with her unawareness that things can go wrong, such as a failed affair and forfeiting her investments if she divorces. Alexandre targets a beautiful female animal, and the trap later assumes an economic form of humiliation.

As it recalls Vadim's film and Zola's novel, *The Game Is Over* film still illustrates a complex, critical *moment* of the naturalist narrative, and all of these film stills function as intertexts to cinematic, literary, and theoretical systems of representation. The experimental method of reading a naturalist film still by locating its "point" has demonstrated a fidelity to Zola's process of observation and informed analysis.

Notes

1. Other French film adaptations of *Germinal* appearing early in the century include Zecca's *La Grève* (1903), Nonguet's *Au Pays Noir* (1905) and Capellani's *Germinal* (1913).
2. The first reel of Jasset's film is not available in the Library of Congress archive.
3. Roland Barthes, *Camera Lucida*, trans. Richard Howard (New York: Hill and Wang, 1981), 18.
4. Ibid., 4.
5. Roland Barthes, *Image-Music-Text*, ed. Stephen Heath (New York Hill and Wang, 1977), 67.
6. Barthes, *Camera Lucida*, 20.
7. Allan Sekula, "On the Invention of Photographic Meaning," *Photography: 1900 to the Present*, eds. Diana Emery Hulick and Joseph Marshall (New Jersey: Prentice Hall, 1998), 41.
8. Ibid., 41.
9. Barthes, *Image-Music-Text*, 68.
10. It should be noted that there are industrial-model publicity shots from films that serve a different commercial function. My article analyzes those film stills that may be read as intertexts that link varieties of narrative experience to specific naturalist texts, such as *Germinal*.
11. Émile Zola, "Le Roman Expérimental," *Le Roman Expérimental* (Paris: Garnier Flammarion, 1971), 77. "perpetual movement, until [a] derangement ... has broken the equilibrium or brought about some trouble or stoppage." Émile Zola, "The Experimental Novel" *The Experimental Novel and Other Essays*, trans. Belle Sherman (New York: Haskell House, 1964), 28.
12. Ibid., 78. "In society, as in human beings, a solidarity exists which unites ... members ... in such a way that if one becomes rotten many others are tainted." Zola, "The Experimental Novel," Sherman trans., 28.
13. Barthes, *Camera Lucida*, 26–27.
14. Stanley Cavell, "Photograph and Screen," *Photography: 1900 to the Present*, eds. Diana Emery Hulick and Joseph Marshall (New Jersey: Prentice Hall, 1998), 206.
15. Georges Sadoul, "Zola et le cinéma français: 1900–1920" *Europe* (Nov.-Dec. 1952): 160.
16. The IMDB lists this title as *Victimes de l'alcoolisme* and the year as 1911.
17. Andrew Sarris, *The American Cinema* (New York: Octagon Books, 1982), 64.
18. I am suggesting there is a dynamic relationship between film noir and select precepts from naturalism, especially the notion of entrapment, and the role of material/genetic causalities (especially alcohol). These factors are evident in the case of *Human Desire* and other noir titles, such as Ulmer's *Detour* (1945) and Wise's *The Set-Up* (1949). Also, although the film was set in the United States, *Human Desire* was largely produced in Canada.
19. Deborah Thomas, "Film Noir: How Hollywood Deals with the Deviant Male," *Cineaction*, no. 12-13 (1988): 25.
20. Louis Giannetti, *Masters of the American Cinema* (New Jersey: Prentice-Hall, 1981), 234.
21. Foster Hirsch, *Film Noir—The Dark Side of the Screen* (New York: Da Capo Press, 1981), 90.
22. Leo Braudy, *Jean Renoir: The World of His Films* (Garden City, N.Y.: Doubleday, 1972), 59.
23. The film still of this *moment* may be viewed in Monica Filimon's article.
24. Although both Renée and Vicki, from *Human Desire*, deceive their husbands, the bourgeois Renée has *some* access to power, capital, as a means to affect her life, while Vicki has only her sexual attractiveness.

Select Filmography

Note: No Zola filmography can assuredly list every production. This filmography was developed from a variety of sources: the list from Braudy's article (1969), the Internet (especially the IMDB), historical sources, articles, and other references. When a question arose concerning dates or director, we include both names and years for consistency, but the IMDB was the final resource. A * denotes a television production.

Year	Title	Director
1902	Les Victimes de l'alcoolisme	Ferdinand Zecca
1903	La Grève	Ferdinand Zecca
1905	Au Pays noir	Lucien Nonguet
1909	L'Assommoir	Alberto Cappellani
1909	Faldgruben	Carl Alstrup
1909	A Drunkard's Reformation	D.W. Griffith
1910	Attack on the Mill	no director listed (USA)
1911	Thérèse Raquin	Einar Zangenberg
1911	Les Victimes de l'acool	Gérard Bourgeois
1911/1912	Le Poison de l'humanité	Chautard/Jasset
1912	Nana	Knud Lumbye
1912	Au Pays des ténèbres	Victor Jasset
1913	Gränsfolken	Mauritz Stiller
1913	Miraklet	Victor Sjöström
1913	Germinal	Alberto Capellani
1913	Au ravissement des Dames	Alfred Machin
1914	L'Argent	Savoia
1914	Per Una Notte d'Amore	no director listed (Italy)
1914	Nana	Camille de Riso
1915	Thérèse Raquin	Nino Martoglio
1915	Destruction	Will S. Davis
1915	Penge	Karl Mantzius
1916	The Marble Heart	Kenean Buel
1916	Nana	Nino Martoglio
1916	La Curée	Baldassarre Negroni

Select Filmography

1917	*Drink*	Sidney Morgan
1917	*A Man and the Woman*	Alice Guy-Blaché
1918	*La Bête humaine*	Leopoldo Carducci
1919	*Travail*	Henri Pouctal
1920	*Die Bestie im Menschem*	Ludwig Wolff
1920	*La Rêve*	Jacques de Baroncelli
1920	*Germinal*	no director listed (France)
1920	*Maddalena Ferat*	Mari/Roberti
1921	*La Terre*	André Antoine
1921/1922	*L'Assommoir*	de Marsan/Maudru
1922	*Zum Paradies der Damen*	Lupu Pick
1923	*Pour une nuit d'amour*	Iakov Protozanoff
1924	*Une Page d'amour*	Pina Menichelli
1924	*Nantas*	E.B. Donatien
1926	*Nana*	Jean Renoir
1928	*Thérèse Raquin*	Jacques Feyder
1928	*L'Argent*	Marcel L'Herbier
1929	*Fécondité*	Evreinoff/Étiévant
1929/1930	*Au Bonheur des Dames*	Julien Duvivier
1931	*La Rêve*	Jacques de Baroncelli
1933	*L'Assommoir*	Gaston Roudès
1931	*The Struggle*	D.W. Griffith
1934	*Nana*	Dorothy Arzner
1936	*L'Argent*	Pierre Billon
1937	*La Faute de l'Abbé Mouret*	Max Haufler
1938	*La Bête humaine*	Jean Renoir
1943	*Au Bonheur des Dames*	André Cayatte
1944	*Nana*	Roberto Gavaldón/Gorsortiza
1945	*Naïs*	Raymond Leboursier
1945	*Pour une nuit d'amour*	Edmond Gréville
1953	*Thérèse Raquin*	Marcel Carné
1954	*Human Desire*	Fritz Lang
1955	*Nana*	Christian-Jacque
1956	*Gervaise*	René Clément
1957	*La Bestia Humana*	Daniel Tinayre
1957	*Pot-Bouille*	Julien Duvivier
1959	*Noc poslubna*	Blomberg/Mozdzenski
1963	*Germinal*	Yves Allégret
1965	*Thérèse Raquin**	Håkan Ersgård
1966	*La Curée/The Game Is Over*	Roger Vadim
1967	*L'Oeuvre**	Pierre Cardinal
1968	*Nana**	(no director listed)
1970	*Nana*	Mac Ahlberg
1970	*La Faute de l'Abbé Mouret*	Georges Franju
1970	*Germinal**	John Davies
1971	*Pot-Bouille**	Yves Hubert
1979	*Thérèse Raquin**	Emanuel Boeck
1979	*Madame Sourdis**	Caroline Huppert
1980	*La Fortune des Rougons**	Yves Hubert

1980	*Une page d'amour**	Elie Chouraqui
1980	*Thérèse Raquin**	Simon Langton
1981	*Nana**	Maurice Cazeneuve
1982	*Nana*	Dan Wolman
1986	*Une femme innocente**	Pierre Boutron
1988	*L'Argent**	Jacques Rouffio
1993	*Germinal*	Claude Berri
1995	*Une page d'amour**	Serge Moati
1995	*Cruel Train**	Malcolm McKay
1999	*Nana**	Alberto Negrin
1999	*Na koniec swiata*	Magdalena Lazarkiewicz
2001	*Nana**	Edouard Molinaro
2001	*This Filthy Earth*	Andrew Kotting
2002	*La Liberté de Marie**	Caroline Huppert
2005	*Thérèse Raquin* (in production)	Charles Stratton

About the Contributors

Russell Cousins lectures in French literature and film at the University of Birmingham. Recent publications include contributions on French cinema to the *International Dictionary of Films and Filmmakers* (2000) and *The Encyclopedia of Stage Plays into Film* (2001). He has also published essays on early cinema and screen adaptations in *Émile Zola Centenary Colloquium* (1995), *Aspects de la Critique* (1997), *French Cinema in the 1990s* (1999), and *New Approaches to Zola* (2003), as well as articles in *Literature/Film Quarterly*, *Excavatio* and the *Bulletin of the Émile Zola Society*. Forthcoming publications include a study of screen versions of Zola's *La Bête humaine* for Birmingham University Press.

Monica Filimon is a graduate student in the liberal studies M.A. program at the Graduate Center, the City University of New York, and is currently employed as a teaching adjunct at the Kingsborough Community College, New York. In 2001 she obtained an M.A. degree in American studies from the University of Bucharest, Romania. She is the author of a book entitled *Windows into Texts: Literary Theory and Critical Approaches to Mark Twain's "Huckleberry Finn,"* published in Romania in January 2004.

Katherine Golsan is professor of French and film studies and chair of the Department of Modern Language and Literature at the University of the Pacific. She has published on Baudelaire, Manet, Stendhal, Flaubert, cross-cultural cinematic adaptations of Patricia Highsmith, and Renoir films. She is currently working on a book on women in Renoir's cinema.

Anna Gural-Migdal is a professor in the Department of Modern Languages and Cultural Studies at the University of Alberta, where she teaches literature and cinema. She has published more than 75 articles on naturalism, French literature of the nineteenth and twentieth centuries, film, and photography. She has published the following works: in collaboration with Filippo Salvatore, *Le Cinéma de Paul Tana* (1997); and *L'écriture du féminin chez Zola et dans la fiction naturaliste*, ed. (2003). At present, she is completing a collection of articles on Zola, to be published by the University Press of the Universidad de Jaén, as well as a book on *Zola and the Visual*, to be published with Editions Honoré Champion at Paris. Additionally, she is president of the Association Internationale Zola et le Naturalism (AIZEN) and editor-in-chief of the review of naturalist studies, *Excavatio*.

Alicja Helman was born in 1935 in Radom, Poland. She received her doctorate and post-doctorate (habilitus) degrees from the Institute of Polish Art at the Academy of Science, where she worked from 1955 to 1973. Presently she is a professor at the Jagiellonian University (director of Film Theory Department) and at the Łódź University. She divides her passions between theory and history of film. She is the author of *O Dziele Filmowym* (*About Filmmaking*, 1970), the two-volume *Historia Semiotyki Filmu* (*History of Film Semiotics*, 1991–1998), and a monograph on Luchino Visconti, entitled *Urok Zmierzchu* (*The Beauty of Duck*, 2002).

Heather Howard is a visiting assistant professor at Allegheny College in Meadville, Pennsylvania. She recently completed her dissertation on images of the reader in the works of Denis Diderot. Her areas of specialization include the epistolary and libertine novels, eighteenth-century French theater, and medical literature and the female body. Current research includes work on images of the comédienne in Diderot and Rousseau's critical texts on theater.

Laurent Marie lectures in French at University College Dublin. He has a Ph.D. in film studies from the University of Warwick. His doctoral research concerned the relationship between the French Communist Party and French cinema between 1945 and 1999. His recent publications include articles on Jacques Tati, the "New Wave," 1950s French cinema (Duvivier, Grémillon), Hervé Le Roux and Bruno Dumont.

Elisabeth-Christine Muelsch is an associate professor of French at Angelo State University, in San Angelo, Texas. Her areas of specialization include nineteenth-century French literature, French children's literature, gender studies and French cultural studies. Her most recent research projects focus on the representation of female reading in naturalist and post-naturalist fiction and on the representation of the female reader in French film.

Robert Singer is a professor of English at Kingsborough, CUNY, and adjunct professor of film studies at the Graduate Center, CUNY. He received a Ph.D. from New York University in comparative literature. He co-edited the *The Brooklyn Film* (2003), and he also co-authored *The History of Brooklyn's Three Major Performing Arts Institutions* (2003). He has written articles on the Faust myth for the Mellen Series in Comparative Literature, the Rodopi Perspectives in Modern Literature, and the *Centennial Review*, as well as articles on film studies for *Film/Literature Quarterly, Griffithiana*, and *PostScript*. Among his professional honors and awards have been PSC-CUNY study grants and the NEH Study Grant for College Teachers. He is the vice-president of AIZEN, and he has written and directed several independent short films.

Klaus Peter Walter is the dean of the faculty of philosophy at the University of Passau in Germany. Prior to this appointment, he was chair of the Romance Philology Department (French and Spanish civilizations and literatures). He was also a lecturer in Romance and German philology at the University of Saar. He studied romance and German philology at the Universities of Saar, Strasbourg, and Paris. His first Ph.D. was about *Ponson du Terrrail* and the *roman-feuilleton*; his second thesis dealt with Realism in "New Wave" cinema. Professor Walter has published articles and a longer work on French serialized novels, fascist novels, and realism in French and Spanish film.

Tony Williams is professor and area head of film studies in the Department of English at Southern Illinois University at Carbondale. Williams is the author and co-editor of numerous books on cinema and literature, such as *Jack London: The Movies* (1992) and *Larry Cohen: Radical Allegories of an American Filmmaker* (1997). He is a frequent contributor to Excavatio, and has recently authored *The Cinema of George A. Romero: Knight of the Living Dead* (2003) *and Body and Soul: The Cinematic Vision of Robert Aldrich* (2004).

Jennifer Wolter is a visiting assistant professor of French at Hillsdale College, Michigan. In addition to her interest in film adaptations of Émile Zola's novels, her research focuses on the theory and practice of naturalism by the group of writers led by Zola and named after their collective publication, *Les Soirées de Médan*. She completed her doctoral studies at the Ohio State University with a dissertation titled *The Médan Matrix: Huysmans and Maupassant Following Zola's Model of Naturalism*. She has published articles on Zola, Maupassant, and the Médan Group in *Excavatio*.

Index

Numbers in *italics* indicate photographs.

Abbé Faujas 35
l'Abbé Godard 17
l'Abbé Madeleine 17
Abbé Mouret 36
Adèle 137, 149
Aimée, Anouk 157
AIZEN 9
Altman, Robert 100
Angelo, Jean 63, *64*
Antoine, Andre 15–26; camerawork 19, 22; editing 21, 22; "fourth wall" 18, 21; lighting 21; *Théâtre Antoine 18; Théâtre libre 18*
Anzin strike 173, 183
Arenberg 171
L'Argent 29, 35, 36
Aristide 36
Artaud Antonin 7
L'Assommoir 8, 31, 54, 132, 142, 199
Assouline, Pierre 164, 165, 169, 172, 183
Au Bonheur des Dames 29, 89
Au Pays des ténèbres 194, *195*
Aunt Phasie 73, 78, 82, 83
Aurenche, Jean 132, 133, 134
Autoportrait 164, 175
Aveline, Claude 7

Baguley, David 89
Bal Mabille 65
Ballet, René 189
Balzac 28, 29, 30; *La Peau de Chagrin* 30
Barbier, Benoît 164, 169, 170, 171, 174
Baron Hartmann 108
Barrois, Marcel 134
Bart, Jean 171
Barthes 196, 197, 198; see also *punctum*
Battleship Potemkin 30, 31, 32, *33*, 34, 37
Baudu, Denise 91–99, 105–113
Baudu, Geneviève 93, 97
Becker, Colette 165–167
Bénard 134
Bentham, Jeremy 69
Berlin Wall 177
Bernard, Claude 198
Berri, Claude 89, 163, 182, 183; *Autoportrait 164*, 175; father figure 175
Berthe 151, 152, 158, 159
Bertin-Maghit, Jean-Pierre 104, 112
La Bête humaine 5, 32, 35, 65, 67, 69–88, *80*, *84*, *89*, 94, 199, 200, 202

Bijard 134
Bizet 194
blackmailer in *Thérèse Raquin* 126, 128, 129
Blond Venus see *La Blonde Vénus*
La Blonde Vénus 49, 51, 54, 65
Bodywork 54
Bolshevik revolution 188
Bordenave 49, 52
La Borderie 17, 23
Bordwell, David 32
Bost, Pierre 132, 133, 134
Bourdoncle 109
Bourgeois, Gérard 199
Bourras 111
Braucourt, Guy 105, 113
Braudy, Leo 5
Bronfen, Elisabeth 55
Brooks, Peter 54
Brother Archangius 35
Brown, Norman O. 36
Burch, Noël 62, 64
Burel, Léonce-Henri 20
Buteau 16, 17, 21, 22

Cabuche 73
Cadine 39
Cain, James M. 122, 127
caméra stylo 96
Camille 120, 121, 123, 124, 125, 126, 127, 128, 129
Camille's mother 120
Camy-Lamotte, M. 73
Capellani, Albert 89
Carné, Marcel 117
carnivalesque 34
Carrel, Dany *150*, 151, *153*
Cartier, Abel 105
Castanet, Paul 20
Catherine 55
Cavanna 184
Cayatte, André 89, 92, 93, 95, 96, 97, 99, 100, 103
Celle Qui M'aime 8
censorship 17
Cézanne, Paul 30
CGT mining union 184
Chabrol, Claude 100
Chaplin, Charlie 63
Charles 196
Charles' brothel 17

Chédeville 17
La Chienne 67
children: in work of Clément 140; in work of Zola 139
Cinderella 105
Le Cinema de Papa 176
Le Cinéma sous l'occupation 112
cinematic poetic realism 130
Claude 40, 137
Claude Bartonio, Eric 168
CLCF 105
Clément, René 89, 133, 134, 139, 140, 142, 177; children in work of 140
Clorinda 35
La Cognette 17, 22, 23
Colom, Joan 197
Colomban 93
Colpin, Françoise 183, 184
Comédie Française 19
Comité de libération du cinéma français (CLCF) 104
Comœdia 113
La Conquête du Plassans 35
Continental Films 104, 105
Count Muffat 47, 50, 52, 53, 54, 56, 57, 58, 63, 65, 66, 67
Coupeau 135, 136, 137, 138, 139, 140, 141, 199
Cousins, Russell 5, 148, 159
La Croix 182
cross-fading 96
La Curée 36, 39, 41, 199, 203

Dabit, Eugéne 118
Dardenne brothers 190
Darrieux, Danielle 152, *153*
Darwinism 90, 91
Daudet, Alphonse 119
Daumier 28, 37, 40
La Debacle 29, 34
Decourcelle, Pierre 15
Degas, Edgar 30, 130
de Lachesnaye, Berthe 73
Delair, Suzy *141*
Delhomme 16
Delpeut, Peter 194, 196
Delphin 22
de Maupassant, Guy 119
Denizet 73
Depardieu, Gérard *164*, 183

derangement 198, 199, 201, 203
Le Dernier Sou 104
Desforges, Henriette 108
de Vivaise, Caroline 168
Dickens, Charles 5
Dictionnaire des idées reçues 45
Dimock, Wai-Chee 152
Dr. Pascal 35
La Donna Delinquente 197
Dos Passos, John 29
Dostoyevsky, Fyodor 34
Dreyfus affair 7, 28, 40
A Drunkard's Reformation 8
Du sollst nicht ehebrechen 121
Duby, Jacques 123, *125*
Duchet, Claude 167
Dumas, Alexandre 119
Dumont, Bruno 190
Duperey, Anny *188*
Duvivier, Julien 89, 92, 93, 94, 96, 97, 98, 99, 100, 148, 149, 151, 154, 156, 159

Eisenstein, Sergei 27–44; in Hollywood 28; *Ivan the Terrible* 40; *Laoccon* 32; *Lessons from Literature* 30; *Non-Indifferent Nature* 34, 37; *On Imagery* 29; *Organic Unity and Pathos in the Composition of Potemkin* 31–32; *Strike* 29, 37; *Thérèse Raquin* 36; Zola's influence on 29
El Carrer 197
El Greco 34
Elodie 17
En avoir ou pas 190
The End of Saint Petersburg 29
Les Enfants de Germinal 184
Les Enfants du Paradis 118
Engels, Friedrich 28, 30
Estelle 17
Étienne 137, 140, 166, 174, 175
Eugène 36
L'Express 182

La Fabrique de Germinal 165, 167
Fanny 16
"the Fats" 39, 40
La Fausse Maîtresse 104
La Faute de l'Abbé Mouret 31, 34, 36, 41
Félicité 37

Feuillet, Octave 119
Feyder, Jacques 121, 122
Le Figaro 16, 182, 189
Figlioni, Evy 165
Film Noir 122, 200, 201
Flaubert, Gustave 6, 9, 45
La Fleur de l'Age 118
Flore 6, 73, 77, 78, 81, 82, 83
Florent 36, 38, 39, 40
focalization 132
Fonda, Jane 203, *204*
Foolish Wives 48
Ford, Glenn 200
La Fortune des Rougons 31, 36, 37, 38
Fouan *see* Fouan, Père
Foucault, Michel 69, 70
"fourth wall" 18, 21
Fowler 37
Françoise 17, 21, 22
French Cancan 49
French Communist Party 175, 182, 188, 189, 190, 191

Gabin, Jean *80, 84*
The Game Is Over 7, 199, 203, *204*
Gance, Abel 96
Garnett, Tay 122
GATT 189
Gautrelet, Sylvie 168
Gaveau, René 20
Georges 49, 53, 54, 57, 65
Germinal 29, 34, 89, 134, 163, *164, 170*, 182, *183, 188*, 194, 196, 197; casting 165; *La Fabrique de Germinal* 165, 167; locations and geographical setting 171; marketing strategies 163; research work 167; reviews of film 184
Germinal Blues: Souvenirs de tournage 164, 169, 174
Germinal, l'Aventure d'un film 164, 169
Gervaise 6, 54, 55, 89, 132–147, *135, 140, 141*, 199
Gideon 17
Gogol, Nikolai 34
Goujet 134, 135
Gozzi, Chantal 140
Grahame, Gloria 201, *202*
La Grande 17

Grandmorin 73, 75, 76, 78, 81, 82, 83, 84
Granoux, Isidore 37
Greed 38
Greene, Graham 30, 37
Greven, Alfred 104, 105
Griffith, D.W. 5, 8
Guy-Blaché, Alice 5

Halles 38, 39, 40
Hamlet 6
Harden, Jacques *135*
Hayward, Susan 22
L'Hebdo de l'actualité sociale-la vie ouvrière CGT 190
Heep, Uriah 6
Henri 81
Henriette 109
Les Heritiers Rabourdin 28
Herzen 28
Hessling, Catherine 46, *47*, 48, 49, 50, 56, 57 63, *64*, 65, 67
Heuschling, Andrée *see* Hessling, Catherine
Highsmith, Patricia 30
Hilarion 17
Hirsch 201
Hitchcock, Alfred 30
Hourdequin 16, 17, 20
How the Other Half Lives 197
Hue, Robert 190
Human Desire 199, 200, 201, *202*, 203; mirrors in 201, 202, 203
L'Humanité 182, 183, 184, 189
l'Humanité-dimanche 183
Hyacinthe 16

International Association for Multidisciplinary Approaches and Comparative Studies (AIZEN) 9
intertextuality 8
Ivan the Terrible 40

Jacques 74, 75, 76, 77, 78, 79, 80, 81, 82, 83, 84, 85, 119, 202
Jasset, Victor 194, 196
Je t'aime je t'aime 36
Jean 20, 21, 22, 107
Jeanson, Henri 154
Jenny, Laurent 8
Jésus-Christ 16, 17, 20, 21
Jocelyn 149

La Joie de Vivre 32, 35, 36
Jospin, Lionel 191
Le jour se lève 130
Joyce, James 6, 29, 32, 41
Juliette ou la Clef des Songes 118
Jullien, Dominique 105
Jurassic Park 189

Kafka, Franz 6
Kammerspiel 122
Das Kapital 29
King Lear 16
Kosma, Joseph 118
Kozintsev, Grigori 29
Krauss, Werner 63

l'Abbé Godard 17
l'Abbé Madeleine 17
Lafargue, Paul 28
Lamartine 149
Lang, Fritz 38, 199, 200, 201, 203
Langmann, Hirsh 175
Lantier 134, 135, 136, 137, 140, 173, 176, 184
Lantier, Claude 40
Lantier, Étienne 6, 165
Lantier, Jacques 6, 200, 201
Last Year in Marienbad 36
Laurent 120, 121, 122, 123, 124, 125, 126, 127, 128, 129
Lenin, Vladimir 28
Léonardini, Jean-Pierre 183, 184
Leprohon, Pierre 57
Lequeue 17
Lestringuez, Pierre 57
Library of Congress 194, 196
Life Against Death 36
Lisa 38
Lise 16, 17, 21, 22
Lison 81
locations and geographical setting 171
Lombroso, Cesare 197
Louis 196
Louiset 53, 55
Lyrisch Nitraat 194

M 201
M. and Mme. Vuillaume 154, 155
MacOrlan, Pierre 118
Macquart, Jean 16, 35

Madame Bovary (novel) 9; Madame Bovary (character) 55, 156
Madame Lecaeur 39
Madame Poisson 139; *see also* Virginie
Madame Raquin 36, 121, 126, 127, 128, 129
Mademoiselle Saget 39
Magdalene, Mary 57
Manet, Edouard 30
Marchais, Georges 190
Un Mariage d'amour 119
Marion 190
Marjolin 39
Marken, Jane 150
Market Day 21
Marx, Karl 29
Masson, Laetitia 190
Maxime 36, 39
McTeague 38
Mélusine 58
Melville, Herman 41
La mère Caca 17
Metropolis 38
Metz, Christian 50
Michel 119
Miette 36
Mignon, Rose 56
Milo, Jean-Roger *183*
Minogue, Valerie 133, 136
Miou Miou 183
mirrors in *Human Desire* 201, 202, 203
Misard 73, 78
Mitterand, Henri 173, 190
Mlle. Desforges 98
Mme. Boche 136
Mme. Bonnehon 73
Mme. Hédouin 152, 153, 154, 159
Mme. Josserand 149, 150, 151, 156
Mme. Lebleu 73, 78, 82, 83
Moby Dick 41
"*moment*" 196, 197, 198, 199, 200, 202, 204
Le Monde 182
Monet, Claude 130
La Moralité en littérature 149
Mortoglio, Nino 121, 122
Le Morvan, Gilles 184
Mother 37

Mouret, Octave 90, 91, 93–99, 105, 106, 108–113, 148, 150–159
Muffat *see* Count Muffat
Mulvey, Laura 35, 50, 70
Murray, Mae 47
myth making 41

Nana 6, 9, 30, 31, 35, 45–68, 47, 65, 89, 134, 136, 139, 142, 172
Le Naturalisme au Théâtre 6, 18
naturalist "*moment*" see "*moment*"
Nelson, Brian 110
Nénesse 22
The New Babylon (1929) 29
Norris, Frank 38
Le Nouveau Roman 36
Nouvel Observateur 182

October 29
L'Oeuvre 32

Pabst 169
Paillencourt 171–172, 174
Palmyre 17
Panopticon 69, 70, 72, 74, 76, 77, 78, 79, 81, 82
Paramount pictures 28
Paris Commune 7, 28, 29
Paris Exposition 52
Pascal 37
Pasolini, Pier Paolo 173
Pauline 107
Pauwels, Louis 189
La Peau de Chagrin 30
Les Pêcheurs de Perles 194
Pecqueux 73, 74, 76, 83, 85
Père Colombe 136
Père Fouan 16, 17, 20, 21, 23
Pétain, Philippe 112
Peter the Great 40
Petrov 40
Philipe, Gérard *150*, 152, 153, 158; *Recasting Zola: Gérard Philipe's Influence on Duvivier's Adaptation of Pot-Bouille* 148
Pichon, Marie 148, 149, 154, 155, 156, 157, 158, 159; parents 156
Pick, Lupu 5
Pickford, Mary 47
Pierre 37, 93
Pierre et Jean 104

Piranesi 34
Pisarev 28
Pisarro, Camille 130
Plekhanov, G.V. 28
poetic realism 130
Le Point 182
"point" of naturalist film 204
Poirier, Manuel 190
Les Portes de la Nuit 118
The Postman Always Rings Twice 122
Pot-Bouille 28, *150*, *153*
Pouille, François 51
Préjean, Albert 110
Prévert, Jacques 118
Proletkult 28
La Promesse 190
Proust, Marcel 6
Pudovkin, V.I. 29, 37, 137
Pulp Fiction 36
punctum 198, 199
Pushkin, Alexander 34
Pyle, Alden 37

Le Quai des brumes 119
Quenu, Pauline 36, 38
The Quiet American 37

Rabelais 34
Raskolnikov 121
Recasting Zola: Gérard Philipe's Influence on Duvivier's Adaptation of Pot-Bouille 148
Renard, Jules 119
Renaud 183
Renée 36, 39
Renoir, Auguste 47, 63
Renoir, Jean 6, 35, 45–68, 89, 130, 201
Resnais, Alain 36
Revolution 183
Riis, Jacob 197
Rocher, Pierre 118
Romains, Jules 28
Le Roman expérimental 27, 197
Romeo 6
Rothwell, Andre 129
Roubaud 74–85
Rougon, Eugène 35
Rougon, Félicité 39
Rougon-Macquart cycle 6, 28, 29, 36, 89, 132, 167, 168, 170, 172

Sabine 50
Saccard, Alexandre 7, 203, 204
Saccard, Aristide 35, 39
Saccard, Maxime 203
Saccard, Renée 203, 204
Sadoul, Georges 199
Saint-Étienne 173
Sand, George 119
Schell, Maria *135*, *141*
Schor, Naomi 51
Séchan, Renaud 166
Sesonske, Alexander 48, 49, 63
Séverine 55, 75–85
Shakespeare, William 5, 16
Shelley, Hugh 37
Sherman, Cindy 199
Siclier, Jacques 154
Signoret, Simone 123, *124*
Silvere 36
Simon, Michel 110
Simon, Simone 76, *80*, 82
La Simple Vie de Gervaise Macquart 133
Sjöström, Victor 5
Sklar, Robert 130
Slotkin, Richard 41
Slott, Kathryn 52, 53
smallpox 55
social circulus 198, 199
Socialist Realism 31, 40, 41
Société des Auteurs et des Gens de Lettres (S.C.A.G.L.) 15
Son Excellence Eugène Rougon 30, 32, 35, 41
Soulas 20
south style 122
Spaak, Charles 117, 118, 127
spatial dynamics 62
Spielberg, Steven 189
Stam, Robert 6
Storer-Clouston 118
Storm Over Asia 37
Strangers on a Train 30
Strike 29, 37
Stroheim, Erich von 38
surveillance 69–88
Suzanne 119
Swanson, Gloria 47

Tarantino, Quentin 36
Tavernier, Bertrand 100

Télérama 182
Le Temps 151
La Terre 15–26, 29, 30, 31, 35, 177; camerawork in 19, 20
Testa, Carlo 117, 118
Théâtre Antoine 18
Théâtre des Variétés 49, 58
Théâtre libre 18
Thérèse 54, 120, 121, 122, 123, 124, 125, 126, 127, 128, 129
Thérèse Raquin 9, 36, 54, 117, *124*, *125*
Thiriet, Maurice 118
Tiny Tim 6
Tissier, Jean 109
Tolstoy, Leo 34
Toubon, Jacques 189
La Tragédie de la mine 169, 177
Trauberg, Leonid 29
Trémois, Claude 136
Tron 17
Trotsky, Leon 28
La Trouille 21, 22

Ulysses 29, 41
Uncle Gradelle 38
L'uomo Delinquente 197
Uriah Heep 6

V.O.—La Vie Ouvrière 190
Vadim, Roger 7, 199, 203, 204
Vallone, Raf 123, *125*
Vandeuvres 48, 49, 54, 57, 63, 65, 66
Venice Film Festival 118
Le Ventre du Paris 29, 31, 34, 36, 37, 39, 41
Vernet, Marc 189
Vicki 201, 202, 203
Les Victimes de l'alcool 199

Les Victimes de l'alcoolisme 132, 199, 200
La Vie de Jésus 190
Vieil Elbeuf 97
Vinken, Barbara 110, 111
Virey-Babel, Roger 58
Virgin Mary 91
Virginie 135, 137, 139, 140
Viry-Babel, Roger 49
Les Visiteurs du Soir 118
Visual Pleasure and Narrative Cinema 35
La Voix du Nord 168
Von Stroheim, Erich 48
Voreux 171, 172, 174

Wagner, Richard 27, 34
Warren, Jeff 200, 201, 202
Whistler, James Abbott McNeill 130
White, Nicholas 158
Whitman, Walt 34
Williams, Alan 62, 63
Women's Death Battalion 29
Wurmser, André 190

Zecca, Ferdinand 132, 199
Zola, Émile: *Celle Qui M'aime* 8; characters 6; children in work of Zola 139; fellow traveler 40; female characters 35; *Les Heritiers Rabourdin* 28; *La Moralité en littérature* 149; *Le Naturalisme au théâtre* 18; *Recasting Zola: Gérard Philipe's Influence on Duvivier's Adaptation of Pot-Bouille* 148; *Le Roman expérimental* 27, 197; seeing 8, 9; symbolism 23
Zola on Film: Ambiguities of Naturalism 5

www.ingramcontent.com/pod-product-compliance
Lightning Source LLC
Chambersburg PA
CBHW032053300426
44116CB00007B/718